Man M

# Man Made Language

## Dale Spender

SECOND EDITION

Pandora
An Imprint of Rivers Oram Press
LONDON AND NEW YORK

First published in 1980
Reprinted in 1981 (twice) and 1982

Second edition published in 1985
Reprinted in 1985

This edition published by Pandora Press
an imprint of Rivers Oram Press Limited
144 Hemingford Road
London N1 1DE

Distributed in the United States of America
by New York University Press
70 Washington Square South
New York NY 10012

Set in 11/12 Singer Plantin
and printed in Great Britain by
Cox and Wyman Ltd, Reading

British Library Cataloguing in Publication Data
A catalogue record for this title is available
from the British Library

ISBN 0 86358 401 2 (pb)

# Women's Talk

what men dub tattle gossip women's talk
is really revolutionary activity
and would be taken seriously by men
(and many women too)
if men were doing the talking

women's talk is women together
probing the privatised
pain isolation exclusion trivialisation
in their everyday lives
if situations were reversed
men would react with identical symptoms
to what women feel in their gut—
worthlessness self deprecation depression

what men call prattle babble chatter jabber blather
gabbing hot air small talk rubbish gibberish verbosity
clearly shows how language reflects
the deep misogyny that's penetrated our lives
and become common sport
but from this day forward
spare me
   I'm sick of being bait

men denigrate our talk at their peril
but that's because they're in ignorance
of its power
our power
those precious few of us who see ourselves
as powerful
    serious
     and deadly.


*Astra*

# Contents

viii

# Preface to
# Second Edition

In 1979 when I first wrote this book, I was wary. I had good reason to be. Most of the research on which it is based had been undertaken for my PhD and at that stage I had not been awarded my degree: I was even ready to accept that I would probably have to revise my dissertation – yet again. I was easy prey for doubts – not just doubts about whether I was 'up to standard' when it came to the requirements of the University of London (for I was an Australian female with only a 'colonial' education), but doubts about the validity of my work.

My thesis was simple, and in my terms demonstrable. I was arguing that men controlled the language and that it worked in their favour. I could demonstrate that men had not only provided themselves with more – and more positive – words but that they ensured that they had more opportunities to use them. There is nothing complex about such a case: society had not found it difficult to accept (*without* the benefit of systematic evidence) that women were the talkative sex, so why should intellectual capacity be strained by coming to accept (*with* the benefit of systematic evidence) that it was men who dominated in mixed-sex talk?

But it was partly because my case was so simple that I could come to doubt the reality of it. Why had it not been put forward before? Why – in the face of so much contrary evidence – had so many experts been able to assert for so long that women were the talkative sex?

And because I had doubts, I was cautious. The book began with a chapter on methodology and I carefully tried to justify the approach I was taking – in the most respectable of terms. I made suggestions rather than assertions; I put forward excuses rather than allegations. Seeking acceptance within the academic community I tried to abide by its rules.

Much has changed since then. I must admit to some embarrassment now as I read over some of my words: they sound so timid and so tame. I draw a parallel between my own tentative steps and those of the women who carried on the campaign for the vote in the nineteenth century – for they too tried to retain the acceptance of the men whose views they were challenging, they too had tried to remain within the bounds of respectability. They had believed that their cause was just and reasonable and that all that was necessary was to make it known to men – who would immediately perceive the error of their own ways and would promptly begin to share power with women!

It was a 'theory of good conduct' – and it didn't work. While the women were 'good' it was possible to ignore their demands – and besides, the conscious efforts to attain respectability were no protection anyway; such women were still ridiculed, mocked – and dismissed. It was the suffragettes who came along and deliberately proposed a 'theory of bad conduct' on the grounds that men would yield power only when they had to, only when they were so inconvenienced by retaining it that it was easier to give it up.

There have been no suffragettes bursting upon the scene in the intervening years since I first wrote this book, but the understandings of the suffragettes have become incorporated in contemporary feminist theory and we are richer and wiser as a result. The conviction that men will not give up power simply because they are asked – however nicely – has grown. Now that we know something about our past we are in a much stronger position. Our doubts have given way to a new-found confidence as we have come to appreciate that women's silence is not just confined to today's mixed-sex conversations but extends to yesterday's spoken and written records as well.

In 1979 when I could find few models for my thesis it was understandable that I should think that in the past women had not speculated on male control of language. But in 1983, when I do know that women of previous generations *did* describe and explain the way language worked in favour of men and that their words have been 'removed from the record', it is not doubt that I feel, but anger. And there is a world of difference between the two.

For women have known for centuries that men have been the underservedly dominant sex, and that their dominance is reflected and reinforced in the language and by language use. Women have known about this form of dominance, and argued (persuasively) against it, and the fact that I did not know of their existence or their protests in 1979 is testimony to the power men have had to silence women. Men have used their power in the past to censor women's challenge and they continue to use it in the present.

There have been times when women have been able to evade the mesh of silence, and one example which I found initially provided me with considerable amusement. Aware of the way women's words can be quickly buried, Elizabeth Cady Stanton, along with Susan B. Anthony and Matilda Joslyn Gage, took upon themselves the daunting task of recording women's activities in the American campaign for woman suffrage, so that future generations of women would know about the magnificent tradition that women had forged.

In *History of Woman Suffrage* (1881, Vol. I) Stanton describes the first women's rights convention held in Ohio at Salem – and where there was a significant difference: 'It was officered entirely by women; not a man was allowed to sit on the platform, to speak or vote. *Never did men suffer so.* They implored just to say a word – but no – the President was inflexible – no man should be heard. If one meekly arose to make a suggestion he was at once ruled out of order. For the first time in the world's history, men learned how it felt to sit in silence when questions they were interested in were under discussion' (p. 110: original emphasis).

In 1850 Elizabeth Cady Stanton had thrown aside the conventional wisdom that would have men as the 'strong, silent types' and had insisted that it was the men who did all the talking, who determined the conversation topics, and who in most situations penalized women who disregarded the man-made rules that favoured men. She relished the opportunity to turn the tables and felt no guilt whatsoever when she witnessed men about to explode from apoplexy. She would not have been susceptible to the suggestion that she was being unfair to the men.

When today men sometimes find themselves in a situation where they are required to hold their peace, and where they have been known to complain about injustice or to protest that women have made 'men's talk' a problem, there can be no doubt about what Elizabeth Cady Stanton's response would have been. For centuries women have been silenced: it does no harm for men on occasion to find out what it's like and to experience the rage and frustration that goes with being a silent subordinate.

All Stanton's writing is liberally sprinkled with her understandings about men's appropriation of women's linguistic resources. She accuses men of stealing women's words and like many women of contemporary times was not unfamiliar with the phenomenon of having her own words and suggestions dismissed or ignored, only to hear them shortly afterwards put forward by a man and greeted with approval, and even enthusiasm.

I didn't know about Elizabeth Cady Stanton in 1979. I do now. And that's the difference. I know now that my thesis about the male control of language is not new. It has just been revived.

But if Elizabeth Cady Stanton's words could disappear, so too can our present insights into male power. It is absurd – and dangerous – to subscribe to the theory that for women there has been uninterrupted progress and that we today are necessarily in a stronger position than were our foremothers. It seems to me that women's history could accurately be described at one level as the pendulum swing from silence to audibility – and back to silence again. Currently we *are* audible, we are being heard in some qurters, but where do we go from here?

That is why I was delighted with Stanton's words about the silencing of men: it is why I have begun to wonder about the permanence of our contemporary voices. Will we have to be reclaimed by some future generation as we ourselves have had to reclaim past generations?

The consideration of this possibility cannot detract however from the strength and certainty we have derived from the knowledge that what we are saying today is not new. We may have to reshuffle some of our assumptions and even abandon the belief that we are radical, but when we are aware that we are part of a long and laudable tradition of women – who have been justly critical of male power – we have a confidence that is difficult to shake.

It is this confidence which in recent years has become part of my fabric which eluded me in 1979 when I tried to argue women's case in terms that were acceptable to men. I now have the lessons of hundreds of years to go by and I have the advantage of the words of my foremothers who, again and again, have said that there are no terms which are acceptable to men if you want to criticize male power. I am now the inheritor of a well-formulated philosophy on the 'theory of bad conduct' and I intend to work sensibly within that tradition. So this is neither a new nor a radical book but just a more recent explanation of male control of language. Whether or not it is erased along with its predecessors while male power persists remains to be seen. But I fervently hope that its insights are most inconvenient and that it helps to contribute to making it easier for men to yield than to continue wielding power over women.

Dale Spender
Coogee, Australia

# Acknowledgments

There is an assumption I wish to challenge: it is that people sit in garrets and write books on their own. I sat in the Women's Resources Center at the University of Utah in Salt Lake City, and I was not on my own. For their help and hospitality I owe a great deal to the staff there. But even before I arrived in Salt Lake City I had many 'drafts' and many tapes, and after I left they continued to multiply, and none of them was produced in isolation. While this book may represent a 'sum total', its many parts have been shaped in many different places and by many different people.

In chronological order there have been my parents who have constantly encouraged, supported and 'dialogued' with me and who gave me an example of living co-operation and sharing, long before we heard the term feminism. There has been my sister, Lou Buchan, my oldest friend; to give full acknowledgment to her contribution would be to have a footnote 'personal communication' on every page. There have also been males who have helped me to appreciate that maleness is not biologically determined: Graeme, my brother, my friend, who has done more than his share of the washing up and coffee-making as well as offering insights and understanding; Ted, who has walked the tightrope between being supportive and critical, between being a source of stability and of independence.

To Cheris Kramarae I owe a special debt; she answered the mail when I wanted to write, and her advice and support have been given generously and they have often been much needed. To the Women's Research and Resources Centre in London I owe another special debt;

it has been a 'home away from home' and, also, often much needed. To my friends who have worked with me, to Elizabeth Sarah, Helen Roberts, Barbara Thomas, who will find some of their thoughts and ideas reflected in these pages, thank-you for all the talking time we have had. To Astra, whose poem made my work less abstract, and to Anna Walters, whose dissertation made it less arduous, I am indebted. To the many women who talked — and were taped — here are my thanks for their inspiration.

To Pippa Brewster who encouraged me, Glynis Butcher who typed the manuscript and wrought order out of chaos and to Camilla Raab who checked my sweeping statements and my references with such care and consideration, I am also grateful.

But if there is one source of energy behind this book, it is the women's liberation movement. Not in isolation in a garret did this book come into existence, but in the co-operative and dynamic context of women's struggle for autonomy.

# Revised Introduction

# The Perpetuation of Patriarchy

A patriarchal society is based on the belief that the male is the superior sex and many of the social institutions and much social practice is then organized to reflect this belief: in one sense a patriarchal society is organized so that the belief in male supremacy 'comes true'. If, in a variety of ways, a community can come to accept that males are superior, that they are more worthy and more deserving (and linguists have been among those who have advanced this case, see p. 147 '*Helman* language'), then the whole community can find it sensible to provide the superior, more worthy, and more deserving sex with more resources, so that males do indeed have a greater chance of appearing superior. And so the system is perpetuated. The supposedly superior males *do* accumulate more resources (UN statistics of 1980 reveal that males own 99 per cent of the world's resources) and because they are in a position to insist on the validity of their own views and values we should not be surprised to find that they continue to insist on their own supremacy, their own worth, their own authority. Given the psychological and material resources they have accumulated, men are indisputably in a position to be heard.

This, unfortunately, is not the case for women in a patriarchal society. Owning less than 1 per cent of the world's resources, being assigned the qualities that men find distressing or disturbing (a phenomenon described by Mary Astell in 1960; see Spender, 1982b), performing the less prestigious tasks in the paid and unpaid workforce, women as a group are not in a position to be heeded or heard. Yet there are many reasons for suggesting that the values and views of women are often very different from those of men.

While the power structure of patriarchy remains undisturbed, there is little space and even less credibility granted to the specific experience of women. Males, as the dominant sex, have only a *partial* view of the world and yet they are in a position to insist that their views and values are the '*real*' and *only* values; and they are in a position to impose their version on other human beings who do not share their experience. This is one of the crucial features of dominance; it is one of the characteristics of patriarchy, for it is the means by which one half of the human population is able to insist that the other half sees things its way. By this process alternative views and values are suppressed and blocked. Women's different experience is outlawed, is seen as unintelligible, unreal, unfathomable.

This process of validating male experience – and it should be noted that male experience includes the perception of their sex as deservedly superior and justifiably dominant – has been described by women as the *male-as-norm* syndrome. It is a feature of our culture which women have recognised – and resisted – for centuries. Women have attempted to label as a problem the way they experience male dominance and the limitations of the dominant view of the world which does not encompass them. But such a problem is, of course, outside male experience, for dominance has been no more a problem to men as a group than it has been to whites, across the centuries: and if it's not a problem for men – whose experience is what counts – then it's not a problem! Yet again and again the issue has been raised by women and the fact that so few members of society even know that women have been protesting for generation upon generation is but more evidence that when women's experience is not the same as men's, it is passed off as non-data in a patriarchal society.

While the male-as-norm syndrome persists, women have a structural problem. So conveniently is the patriarchal system arranged that we are damned if we go along with it, and damned if we do not. If we indicate that we have learnt the rules for making sense of the world in our patriarchal society and have become 'full' members of our community, then we demonstrate that we accept the dominant view of the world, we accept the authenticity of male experience, we accept our 'inferiority'. For many reasons this is not therefore a course of action that I would recommend!

But what if we object? What if we refuse to learn the rules for making sense of our patriarchal society, if we refuse to subscribe to our own subjugation, if we refuse to see men as deservedly dominant? There are penalties for this stance as well: the history of women is littered with the patriarchal response to such recalcitrant women who have been described not as disobedient, but as *failures*. They have failed to become full members of society, failed to see the world the way they should, failed to behave in a fitting manner. The more women have resisted the more it has been suggested that there is something wrong with us: in the view of the dominant group we are abnormal, neurotic, frigid or hysterical, or even bitter and twisted. We are man-haters, and there is the clinching argument that we even fail to have a sense of humour.

While this is no doubt evidence that the dominant group does not take kindly to criticism, nor does it find its own antics amusing when described by women, it also indicates that such forms of resistance on the part of women have little to recommend them either.

Neither acceptance nor persistent protest appears to have disturbed the patriarchal structure, so, what to do? Obviously it is no solution to suggest that 'ye who enter patriarchy abandon all hope.'

For me, a priority is to find out how patriarchy functions: in the words of Liz Stanley it is to find out *how* men *do* dominance, how they do oppression. This means finding out how the rules for making sense of the world are encoded and used; it means finding out how our social reality is constructed so that men achieve dominance in our daily lives; and this means finding out about language for it is a major and crucial part of the process.

Language helps form the limits of our reality. It is our means of ordering, classifying and manipulating the world. It is through language that we become members of a human community, that the world becomes comprehensible and meaningful, that we bring into existence the world in which we live.

Yet it is ironic that this faculty which helps to create our world also has the capacity to restrict our world. For having learnt a particular language and had access to being 'humanized' we have also been 'socialized' in the process, we have also learnt to confine our way of looking at the world to a particular cultural world view. Having learnt the language of a patriarchal society we have also learnt to classify and manage the world in accordance with patriarchal order and to preclude many possibilities for alternative ways of making sense of the world.

Through my language and socialization I did learn to see as *sensible* many arrangements in my society which an 'outsider' (who did not share my socialization) would find absurd. So at one stage I did learn, for example, that it was sensible to give the least educational experience to those who appeared to take longer to learn. I did learn that it was sensible to classify some forms of skin pigmentation as possessing mystical powers. I did learn that it was sensible that one half of the population should be paid for their work while the other half should not. I did learn that it was sensible to ensure the survival of the species by amassing a vast arsenal that could destroy the planet many times over. And I did learn that it was sensible to see men as superior.

Such lessons, however, can be unlearned. It may not be easy to break out of the patterns of thinking and believing into which our society and language have led us, but it is possible. Language is a human product, it is something which human beings have made, and which can be modified. We can – with perseverance – posit alternatives to those which are readily available within our society. We can make the effort to formulate possibilities at the periphery of our cultural conditioning and to reconceptualize our reality: we can generate new meanings – and we can validate them.

And this has become my second priority. If and when sufficient women agree that they no longer subscribe to the rules and patterns of patriarchy, then the rules and patterns are likely to be transformed. While I hold the personal view that Sigmund Freud would probably have declared all women *abnormal* before he revised his theories on women, it is possible that not all males are as intransigent, or as resistant to the evidence. It did not take *all* women to confound some of the cherished patriarchal beliefs when the suffragettes took to militancy: there was considerable difficulty in attempting to reinforce the rule that women were naturally docile and demeaning when a significant percentage of them went around demonstrating that they could quite naturally be disagreeable and defiant.

When women acted together and validated each other's actions, men had little choice but to change their minds – marginally, anyway. For centuries men may have been checking with each other and confirming the accuracy and adequacy of their descriptions and explanations of the world – and women – and without any consultation with women. So they may have agreed on the soundness and suitability of describing and explaining women as innately passive and polite, despite the protests of individual women that they did not feel innately passive and polite (and on the contrary could testify to the struggle they had to acquire this supposedly innate state – as did Mary Wollstonecraft, for example). But any appeal to men to revise their rules brought no great changes: after all, by the time the suffragettes came upon the scene women had been appealing for sixty years or more.

But it was a new development when women ceased to look to men for support and confirmation, and instead started looking to themselves. Women took the initiative and men were obliged to react.

And women can still take the initiative. We can choose to dispense with male views and values and we can generate and make explicit our own: and we can make our views and values authentic and real. Rebecca West has said that we take men too seriously, we accord them too much power, and that we should be more interested in what women think than in seeking approbation from men (Spender, 1983b).

Much depends on the way you look at it. It is all very well for the dominant group to suggest that its knowledge is objective while that of women is subjective, that its concerns are mainstream while those of women are marginal, that 'men's studies' are central while women's studies are a ghetto. When women start validating women's experience we have the numbers to call a reversal if we so desire. We have the power to obstruct patriarchy and we can use it.

This is not to suggest that there are no problems. In 1909, Cicely Hamilton stated the issue simply when she declared that if all women were to become 'disagreeable' tomorrow (that is, to practise the theory of bad conduct and to defy the patriarchal order), then the day after, men would learn to live with disagreeable women – or do without! But for many reasons, many women may find it difficult if not impossible to engage in disagreeableness – and not just because of their socialization!

Patriarchy is an interlocking system with its psychological and material components, and while women's consciousness may indicate the desirability and even necessity of practising 'disagreeableness' in order to undermine patriarchy, material circumstances may prevent them from doing so. It was a tenet of the nineteenth-century (and early twentieth-century) women's movement, that there could be no autonomy for women until women were economically independent, and it is a tenet that is no less relevant today than it was then. For it is not just that men earn more than 90 per cent of the world's wages and own more than 99 per cent of the world's resources, it is that the gap between women and men grows greater every year. So significant is the growing discrepancy that in a forthcoming book, Hilda Scott alleges that by the year 2000 poverty will be exclusively a female problem.

Women are economically deprived and this has consequences: it is patently obvious that less than 10 per cent of the world's wages and less than 1 per cent of the world's worth is simply not enough to go around among more than half the world's population, so women must turn to those who control the resources if they are to survive. Women must turn to men: as Cicely Hamilton stated in 1909 women must trade themselves in order to earn their bread.

While many women if free to choose might choose not to trade, might choose to defy patriarchal order and to validate women's experience rather than seek the approval of men, in practice few women have the privilege of choosing the rules by which they live their lives. The choices for women are often constrained by the necessity to earn their bread and they are obliged to cultivate the good will of their masters, to support the view of the males as the superior sex, to be 'agreeable' to employer, husband, father. This pattern of behaviour is one which girls have been taught for centuries and it is a pattern which helps to perpetuate patriarchy. Part of the structure of male power and female subservience is that for most women who want their supper there is the requirement that they must first sing.

To be 'disagreeable', to defy patriarchy under these circumstances, to look to women rather than men is 'to bite the hand that feeds you' – and could well lead to being deprived of your supper.

So when men may argue for the authority for their meanings and insist on their right to 'take the floor' and control, in mixed-sex conversation, many women have no choice but to agree. Many women must be seen to give consensus to this sytem in which males *do* dominance, despite the fact that they may find it odious. This is one of the ways that women's linguistic resources are appropriated by men. Yet it does seem that the only means which we have as women to disrupt this neat process is to cease making our linguistic resources available, to cease giving our consensus to a system which denies us.

Instead of acquiescing we will have to invest the language with our own authentic meanings, and repudiate many of those which are currently accepted as accurate: we will have to insist on our own forms of language use, on listening to others and on being heard, on 'taking a turn' rather than 'taking the floor' and on doing it without use of imposition, control, or devaluation of 'others'.

And because such a strategy is likely to be effective, because it is likely to be disruptive, it won't be easy. No doubt we will be vilified – for this is what has happened invariably in the past. It is no coincidence that the language encompasses many meanings – for which there are no male equivalents – which are designed to quickly put us in our place: embittered, hysterical, nagging or shrill, spinsterish, strident. These are precisely the responses we can expect under patriarchy and which we must be prepared to dispute. 'Bitch' and 'witch' and even 'spinster' have been used against us in this way in the past but we have been partially successful in reclaiming them, in investing them with our own meanings, in validating them among women so that they no longer mean what they were intended to mean and no longer work as they used to.

Investing the language with one's own different and positive meanings is a priority for all oppressed groups. The English language contains almost as many derogatory words for blacks as for women and it is a constantly undermining task to structure one's world with a language that daily and deliberately denies one's humanity, and to use language in a manner that the dominant white group deems appropriate. So the language and its use has to be changed; there is no alternative if one seeks to throw off one's oppression.

However, not for a minute would I want to suggest that new meanings and new forms of language use lead directly to a redistribution of wealth. That 'bitch', 'witch' and 'spinster' no longer mean what they used to does not lead to increased employment opportunities for women or help to reduce women's economic dependence. And it is no solution – and it is an insult – to suggest that women who are struggling for food and shelter – or to avoid violence – would be better off if they thought more about language and used it with greater perception and perspicacity.

But it is to suggest that as human beings – with consciousness and with the ability to construct reality – bread alone is not sufficient. We may be well fed, warm and free from physical violence but we are liable to become insane in solitary confinement or when deprived of the opportunity to communicate and create our world through language. It is to suggest that economic independence of its own is no guarantee of psychological independence, that it is no guarantee of women's liberation. It is possible that if all women were financially liberated, patriarchy could still prevail. The colonization of our minds is not necessarily overthrown by an increase in material resources: we have the evidence of some women who are economically independent and who are influential within the male-defined system and reality, and not a few of them show signs of perpetuating that system and reality which has rewarded them, instead of using their power to change, so that women are accommodated on equal terms with men.

It is not a case of either/or: of either linguistic determinism or economic determinism. It is that both language *and* material resources have been used by the dominant group to structure women's oppression, and they are interconnected. One cannot be transformed without the other if women are to be liberated and patriarchy is to be prevented from persisting.

## · I ·

# To Believe or not to Believe ... Language/Sex Research

### The deficient woman

As with so much of the knowledge we have inherited, women appear as deficient – or deviant – in studies of language and sex. And, as with so many other research areas in the social sciences, when the assumptions on which this knowledge has been constructed are examined, it becomes increasingly clear that this female deficiency often has its origins in the research premises and procedures themselves. By beginning with the initial assumption that there is something *wrong* with women's language, research procedures have frequently been biased in favour of men. The presentation of skewed findings has helped to establish the deficiency of women's language and in conveniently circular logic has thereby helped to confirm the validity of the initial premise that women's language is inferior.

Susanne Langer (1976) has emphasized that the way a question is formed determines in part the answer that can be given; in language/sex research there are numerous questions which have been formulated in terms of the inadequacy of women's language, with the result that many of the 'answers' are confined to measurements of that inadequacy. It seems that all that is necessary is a basic assumption that there is something *wrong* with women and it is possible to find in their language – by legitimated, 'objective' means – a vast array of peculiarities which help to justify their subordinate position in society. One of the contributions that feminism has made to language/sex research has been that of exposing this bias against women ('bias'

7

hardly seems an appropriate term given the degree to which research has been geared to find in favour of men) and of framing questions which are *not* conceptualized in terms of deficiency, and which, therefore, will not automatically lead to answers which support the case that there is something *wrong* with women, and their language.

It is political choice on the part of feminists to find in favour of women but this is no different from non-feminist researchers who have exercised their political choice by almost always finding in favour of men. The difference is that feminism acknowledges its politics.

Social beliefs about women have been brought into the research process and in traditional studies there are few unexpected entries in the inventory of women's linguistic deficiencies. Robin Lakoff (1975) has outlined what she thinks are the commonly held salient characteristics of women's language, and she states that women *lack* authority and seriousness, they *lack* conviction and confidence. In her view, in comparison with the (ostensibly) forceful and effective language of men, women are tentative, hesitant, even trivial, and are therefore 'deficient'.

It would be unfortunate − and unjust − to be unduly critical of Lakoff's findings on women's language for she was one of the early feminists who began to explore − and to make acceptable − such research. Her study, *Language and Woman's Place*, has been influential; it has also been constrained by some of the sexist assumptions of the linguistic paradigm in which she worked. But as her hypotheses and theories serve to illustrate some of the ways in which the deficiency of women's language has been constructed, I am using them to generalize about the deficiencies of language/sex research.

For example, Lakoff accepts that men's language is superior and she assumes that this is a feature of their linguistic performance and not of their sex. She also compares women to a male standard. She takes male language as the norm and measures women against it, and one outcome of this procedure is to classify any difference on the part of women as 'deviation'. Given these practices, it is unlikely that Lakoff could have arrived at positive findings for women, for any differences revealed, whether a product of language or of sex, would be predisposed to interpretation as yet more evidence of female deficiency.

Perhaps one of the best illustrations of language/sex research in action is that of the work which has been undertaken on the use of the tag question. When the starting premise is that women lack the forcefulness and effectiveness of men's language, then hypotheses and explanations are formulated to account for female hesitancy. The search to locate the vehicle which carries these features begins and Lakoff speculated that it was the tag question which permitted women to exercise hesitancy and qualification.

Linguistically there is some difficulty in defining a tag question: it is supposed to be a form which is half-way between a declaration and a question. It is a question which is added on to the end of a statement, as in 'It's a nice day, *isn't it*?' or 'I'll be home by midnight, *all right*?' and it is supposedly a means whereby the user can make a declaration without being assertive. (One of the difficulties with tag questions is that it is almost impossible to differentiate grammatically the 'tentative' ones from the 'forceful' ones, as in, for example, 'You won't do that again, *will you*?') However, despite the inherent difficulty in categorizing tag questions, it appears that some researchers were sufficiently convinced of the merits of the argument to investigate empirically women's use of the tag question. The results were disappointing. In those studies where the results were reported, men were found to use more tag questions than women (Dubois and Crouch, 1975).

It is at this point that some of the distortions in the research process become even more interesting. First, it is possible that we do not know just how frequently women were tested for tag questions and found wanting, for it is possible – even probable – that to some researchers such results might have been considered 'unhelpful', the study deemed to be a failure, and the findings unreported. Like many other disciplines, linguistics is not known for its abundance of publications on unconfirmed hypotheses. Second, there is the distinct possibility of a double-standard at work here and that a tag question is being defined as the *female* use of a particular form; when men use the same form it is called something else. This would help to explain the discrepancy between the beliefs about women's language and the empirical reality. But it is the third point which I find the most fascinating and the most revealing.

Although the initial hypothesis was that tag questions contained the key to hesitancy and tentativeness, the discovery that men use more of them has not been accompanied by a single suggestion that it is *men* who might lack confidence in their language.

In a society which exercised no bias on the grounds of sex, the finding that men used more tag questions than women could have been seen as significant, could have been enthusiastically reported in the literature as a breakthrough and could have resulted in numerous hypotheses about the deviancy or deficiency of men's language. This exposes one of the most serious flaws in language/sex research. Experiments and theories have been constructed on the premise that women's language is inferior and by some strange 'logic', where this premise has remained unproven, the result is *not* the rejection of the initial premise, but the 'explanation' that researchers have been 'looking in the wrong place'. The belief in the deficiency of women's language can remain unchallenged *regardless* of the research outcome.

The belief that there is something wrong with the language of more than half the members of society has been reinforced rather than refuted in language/sex research despite the paucity of empirical findings to support such a contention (Kramer *et al.*, 1978). In a society where women are devalued it is not surprising that their language should be devalued, but few have suggested (apart from feminists) that this might be a function of judgments based on sex and not on language. Because of the deficiencies in research – and not in women – the findings in this area need to be treated with considerable caution.

Language is not an insignificant dimension. To be inferior when it comes to language is frequently to be discounted. In a hierarchical society predicated on divisions and inequality and constructed on a concept of 'leaders' (and necessarily 'followers'), it is not coincidence that the language of women is held to be lacking in authority, forcefulness, effectiveness, persuasiveness. Language is one means by which women may be disqualified on ostensibly 'objective' grounds and their oppression translated into 'rational' argument. Whether sex differences in language are real or imaginary, or whether they are products of sex or society, have not been priority questions in language/sex research, and it needs to be noted that it is in the interests of a male supremacist society to promote prejudice against women's language. Some linguists have been more than helpful in this enterprise.

Almost since the acceptance of linguistics as a respected field of study it has been possible to quote 'authorities' – whose claims have been legitimated and are therefore enshrined in the literature – on the deficiencies of women's language. Otto Jespersen (1922), for example, detailed these deficiencies in disparaging terms and claimed that women, by virtue of their sex 'shrank from coarse and gross expressions' and had a 'preference for ... veiled and indirect expressions' which precluded them from being as effective as men. But it appears that it was not sufficient to itemize women's inadequacies: it was also necessary to protect the language – and one must ask *whose* language it is in this frame of reference – from their influence.

According to Jespersen, women had a debilitating effect upon the language (p. 246) and it was reasonable for men, 'certainly with great justice [to] object that there is a danger of the language becoming languid and insipid if we are to content ourselves with women's expressions'. Jespersen maintained that 'vigour and vividness count for something' and because, in his opinion, women lacked such qualities and could make no such contribution, their language was perceived as a threat.

Jespersen, an esteemed and still oft-quoted linguist, offered no convincing evidence for his forceful and authoritative pronouncements but his own deficiencies have been largely overlooked by many of his modern counterparts who have continued the quest to document the negative features of women's language and to assume that *the* language is the particular preserve of men.

Some male linguists have been quite explicit in their assertion that the language (or parts thereof) belongs to males. Stuart Flexner (1960) for example, confined himself to a study of vernacular words coined by men (slang) and then concluded that it was males who were the makers and innovators of language. For his purposes, women had no claim to language and as he made no attempt to study women – and any possible coinages they may have produced – there was little likelihood of his assumption being challenged. Brian Foster (1976) also reveals a significant 'slip' when he documents some of the changes which have occurred in English and states that 'Some psychologists should really tell us what envies and unfulfilled longings cause women to steal the names of men's clothes' (p. 142). His case that women have stolen the names of clothes that manifest little sex typing is unconvincing, but his assumption that the language is owned by men – for one can only steal from an owner – is quite revealing.

Although, on one hand, it is justifiable for women to protest that these assumptions about language as male property are the manifestations of sexist bias, on the other hand the case for the English language being male property can also be justified. It does not, however, take the form which gives consensus to the property rights of males but rather exposes their appropriation of language.

## A man's language

To suggest that English is a man's language is frequently to arouse the indignation of some people who feel secure in stating the obvious; that is, because women use the language it cannot therefore be the property of males. But it is perfectly feasible to suggest that women have been obliged to use a language which is not of their own making. For example, Cora Kaplan (1976) has pointed out that even though advantages would accrue to men in a patriarchal society if women were not permitted to use the language at all, there would also be disadvantages, and the compromise – constructed by males – has been to allow women to express themselves, but only in male terms. In this way, women remain 'outsiders', borrowers of the language. This analysis is shared, in differing degrees, by many feminists, among them Sheila Rowbotham (1973a) who has said that this borrowing restricts women 'by affirming their own dependence upon the words of the powerful' (p. 32), and male property rights to the language are reinforced rather than weakened by women's use of language. So although it is readily demonstrable that both sexes use the language, this cannot be taken as sufficient evidence that both sexes stand in the same relationship to that language. On the contrary, it is also demonstrable (though for many reasons not quite as evident) that language is primarily the product of male effort and that historically – and currently – men have held greater 'rights' to language.

That the English language has been literally man made and that it is still primarily under male control is the substance of this book. This monopoly over language is one of the means by which males have ensured their own primacy, and consequently have ensured the invisibility or 'other' nature of females, and this primacy is perpetuated while women continue to use, unchanged, the language which we have inherited. Rather than unmask some of the mechanisms whereby the male supremacist (or, in Kaplan's terms, patriarchal) society is maintained through language, research has sometimes assisted in securing and sustaining these mechanisms. Studies on sex differences in language use have too frequently supported male supremacy and studies on sexism and language have too seldom seen through the mechanisms. But research is also a social product and it is therefore not surprising that a male supremacist society should design research which is bound to male supremacist considerations. The parameters of the question help to ordain the parameters of the answer.

# The legacy

Language/sex research has been split into two discrete and usually unconnected areas and this split has not aided feminist analysis of language. It is not surprising that this division should have arisen, for historically there has been a linguistic tradition of separating the language as a system from the people who use it, and this tradition is reflected in the development of the dual areas of sexism in language (where language is studied as an abstract system without reference to the context) and sex differences in language (where language use is examined). The relatively recent growth of sociolinguistics has been a response to the inadequacies and inaccuracies which are bound to occur when this division is maintained; it was because this division was no longer considered helpful that sociolinguists began to collapse the traditional dichotomy and to focus their attention on the social context in which the language is used. Out of this came new insights into Black language and language and class.

It is worth noting that approximately ten years ago there was widespread belief that there was something *wrong* with the language of Blacks and of the working class, but that within those ten years the explanations have shifted so that there is now general consensus that the 'deficiency' lies not in Blacks or the working class but in society. We can now appreciate that what has been termed 'correct' English is nothing other than the blatant legitimation of the white middle-class code. Harold Rosen (1975) has made it clear that requiring working-class people to use the middle-class code is tantamount to requiring them to use an alien language – a language not of their own making. Chris Searle (1973) has made the point equally clearly in relation to Blacks who are required to use 'the white man's language' which consistently denies and denigrates them.

The outcome of these studies concerned with class and ethnic considerations has been twofold. They have helped to foster appreciation for the codes of different groups and they have also helped to expose some of the means by which dominant group(s) construct and perpetuate their power. There are no studies which I know that separate classism and racism in language from class and ethnic analyses of society, and this is where they stand in sharp contrast to language/sex research where in general this duality and separation still exist.

It is something of a puzzle that language/sex research should have persisted with these hindering divisions. Certainly they have been unprofitable from a feminist point of view. While these divisions are maintained and while there is virtually no cross reference between them, many of the crucial questions which relate language to society go unasked and unanswered. Whether the English language is a *man's* language – in the same way that it is the language of the white middle class – remains a question which cannot be answered fully within either area. Whether the language itself plays a role in any possible sex differences in language use also remains outside the province of either area and therefore shares a similar fate. Questions of the relationship between language and power hover at the periphery of research, unable to become central as they do not conveniently fall into one or other research area.

Because I am not convinced that any useful purpose is served (from a feminist point of view) in keeping the two research areas apart, I propose to collapse them and bring them together. The pattern of male control of language emerges more clearly when they are integrated. But as existing research findings are presented in the divided form I am obliged to review them separately. Wherever possible I will make the cross references which indicate what has been 'left out' primarily as a result of what I would term the 'divide and rule' strategy which has characterized language/sex research.

## Sexism in language

One of the basic principles of feminism is that society has been constructed with a bias which favours males; one of the basic principles of feminists who are concerned with language is that this bias can be located in the language. The claim is that 'English is biased in favour of the male in both syntax and semantics' (Schneider and Foss, 1977:1). Broadly speaking, semantics refers to the meanings available within the language, while syntax refers to the form (the sentence structure) in which those meanings are conveyed. In this section I am primarily concerned with semantics and am leaving the discussion of syntax for chapter 5.

This bias in favour of males has most frequently been referred to as *sexism* in language but other terms have also been used. Ann Bodine (1975) for example makes use of the term *androcentric* (male centred) in her effort to expose the male bias in the formulation of some of the rules of the prescriptive grammarians, and Joan Roberts (1976) uses the term *masculist* to label the male bias in language and culture.

In designating the world view, the order under which we live and in which language is integral, Cora Kaplan (1976) uses the term *patriarchal*. Although all of these terms share common features and all are attempts to label a previously unnamed and uncategorized phenomenon, they do possess subtly different shades of meaning and, for clarification, I am going to indulge in a semantic exercise and outline what I mean by my usages of them. The two terms which I favour and which represent distinctions are those of *sexism* and *patriarchy*. I accept Kaplan's concept of patriarchy as the order under which we live, an order characterized by male dominance and the means – both actual and symbolic – of perpetuating that dominance. I use sexism to denote particular manifestations of that order so that examples of the bias in favour of males – in language or sociology for instance – is sexism.

That there is sexism in the English language is now well substantiated and generally accepted although there are of course some individuals who will dispute – or more often trivialize – its existence. Currently, the question is more one of degree – and significance – than acceptance. Various definitions have been put forward and one criterion which has been used is that 'the English language is sexist in so far as it relegates women to a secondary and inferior place in society' (Berger and Kachuk, 1977:3). This criterion can be readily met by the simplest exercises since all that is required is a list of terms which relegate women to a subordinate position. Some of the early research on sexism and language was of this order as inventories of words were compiled which indicated that not only were there more words for males but that there were more positive words; Julia Stanley (1977) pointed out that there was no linguistic reason for this to be the case. Stanley also found that many of the words for women had sexual overtones and despite the fact that there were more words for men, of the smaller sample assigned to women there were 220 words for a sexually promiscuous female and only 20 for a sexually promiscuous male (Stanley, 1973). This would seem to indicate that the language – as a system – embodies sexual inequality and that it is not women who enjoy the advantage.

Such word counting was a necessary and important task in the preliminary research aimed at documenting the existence of sexism in language, but it is also limited. Such activities – despite the number of lists and the number of items – afford few new insights after the establishment of the fundamental inequities in terms of resources. Having documented the existence of sexism in language what was required was an explanation of the origin and function of these terms, and unfortunately this has not always been the direction which research has taken.

What is the relationship between women's devaluation in language and their devaluation in society? What role have women played in the construction of terms which demean, deny and diminish them? Have women been instrumental in constructing sexism in language, in coining sexually debased meanings for themselves? These questions have often remained peripheral to research on sexism and language. The emphasis has been on description rather than analysis, and references to the social (in our case, patriarchal) order in which they have arisen have often been confined to the last paragraph of a report, where they have been accompanied by the suggestion that 'more work is required in this area'. By and large the discussion of the significance of sexism in language has been superficial.


## The semantic derogation of women

Muriel Schulz (1975a) took one of the first steps in relating sexism in language to society when she incorporated both descriptive and analytical frames of reference in her investigation and suggested that there was a systematic basis to linguistic sexism. To Schulz, it was not mere coincidence that there were more positive words for males in the language, nor was it an accident that there were so many negative words for females with no semantic equivalent for males. These manifestations of a patriarchal order were rule governed and the rule is that words which are marked for females, which are used in association with females, become 'pejorated'. Because, irrespective of origin, or intent, words which are marked female are marked negative, Schulz referred to the systematic, semantic derogation of women.

Others had already noted the way in which words become negative when they shift into the female sphere, but their efforts had often stopped short at observation. Few attempts had been made to link the examples of sexism with patriarchal order. Miller and Swift (1976), for example, observed that once a boy's name became popular as a girl's name it lost its appeal and usually ceased being used for boys. Names such as Shirley, Leslie, Beverley, Evelyn and Sidney all began as boys' names (and were positive), were then used as girls' names (and became negative), and now are rarely used for boys. Miller and Swift argue convincingly that 'once a name or a word becomes associated with women, it is rarely again considered suitable for males' (p. 6) and they also observed that there is no reciprocity: the process does not operate in reverse.

The word for women assumed negative connotations even where it designated the same state or condition as it did for men. *Spinster* and *bachelor*, for example, designate an unmarried adult but when this word is marked for males it is positive while when it is marked for females it is negative. The only variable is that of sex and this variable is crucial to the semantic system.

Whereas other studies made random reference to this 'double-standard' Schulz made the connection between sex and semantics. She documents the working of this semantic rule – which of course did not descend from the heavens 'ready made' but which was evolved by the human beings who constructed the language.

The relationship between sex and semantics is not occasional; it is not confined to such blatant examples as that of spinster and bachelor but is all-pervasive, extending to *all* words that are marked female. To illustrate this point, Schulz takes the case of *man* and *woman* and says that no insult is implied if you refer to a female as an *old man*: it is inaccurate but the assumption is that there has been a mistake in identity. This is not the case if you call a male an *old woman*; it is also inaccurate but the assumption is that you intend insult. *Woman* does not share equal status with *man* (linguistically or otherwise) because, in accordance with the semantic rule, *woman* has become pejorated while *man* has remained pure and untainted, protected by its semantic association with the male.

Schulz makes use of many comparable terms to illustrate the working of this semantic rule. She investigates the use of titles and shows that while male titles have retained their original positive meanings, female titles have frequently undergone a dramatic 'downhill slide', ending more often than not with sexually debased meanings. It is by this process that more positive words are created for males.

Although *Lord* still preserves its initial meaning, *Lady* has undergone a process of 'democratic levelling' and is no longer reserved for women of high rank. (Robin Lakoff (1975) makes a case for *lady* having become a term of insult but her argument appears to be relevant only for American usage.) *Baronet* also functions in its original sense whereas its equivalent, *Dame*, has come to be used derogatively (again, particularly in American usage). There has been some pejoration of *governor* – in cockney usage for example – but it still serves in its original meaning whereas *governess* has come to be used almost exclusively in the context of young children and not in the context that Queen Elizabeth I used it to denote her own power and sovereignty.

Little stigma seems to have become attached to *courtier*, while it is almost surprising to find that *courtesan* was once an equivalent term, so extensive are the sexual connotations it has acquired. *Sir* is still used as a title – and as a form of respect – and, unlike *Madam*, does not refer to someone who keeps a brothel. *Master*, too, has lost little of its force whereas *Mistress* has acquired almost exclusively sexual connotations and is no longer associated with the person who accepted responsibility and exercised control over the varied and essential tasks of a household. In drawing attention to the loss of parity between these terms, Robin Lakoff (1975) has pointed out that there is considerable discrepancy in meaning between an *old master* and an *old mistress*.

With these titles it can be argued that such terms did *not* have parity to begin with partly because females have always been inferior to males and therefore few insights can be gained from the documentation of contemporary asymmetry. Because of the historical subordination of women and the social (patriarchal) practice of inheriting through the male line, it was the *Lord* who inherited the title and who took his *Lady*. But leaving aside these considerations (and their ramifications for female family names), there are still instances – past and present – where it was the female who was the 'genuine' title-holder (usually in the absence of a male heir) and who conferred *her* status on her spouse. Elizabeth II is no less a 'genuine' monarch than her father, but whereas *King* retains its positive meanings, *Queen* has also developed debased sexual connotations.

The case for the systematic pejoration of female terms does not, however, rest solely on titles. Muriel Schulz uses this as but one example of her thesis. All words – regardless of their origin – which are associated with females acquire negative connotations, because this is a fundamental semantic 'rule' in a society which constructs male supremacy. When the same word shifts from being positive to being negative once it has moved from referring to a male to referring to a female, then the 'logic' lies not in the word (and what it represents) but in the sex. The way meaning is created in our society depends upon dividing the world into positive-masculine and negative-feminine.

Schulz provides numerous examples of this semantic rule at work and although Robin Lakoff (1975) does not posit the same underlying thesis as Schulz, her documentation supports Schulz's theory. Lakoff has noted that whereas metaphors and labels are more likely to have a wide frame of reference when applied to men, the same metaphors and labels are likely to narrow and assume sexual connotations when applied to women. One of the examples which Lakoff quotes is that of *professional*: the use of such a term, be it applied to men or women, should on 'logical' grounds be 'completely parallel semantically'. But when the sex changes, so too does the meaning, indicating the sex dimension of semantics (1975: 30):

(a) He's a professional
(b) She's a professional

Hearing and knowing no more about the subject of the discourse than this, what would one assume about them in each case? Certainly in (a) the normal conclusion the casual eavesdropper would come to was that 'he' was a doctor or a lawyer or a member of one of the other professions. But it is much less likely that one would draw a similar conclusion in (b). Rather, the first assumption that most speakers of English seem to make is that 'she' is a prostitute, literally or figuratively speaking.

The only way to 'make meaning' of these discrepancies in meaning is to posit the existence of a semantic rule which determines that *any* symbol which is associated with the female must assume negative (and frequently sexual — which is also significant) connotations. Even with words such as *tramp*, for example, there is a shift to negative and sexual meanings when it is applied to females.

## Plus and minus male

Julia Stanley is among the feminists who have developed a theoretical framework for this phenomenon in language, and she has suggested that this difference which is manifested in the language is the outcome of differentiating the sexes in semantic terms on the basis of plus and minus. Stanley has good evidence for this hypothesis: one linguist, Geoffrey Leech (1968), in developing a set of categories for English, actually uses *plus* male and *minus* male to distinguish masculine from feminine. Stanley outlines this semantic rule (1975: 29):

In the case of gender, [minus male] must be the significant feature of girl and woman, because females are defined traditionally as 'non males' since males are the standard of comparison for the entire species, and women are the beings who contrast with them.

Leech's analysis, that the world can be divided into male and minus male, has been justified on the grounds of simplicity because almost all animate nouns in English are masculine. This being the case, there are implications for females for it means that most of the semantic space of the language is occupied by males.

Masculinity is the unmarked form: the assumption is that the world is male unless proven otherwise. Femininity is the marked form: it is the proof of otherwise. Numerous feminists have also claimed that the male is the unmarked or assumed form (Toth, 1970) and the writers of the poster, 'The Feminist English Dictionary' (1973), indicate what role the male lexicographers (dictionary-makers) have played in reinforcing this semantic rule. It was men who made up the language and recorded it, says Alleen Pace Nilsen (1977:34), and they persistently defined themselves as occupying the positive semantic space.

This accumulated evidence led Julia Stanley (1977) to posit the theory of negative semantic space for women. It is not just that the vocabulary is divided into two unequal portions with *less* nouns to refer to females, argues Stanley, but that this smaller number of words also encompasses that which is of *lesser* value. Words which are marked for female refer to specifically female activities which are evaluated from a male point of view (p. 66):

When women attempt to move outside the lesser spheres which have been allocated to them they do not join the ranks of those who enjoy positive status because they carry their femaleness, their minus maleness, with them. This is what Stanley has referred to as negative semantic space for no matter what women do they are still branded as women and therefore cannot develop positive meanings and definitions of themselves. According to Stanley, semantic space does not exist for women because it is already occupied by the male sex. 'When a woman becomes a professional in one of the fields usually reserved for males,' says Stanley, 'she does not move into the corresponding semantic space covered by the noun conventionally used as its label.' Instead, she must signify that the norm, the positive, does not apply and so she becomes a *lady* doctor, a *female* surgeon, a *woman* lawyer, or else, in less prestigious occupations, a *waitress*, a *stewardess*, a *majorette*. There is no space for a woman to be positive. This problem is appreciated by many women and the following transcript from a discussion of women writers illustrates their recognition of the difficulty:[1]

> 'It's useless trying to say I'm a writer ... and a good one. I nearly said "as good as a male". And that's what I'm talking about. By definition you can't be a good *female* writer, it's a contradiction of terms. And the more you try to establish yourself as a writer the more you have to move towards being "as good as a male". That's exactly what I want to get away from. What happens if you are as *good* as a female? It's laughable isn't it. It pisses me off ... [mimics] "Excuse me, I want a job on your paper. I'm an excellent *female* writer. I have all the *female virtues* ... in abundance. I'm silly, irrational, irresponsible ..." etc., you know the rest. You just can't capitalize on being female. That way no good lies, you have to show that you have *male virtues*, and then, of course, you're trapped. Because you are *not* a male! You're a substitute male.'(1)

For women who do not wish to be compared to men there is 'nowhere to go' in the language. This is one way of expressing the concept of negative semantic space for women.

Julia Stanley's thesis fits comfortably with Muriel Schulz's analysis as both recognize that regardless of origin words which are marked for females are marked negatively: and women – no matter what they do, no matter what names they coin to describe themselves or their activities, cannot step outside this classification of themselves as negative. Even where they venture into areas which have ostensibly conferred high status upon males, females find themselves still labelled negative, as minus males, as 'not the real thing'. There is only negative semantic space for females in the English language.

Establishing that this classification system of plus male/minus male is at the root of divisions structured by language is not often a task which lends itself to empirical observation. It is difficult to 'observe' language in the process of production. But there is one language where this is not the case, and that is Esperanto. Esperanto was devised with the intentional aim of constructing a new language which – ideally – could encompass the meanings and meet the needs of *all* human beings. Susan Robbins (1978) has pointed out, however, that it was also an attempt to reserve positive semantic space for males because it was

1 The numbers in parentheses refer to the transcripts at the end of the book.

based on the assumption that the normal human being was a male one.

In Esperanto all nouns end in 'O', but 'O' also signifies *male*. If the name refers to a female then it must be marked to show a deviation from the norm (in the same way that suffixes like *ess*, *ette*, etc. signify deviation from the norm in English). So *patro* is father, and with the inclusion of '*in*' – the female marker – becomes *patrino* the mother; *fratro* is brother and *fratrino* is sister. The normal or 'full' category is a male one, which with additional information signals that the norm does not apply and that this is a lesser entity.

Of the creator of this language, Zamenhof, Susan Robbins states:

> Since Zamenhof was a dedicated humanist I can only conclude that the sexism in Esperanto was not apparent to him; he, like many speakers of Indo-European languages, simply assumed that the basic form of nouns of course indicates males since males *are* the paradigm for humanity. Femaleness is a marked trait; in Esperanto females are always in negative semantic space (1978:9).

There are many reasons for suggesting that the rules are the same in English. The semantic derogation of women is the result of females being classified as minus male and consigned only negative semanitc space.

The evidence which has accumulated in the area of negative semantic space and the pejoration of female terms cannot be ignored. Arguing that there are currently some positive words for women does not refute the existence of the semantic rule; it is also debatable whether such words are indeed positive (Stanley (1977) and see chapter 5), for history suggests that they will not remain positive. Some words in our language – such as words of endearment for women – were presumably coined with the intention of portraying women positively but they too reveal that they have been consigned to negative semantic space and have been systematically pejorated.

Words such as *biddy* and *tart* have shifted dramatically in meaning since they were first used positively as terms of endearment. *Tart* meant a small pie or pastry and its first metaphorical application was as a term of affection and warmth. Not surprisingly in a society where women are evaluated as sexual objects, the meaning shifted to that of a young woman who was sexually desirable, and then – of course – to a woman of careless morals. Finally and currently it refers to women of the street. *Whore* once meant a lover of either sex (and was not negative) and *slut* and *slattern* referred to 'a person who is negligent of *his* appearance' (Schulz, 1975a:68–9). *Harlot* was 'a fellow of either sex' and in Middle English the reference was more frequently to males, and *wench* was also 'a child of either sex' (p. 70). Be they affectionate – or even neutral terms such as *child* – the crucial factor in determining whether they represent positive or negative values is sex.

The semantic rule which has been responsible for the manifestation of sexism in the language can be simply stated: there are two fundamental categories, *male* and *minus male*. To be linked with male is to be linked to a range of meanings which are positive and good: to be linked to minus male is to be linked to the *absence* of those qualities, that is, to be decidedly negative and usually sexually debased (for further discussion see chapter 5). The semantic structure of the English language reveals a great deal about what it means to be female in a patriarchal order (note that female is not even an autonomous category but a derivation of the male: it is minus male) because *by definition* males are assigned the positive attributes.

Unless irony or insult is intended it is usually a violation of the semantic rule to refer to males with terms that are marked for minus males. There is a jarring of images if and when people make such a mistake. It is all right, for example, to call a mixed sex group 'guys' or 'men' but it is a mistake – and an insult – to refer to a group which contains even one male as 'gals' or 'women'. You 'may call a woman a *bachelor* without implying abuse', states Muriel Schulz, but do the opposite and 'call a man a *spinster* or *an old maid*' and you are violating the semantic rules – perhaps deliberately if you intend abuse – for you are saying that 'he is a prim, nervous person who frets over inconsequential details' (p. 65).

There are numerous examples of the way in which there is no loss of prestige when females are referred to in male terms but there is a loss of prestige when males are referred to in female terms. In a society where male primacy must be carefully cultivated, semantics makes a substantial and significant contribution in structuring this supremacy.

The semantic derogation of women fulfils a dual function: it helps to construct female inferiority and it also helps to confirm it. The process is not a simple, linear one, but a more complex, interactive and dialectical one. In a society where women are devalued the words which refer to them – not surprisingly – assume negative connotations. But because the options for defining women are confined to negative terms, because their meanings are primarily those of minus male, women continue to be devalued. By such an interrelated process is the subordination of women in part created and sustained. It is a semantic contradiction to formulate representations of women's autonomy or strength and so it remains unencoded and women are deprived of the opportunity to formulate positive representations of themselves.

It is unlikely that women were instrumental in achieving this end.

## The male line

Studies of language have revealed that semantics is only one of the forms through which sexism operates (for the role played by syntax, see chapter 5). One of the other features of English language practices which is inherently sexist is the use of names. In our society 'only men have real names' in that their names are permanent and they have 'accepted the permanency of their names as one of the rights of being male' (Miller and Swift, 1976:14). This has both practical and psychological ramifications for the construction – and maintenance – of male supremacy.

Practically it means that women's family names do not count and that there is one more device for making women invisible. Fathers pass their names on to their sons and the existence of daughters can be denied when in the absence of a male heir it is said that a family 'dies out'. One other direct result of this practice of only taking cognizance of the male name has been to facilitate the development of history as the story of the male line, because it becomes almost impossible to trace the ancestry of women – particularly if they do not come into the male-defined categories of importance.

Very little is known about women, says Virginia Woolf (1972), for 'the history of England is the history of the male line' (p. 41); this point was brought home to Jill Liddington and Jill Norris (1978) when they undertook to document the story of women's suffrage in Lancashire for 'this vital contribution had been largely neglected by historians' (p. 11). They had difficulty with sources, and one difficulty was not one which would be encountered in tracing men (1978:17):

Sometimes we seemed to be forever chasing down blind alleys. For instance, one of the most active women, Helen Silcock, a weavers' union leader from Wigan, seemed to disappear after 1902. We couldn't think why, until we came across a notice of 'congratulations to Miss Silcock on her marriage to Mr Fairhurst' in a little known labour journal, the *Women's Trade Union Review* ... it was an object lesson for us in the difficulties of tracing women activists.

It is also an extremely useful device for eliminating women from history and for making it exceedingly difficult to perceive a continuum and develop a tradition.

When females have no right to 'surnames', to family names of their own, the concept of women as the property of men is subtly reinforced (and this is of course assisted by the title *Mrs*). Currently many women are changing their names and instead of taking the name of either their father or their husband they are coining new, autonomous names for themselves; for example, Cheris Kramer has become Cheris Kramarae, Julia Stanley has become Julia Penelope – there are almost countless examples of this change. A common practice has become that of taking the first name of a close female friend or relative – such as mother – as the new family name (for example, Janet Robyn, Elizabeth Sarah). When asked why she had legally dropped her surname and retained her first two given names, Margaret Sandra stated that a 'surname' was intended as an indication of the 'sire' and was so closely linked socially with the ownership of women that there was no 'surname' that she found acceptable.

Although attempts have been made to trivialize these new naming activities among women, such activities are serious and they do undermine patriarchal practices. At the very least they raise consciousness about the role men's names have played in the subordination of women, and at best they confound traditional patriarchal classification schemes which have not operated in women's interest. I have been told that it makes it very difficult to 'pigeon-hole' women, to 'place' them, if they persist with this neurotic practice of giving themselves new names. One male stated quite sincerely that it was becoming 'jolly difficult to work out whether women were married these days because of the ridiculous practice of not taking their husband's names'. In order to operate in the world, however, it has *never* been necessary to know from a name whether someone is married or single, as women can testify. Men have not thought that *not* changing their name upon marriage should present difficulties to women and once more the bias of language practices is revealed.

But many males are confused, and not without cause. The language has helped to create the representation of females as sex objects; it has also helped to signal when a sex object is not available and is the property of another male. The patriarchal order has been maintained by such devices and when women consciously and intentionally abolish them men have reason to feel insecure; they do not however have reason to protest.

There are also other 'by-products' of this process of permitting the permanency of names only to males. Miller and Swift (1976) ask whether it is because of the unenduring nature of female family names that much more emphasis is placed on their first names. Whatever the reason, it is clear that males are more frequently addressed by their family name (and title) and women by their first name. Psychologically this can also work to produce sexual asymmetry.

The use of first names can be evidence of intimacy or friendship but in such circumstances the practice, generally speaking, has to be reciprocal. When one party is referred to by the first name, and the other by the family name and title, it is usually evidence that one has more power than the other. So, for example, the employer may be Mr Smith and the employees Bill and Mary. The practice of those 'in power' referring to those 'out of power' by their first names – while still retaining the use of their own title and family name – is widespread and applies to both sexes in a hierarchical society. But there are still instances where both sexes occupy comparable positions but where males are referred to by their family names and women referred to by their first names, indicating the operation of yet another hierarchy.

This is frequently illustrated in the media. Even where there are both male and female contestants on some 'quiz' shows, the women are more likely to be addressed by their first names. Interviewers are also more inclined to use women's first names. News items are more likely to make reference to women by their first name (and of course their colouring, for example, blonde or brunette, and their age and marital status) and the usually male presenter of 'talk-back' shows indicates a decided disposition to discriminate between the callers in this way.

But it is not confined to the media. I have never heard a male complain that a medical practitioner addressed him (perhaps patronizingly) by his first name at the first consultation, yet this protest is often made by women. It would, however, break the social rules which govern subordination if women were to respond by addressing medical practitioners by their first names. This is precisely why I think they should do so.

Regardless of the reason for the development of this practice of calling women by their first names in formal situations, it assists in making 'visible' the subordination of the female.

The practice of labelling women as married or single also serves supremely sexist ends. It conveniently signals who is 'fair game' from the male point of view. There is tension between the representation of women as sex objects and the male ownership rights over women and this has been resolved by an explicit and most visible device of designating the married status of women. As women do not 'own' men, and as men have many dimensions apart from their sexual ones in a patriarchal order, it has not been necessary to make male marital status visible. On the contrary, it could hinder rather than help male operations in the world so it has never appeared as a 'logical' proposition.

Contrary to the belief of many people, the current usage of *Miss* and *Mrs* is relatively recent, for until the beginning of the nineteenth century the title *Miss* was usually reserved for young females while *Mrs* designated mature women. Marital status played no role in the use of these terms. How and why this usage changed is a matter of some speculation,[2] but there is nothing speculative about the ends that it serves.

It labels women for the convenience of men. It also labels those whom men do not want. To be over thirty and *Miss* Jones in times but recently passed was an advertisement of failure and an invitation for ridicule.

The question arises as to why more women have not objected to this offensive labelling in the past. Why was there not greater protest when in the late nineteenth century women were required to surrender even

2 Miller and Swift (1976) suggest that the use of *Miss* and *Mrs* to designate marital status was a response to some of the pressures created by the industrial revolution, which disrupted the familiar patterns of small communities in which relationships were readily known. There was no need for this usage prior to the industrial revolution for a woman's marital status was already known in the community in which she lived, but with the migration of population that occurred at the onset of the revolution and with women's entry into the workforce outside the home or local community,

a simple means of distinguishing married from unmarried women was needed [for men] and it served a double purpose: it supplied at least a modicum of information about women's sexual availability, and it applied not so subtle pressure toward marriage by lumping single women with the young and inexperienced. Attached to anyone over the age of eighteen, Miss came in time to suggest the unattractive or socially undesirable qualities associated with such labels as *old maid* and *spinster* or that dreadful word *barren*. So the needs of patriarchy were served when a woman's availability for her primary role as helper and sexual partner was made an integral part of her identity – in effect, a part of her name (p. 99).

more of themselves and their identity and to become not just Mrs *Jane* Smith, but Mrs *John* Smith? (Casey Miller and Kate Swift point out that there would have been bewilderment if a letter had ever arrived addressed to Mrs *George* Washington.)

It is I think a mark of the identity options open to women in a patriarchal order that so many women voluntarily and even enthusiastically seek to be labelled as the property of a male. The title *Mrs* and the abandonment of their father's name (a name which required no effort on their part and could not be construed as an achievement) for their husband's name, appears to confirm their identity. In a patriarchal society it is not unrealistic to perceive that security lies in marriage – even if this is eventually revealed as a myth. That so many women continue to choose to be Mrs Jack Smart and to become 'invisible' is an indication of the success of patriarchal ideology.

This is why the refusal of some women to be designated *Mrs* is significant. To insist on the title *Ms* (if titles are unavoidable) does undermine some of the patriarchal practices. If the strength of the resistance is proportionate to the danger posed by the strategy then it is clear that some individuals are aware of the subversive influence of the use of *Ms*.

Numerous arguments other than the fundamental one have been advanced to substantiate the undesirability of the term *Ms*, and they share the common features of being inadequate and illogical – and even absurd. For example, one reason that has been given is that the pronunciation of *Ms* cannot be determined by its spelling. This is a non-starter in English. If we were to find unacceptable all those words which do not reveal their pronunciation from their spelling we would have to dispense with a sizeable number and we could begin with *Mr* and *Mrs*.

The (unstated) reason for the undesirability of *Ms* is that it is of no assistance in the maintenance of the patriarchal order and it can even be problematic for males. Again, this is why I think it extremely important that all women should make use of it as a title – if we are to persist with titles.

## Language change and social change

This has been but a brief review of a partial area of the body of research on sexism in language (for discussion of sexism in syntax, in the use of pronouns, for example, see chapter 5). It is however illustrative of the basic problems.

Traditionally, research on language as a system has been confined to the language itself and so descriptive studies have been in order, but feminism needs more than descriptive studies and documentation. No more evidence is necessary to convince feminists that the language is sexist. What is needed now is an analysis of this sexism.

How and when did such sexism evolve? How does it work? How can it be transformed? These are the questions which feminists need to answer and to do so demands that they go beyond the traditional boundary lines that have been imposed upon language research. The definitions of what constitutes 'proper' linguistic study have (conveniently?) acted as obstacles in pursuing feminist based questions.

From this area of research has come the proposal that all sexist words in the language should be 'eliminated' and although well intentioned it is hardly feasible. As Muriel Schulz and Julia Stanley have indicated, words which are associated with females occupy negative semantic space and become pejorated and are therefore sexist in that they do not afford parity. It would be necessary to eliminate most words which refer to women — or of course, most words which label men, because parity could also be achieved if the artificially enhanced images of the male were to be abolished. What is clear is that it is necessary that we know how sexism in language operates if we are to deal with it, otherwise we are likely to develop ineffectual strategies.

Another factor which we must bear in mind is that women need more words — and more positive words — not less. The removal of sexist words would not leave a large repertoire of words for women to draw upon! Such strategies as the elimination or addition of words are basically short-sighted, for the problem lies not in the words but in the semantic rule which governs their positive or negative connotations. We have seen that the same word has negative connotations when applied to women and positive connotations when applied to men, and any strategies which are predicated on the removal of sexist words are unable to deal with this phenomenon. Words such as *aggressive*, for example, (not being seen as essentially sexist) would still remain, although the meaning when applied to women is very different from the application to men. And there are fundamental problems with the creation of new words because while they are also subjected to the existing semantic rule that male is positive and minus male is negative, there is reason to believe that when consigned to negative semantic space they too will become pejorated and sexist. It is the semantic rule which needs to change, not the words themselves, yet this suggestion has rarely arisen in language/sex research.

The message is already there. Some attempts have been made to modify sexist words and there are signs that this on its own is insufficient to reduce sexism in language. Words such as police *officer* and chair*person* have been an attempt to break away from the negative value which female words acquire by the creation of sex-neutral terms. But sex-neutrality is not a meaningful category in our society and, while the world is obsessively divided into masculine and feminine, people have a genuine need to know whether the chairperson or the police officer is a man or a woman: only then are they able to decide whether the appropriate classification is positive or negative. It is not idle curiosity which prompts them, but necessity, in a patriarchal order, for if we are to make sense of the world we inhabit the distinction between masculine and feminine is a crucial one.

It seems that, with the exception of providing positive images for females, the English language has rich and flexible resources for meeting people's needs and this is clearly illustrated in the need to make sexual discriminations. The United States Department of Labor has attempted to overcome the exclusion of women from job categories and has revised the titles of almost 3,500 jobs so that they are no longer male-designated but sexually neutral (Berger and Kachuk, 1977). But speakers of English have found new and ingenious ways of marking such jobs for sex. We will probably witness the rise of such usages as *female flight attendant* (since steward/stewardess has been abolished), *woman sales person* (since salesman/saleswoman has been outlawed), as well as *lady police officer* and *madam chairperson*. They may be cumbersome usages but they will do the job: they will allow the sexist semantic rule to continue to function. The allocation of negative semantic space to women will go unchallenged.

The alternative proposal which has come from research is that sexism in the language is a reflection of sexism in society and the language will not change until society does. I do not think it realistic simply to wait for society's needs to change — that is, for the patriarchal order to 'evaporate' — in the hope that this will produce changes in the language. I do not think society can be relied upon somehow to automatically change in a direction which feminists would find acceptable.

Unfortunately there has been a division — often based on a fairly simplistic analysis — among those who advocate the demise of sexism in language. Broadly speaking there are two camps – those who think it more important to change the language, and those who think it more important to change society.

To me, both tasks appear to be equally important and neither will lead to success on its own.

Words help to structure the world we live in, and the words we have help to structure a sexist world in which women are assigned a subordinate position (Chapter Five). As Schulz has stated: 'words which are highly charged with emotion, taboo, or distaste, (as so many words for women are) not only reflect the culture which uses them. They teach and perpetuate the attitudes which created them' (1975a:73). Obviously the meaning of these words must be changed. We cannot trust to luck that women will be able to formulate positive definitions of themselves (an objective in the women's movement) while they are confined to the present semantic sources. But just as previously initially positive usages enjoyed only a short life-span and became devalued because the object to which they referred was devalued, so will present positive coinages be pejorated (the women's libber?) unless women are valued. Society must change if positive meanings which are being coined are to be sustained.

The process is a dialectical one. As more meanings are changed so will society change and the sexist semantic rule be weakened; as society and the sexist semantic rule changes so will more meanings change – even without deliberate intervention. To concentrate on either word meanings or social organizations – to the exclusion of the other – is to invite failure.

Sadly, researchers into sexism in language have not always come to appreciate the dimensions of this issue and too frequently, where it is felt 'proper' to make suggestions for possible strategies, the proposals are in terms of whether there should/should not be intervention in the language or whether the focus should/should not be on changing society. Effort has been expended on the futile debate on which comes first, the chicken or the egg.

The absence of an analysis of the patriarchal order is glaringly obvious in this research area. Language is a cultural artifact which has been invented by human beings; because males have primarily been responsible for the production of cultural forms and images (Smith, 1978) it would be surprising if language were to be an exception. But this line of inquiry – this thesis of English as a man's language – has not been pursued. Few researchers have asked who made up the language and how did these people see themselves and define themselves? Few have asked whether women have played any part in encoding the meanings of society. Few have asked whether sexism in language is a result of women's exclusion from the production of cultural forms.

It is a mark of the sexism of linguistics as a discipline that in all the research which has been done on the history of the language the question of the role played by women in its production and development has received virtually no attention; indeed such a question has not even been asked!

When it can be seen that the image of one sex is enhanced by the language while that of the other is diminished it seems that it would be necessary to explain this situation. The hypothesis that one sex might have greater linguistic rights would seem to be appropriate. But of course such questions would have moved research in very different directions – which while they may have been profitable for feminism would not necessarily be in the interests of the patriarchal order.

It is ironical that one of the reasons for not taking up such questions is that, within the patriarchal framework of discipline division and methodology, it is not considered in order for linguists to move into such suspect territory as the analysis of patriarchy. Such an analysis would not exclude the construction of the research area itself and such an examination could give rise to a disparaging critique.

Currently, research on sexism and language has not always provided the evidence which feminism needs: lists of sexist words pose little threat to the patriarchal order. Interesting, but not threatening, these inventories can be absorbed relatively easily without necessitating any modification in the semantic rule that women are negative because they are minus male. Patriarchal order rests on such a concept and it is this concept which feminists must challenge, linguistically and socially, if the patriarchal order is to be transformed.

## Sex differences in language

One indictment of this research area is that so many of the hypothesized differences that have been tested have not been found. This is not necessarily because research techniques are unsophisticated and inadequate and therefore incapable of locating sex differences in language use: it is primarily because research procedures have been so embedded with sexist assumptions that investigators have been blinded to empirical reality. Sexist stereotypes of female and male talk have permeated research and often precluded the possibility of open-ended studies which may have revealed sex differences – and similarities – in language use.

English speakers believe – and linguists appear to be no exception – that men's speech is forceful, efficient, blunt, authoritative, serious, effective, sparing and masterful; they believe that women's speech is weak, trivial, ineffectual, tentative, hesitant, hyperpolite, euphemistic and is often marked by gossip and gibberish (Kramer, 1977). The extent and rigidity of people's beliefs has not always been accepted as an index of accuracy in research – people have believed many strange things throughout history – but in sex differences and language, research is not remarkable for the challenge it has made to belief – and prejudice. Instead we have the focus on small segments of female speech and the conviction that if investigators look long enough and hard enough – and in the 'right' place – they are bound to find these hypothesized deficiencies in female speech. Unfortunately this has constituted a blind spot since not only have they frequently failed to find what they were looking for (Kramer *et al.*, 1978), they have often found little else either. Without looking at the society in which these sex differences – real or imagined – originate, there have been few insights presented.

## The 'lesser' value of women's words

One of the first places selected for research in the quest for locating the elements of female inferiority was the area of vocabulary. Prior to the rapid expansion of research in language/sex in the late 1960s there were numerous (untested) references in the literature to sex differences in word choice and it was generally believed that 'slang' was the exclusive property of males (Flexner, 1960), while females were disposed towards the choice of 'euphemisms'. With the new interest in sex differences in language, it is not surprising then that attention should focus on the female use of deviant/trivial/euphemistic terms.

But this is where the need for caution arises, for to accept some of the legitimated findings in this area would be to become victims of yet another (patriarchal) myth. Individuals generally acquire and use more words associated with their daily tasks – so a schoolteacher for example would probably use a different repertoire from a truck-driver – and in a society which practises a sexual division of labour – and of interests – it would not be surprising to find that women have a different vocabulary from men. Within a patriarchal order, however, even this can be interpreted in the interests of male supremacy.

For example, Moore (1922) found that men talked about their work far more frequently than did women: he did not seem to be perturbed that he had defined work implicitly as 'something which men do' and therefore had skewed his data in favour of males. In his terms, men worked, so the vocabulary associated with their work was serious: women did not work, so their vocabulary was trivial. He could not have reached the conclusions that he did, if he had classified *both* sexes as *workers* for then there would have been no sex differences: men and women would have both talked about their work and the vocabulary of both would have been regarded as serious.

Sometimes the interpretation placed on the data is a little more subtle. Hartman (1976), for example, studied the language of women and claimed to have located some of its euphemistic qualities. She described their language as 'flowery', 'tentative' and 'qualified' (p. 89) and therefore a lesser or deficient form. But I would suggest that *if men spoke in exactly the same way* as the women did in Hartman's sample their language would have been evaluated positively (the operation of the sexist semantic rule) and would no doubt have been described as polished, thoughtful and balanced. I am not (necessarily) disputing Hartman's evidence (though it is open to challenge) but I am stating unequivocally that the interpretation imposed upon it is sexist and unacceptable. I reject her conclusions – and many other conclusions in this research area, on the same grounds.

I also reject some of the evidence which is based on determining what people *believe* to be sex differences in language, and then by sleight of hand – presenting these beliefs as 'facts'. Robin Lakoff (1975) claims that everybody – including young children – knows that 'shit' is part of male vocabulary, while 'oh dear' (in the same context) is part of female vocabulary. While it is perfectly possible that most English speakers believe that men use 'shit' and women use 'oh dear' this does not constitute evidence that males and females use these terms. All it proves is that the speakers are familiar with sexist stereotypes and given their pervasive nature it would be amazing if they did not know what vocabulary was 'appropriate' for a woman and what was 'appropriate' for a man.

The case for women's use of 'lesser' words – be they deficient, trivial or ultra euphemistic – cannot be proven. Lakoff inadvertently undermines her own case when she says that women are likely to use more trivial words for colour (for example, mauve or beige) and that if a man were to use such terms one would assume that he was being sarcastic, or that he was an interior decorator! (Lakoff, 1975:8–9). One might also conclude that for *anyone* engaged in tasks of colour discrimination, mauve and beige might be useful terms. In our society in which women are more frequently engaged in interior decorating – or even in the choice of fabrics – it would not be unlikely that they acquired these discriminating terms. Even if women do use *mauve* and *beige* more frequently than men (and Lakoff offers no convincing evidence that they do), it is but another indication of the sexual division of labour and interest, and it requires a patriarchal frame of values to interpret this as evidence of the triviality of women's vocabulary.

My criticism of research procedures and findings would become repetitious if I were to list the deficiencies of studies that have claimed to locate female deficiency. There has often been a double dose of sexism for hypotheses have been framed in terms of female deficiency (thereby increasing the possibility of finding in favour of males) and the data which has been gathered has then been interpreted so as to find in favour of males. Research has frequently been 'rigged'.

Take the case of *qualifiers*, for example. As with tag questions there is some difficulty associated with defining a qualifier, which generally speaking is 'a term which qualifies' and, presumably because female speech was believed to be more tentative and hesitant – and qualified – it was hypothesized that females used more qualifiers. Hartman (1976) stated that in her study females did use more qualifiers, but she adds an extra bit of information as well. She claims that men used more absolutes. I envy her such assurance and confidence for it seems to me that the use of the same term could be interpreted as a qualifier if used by females and an absolute if used by males; for example:

> '*Perhaps* you have misinterpreted me.'

> '*Maybe* you should do it again.'

I think the determining factor is more often the sex of the speaker rather than the speech, so that when females use *perhaps* or *maybe* it is interpreted as a qualifier: when males use the same terms the interpretation is that they are using absolutes.

The same criticism applies to studies of *intensifiers*. Again, conveniently, an intensifier seems to be defined as a form used by women and this helps to bias findings in favour of males. Women are supposed to use hyperbole more often than men and Jespersen (1922) stated that it is the use of intensifiers which is responsible for the lack of precision in women's speech; he cites the female usage of vastly — completely untested of course — as the example (p. 279). Contemporary linguists have followed in his footsteps with Lakoff claiming that women use *so* more often (for example, 'it was *so* nice of you to invite me') and Mary Ritchie Key (1972) claimed that they use *such* more often (for example, 'it was *such* a nice party').

But isn't there a double-standard at work here? When men use hyperbole it is frequently classified as slang and designated as a male realm. When women use it, it is an intensifier and it is therefore a lesser form.

A female may say 'It's such a nice party' while a male may say 'Damned good party' (I am not suggesting that this is the case, only that it might be) but whereas the female usage is taken as evidence of her imprecision, the male usage is taken as evidence of his forcefulness. *So* much for *such* 'objectivity' of linguistic research.

These studies, because of their inherent sexism, simply do not substantiate the hypothesis that the language of women is a lesser form. Perhaps the only contribution they make is to provide evidence that women and their language have been devalued — though this has rarely been the explicit conclusion outside feminist research! In many cases, all that has been measured is the extent to which the patriarchal order imposes it values upon research. In the interests of credibility it is both desirable and necessary that this bias be transformed and that research be conducted on the premises that: (a) there is nothing wrong with women's language; and (b) that any sex differences in language could — or even should — be interpreted in favour of females at least 50 per cent of the time. This would be a very different bias and would give rise to some very different results!

## Politeness and servility

That women are more polite than men is a finding which has frequently been put forward and which has not been refuted. This finding is hardly surprising for there is a social expectation that 'subordinates' should be more polite than their 'superiors'; the onus is on the waiter, not on the customer to be polite, it is on the employee and not the employer, the student and not the teacher. It is nothing less than consistent that women should be more polite than men!

People who have power expect — and often have the capacity to exact — politeness from their 'subordinates', and though this operation may be more masked in the case of women and men than it is in the case of privates and generals, there is no reason to suspect that it is in any way intrinsically different. However, even given my readiness to believe that it can be found that women are more polite than men, I need more than some of the existing data in the area if I am to accept this finding.

It can be substantiated that females use so-called status linguistic forms more often than males and Barrie Thorne and Nancy Henley (1975) have said that 'women, compared with men of the same social class, age, and level of education, more often choose the form closer to the prestige, or "correct" way of talking' (p. 17). But I have a few reservations about accepting this. First, I would challenge the assumption of control for I cannot accept that it is possible to 'make all things equal' between the sexes. I do not think it possible to speak categorically of men and women of the *same* social class (see p. 71 for further discussion) or with the *same* education. Also, I cannot uncritically accept the 'leap' which is required between the use of prestige forms and politeness. They are not necessarily the same thing. Members of the upper class may use more of the prestige forms than anyone else but their usage is not always construed as politeness.

Peter Trudgill (1975b) has undertaken research in this area and he claims that women 'consistently produce linguistic forms which more closely approach those of standard language or have higher prestige than those produced by men' (p. 89) and if this is the case then it is indeed interesting to speculate on the reasons for it. However, many of the explanations which are offered are unsatisfactory.

Trudgill maintains that there is a feminine and a masculine linguistic variety, and says: Using a female linguistic variety is as much a case of identifying oneself as a female, and of behaving 'as a woman should' as is say, wearing a skirt. What would happen to a man in our society who wore a skirt? (1975b: 94–5). The question may be rhetorical but the answer would be obvious to any 'reasonable' person in our society: if a man wore a skirt, or 'talked like a lady' he would be identifying himself with all that is negative and undesirable in our society and would be open to ridicule or abuse. To Trudgill, linguistic variety helps to maintain the demarcation lines between the sexes, to prevent contamination – for men – and, implicitly then, is to be upheld. This seems to me insufficient reason for maintaining different linguistic varieties – assuming of course that they do exist and are not merely in the eye (or ear) of the beholder.

The explanation that women are more status conscious than men (Trudgill, 1975b:94) is not without its inadequacies either. Since women 'are not rated by their occupations', declares Trudgill, 'other signals of status, including speech are correspondingly more important' (1975a:92). Perhaps it should be pointed out that if women are not rated by their occupations (and whose value is this anyway?) it is not always because they do not have them. That Trudgill does not take women's work into account and does not value it does not mean that women don't, or that they are trying to compensate for their own deficiency and invisibility by using more prestigious forms of English.

Trudgill suggests that it is not just that the poor women choose to use prestigious forms but that the secure men choose to use non-prestigious forms. This is a 'signal of group solidarity and personal identity' (1975b:94) on the part of men and once more we confront the supposed male linguistic variety as the norm while the female linguistic variety (which of course does not serve to 'bond' females) is the deviation from that norm. That females have no identity and cannot develop solidarity is an 'explanation' which is not inconsistent with patriarchal order; it is an 'explanation' which I do not accept.

It might be possible that women do speak 'better' than men, and that this 'better speech' is a form of politeness or subservience, but at the moment the available evidence is not convincing. That the findings of women's politeness have not been refuted could be an indication of the pervasiveness of patriarchal assumptions rather than proof of women's 'politeness'.

## Pitch : fact or fiction

Pitch has also been used as an index for the measurement of women's language inferiority. Women, as it is well known, have very high pitched voices which are aesthetically unpleasing. Their shrill, often whining, voices are difficult to listen to for a long time and they do, so it is believed, make it difficult for women to be taken seriously. However, like so many other sex differences in language, investigators have found it very difficult to locate this unacceptable high pitch.

Ruth Brend (1975) carried out a study on sex differences in pitch and found evidence which can both support and contradict the stereotype. First of all she suggests that women make greater use of pitch (and this is very different from suggesting that women are cursed with high pitched voices) in that they use four contrastive levels, whereas men – for some 'inexplicable' reason – do not utilize their highest level of pitch but confine themselves to three contrastive levels. In some respects then Brend's findings do support the stereotype of women's language as high pitched in that women use high pitch more often than men; but her findings also undermine the stereotype because she says that this is not biologically determined but that women 'choose' to make use of high pitch while men 'choose' not to.

It is not that men do not have the capacity to engage in high pitched utterances but that they refrain from presenting such incriminating evidence: this casts a new light on the 'naturally' deeper voices of men. It is not a mystery why men choose not to speak in the high pitched tones which are available to them in a society which links low pitch and masculinity, and high pitch and femininity; males who did produce high pitched utterances would be venturing into that negative realm and violating the gender demarcation lines. They would be ridiculed – as many adolescents whose voices have been late in breaking could testify.

This introduces the question of the degree to which pitch differences are learned. Traditionally the assumption has been that these pitch differences are 'natural' – why else were young boys castrated in order to preserve their high pitched voices? – but recent evidence suggests that pitch is not solely the product of physiology. After considerable research, Mattingly (1969) concluded cautiously that sex differences in pitch 'though doubtless related to typical male and female vocal tract size is probably a linguistic convention' (p. 1219), while Jacqueline Sachs *et al.* (1973) reached a similar conclusion and contended that anatomical difference alone is insufficient to account for pitch differences between men and women (pp. 80–1).

One must also 'explain' why it is that some congenitally deaf males – that is, those who are born deaf and never hear sex differences in pitch – have voices which do not break at puberty (Luchsinger and Arnold, 1965). This raises interesting questions about the role of voice breaking in adolescent males and the 'visible' (or audible) entry to 'manhood' which it constitutes: it also raises questions about females learning or 'choosing' to use high pitch.

Robin Lakoff has claimed that women are required to learn specific linguistic 'skills' – although skill is hardly an appropriate term – which can then be used against them. She argues that women are encouraged/ obliged to talk in a particular way which is then easily discredited. Perhaps pitch is an example of this: it could be that for women to talk in a socially acceptable way it is necessary for them to cultivate the use of high pitch, but having acquired high pitch they may then have their voices – conveniently – rejected as unacceptable. This could be one means of constructing asymmetrical sex differences.

I am, however, wary of accepting this explanation for it is based on the assumptions that (a) there is something inherently good about low pitch and inherently bad about high pitch; and (b) that the judgment is based on linguistic features (in this case, pitch) and not on sex. Because so frequently the judgments made about sex differences in language have not been based on the language at all I am more inclined to question the validity of pitch variation. It could be that pitch – like word choice – is irrelevant and that it is *women* who are being devalued while the ostensible high pitch of their voices simply serves as an 'objective excuse' for such devaluation.

Despite some evidence I am not convinced that the voices of women are more highly pitched than men's (be it by nature or nurture), but I am convinced that the *belief* that women's voices are high pitched and shrill is one way of disqualifying women from public speaking. This is certainly what Cheris Kramarae (Kramer, 1978) discovered when she investigated the reasons the BBC gave for finding the voices of women unacceptable – for talking about 'serious' topics to men!

The high pitch of women's voices has not excluded them completely from the media, for their delivery was acceptable on women's programmes. Their deficiencies – as outlined by various BBC officials – have consisted of having inappropriate voices for carrying the 'serious' topics which are addressed to men, namely television news programmes and (male) sporting programmes. It is interesting to note the exception to this rule: during World War II for those men who were 'in monastic conditions of service life' (Kramer, 1978:8) it was quite appropriate – and even desirable – that women should have been the newsreaders for men deprived of female company.

There is no basis for the exclusion of women from the delivery of serious topics in the media; the argument of their unsuitable high pitch will not stand up to scrutiny. Like so many other presumed deficiencies in women's language, I would suggest that high pitch and its undesirability is based on the sex of the speaker and not the speech itself. I think it would be perfectly possible for a woman to be speaking in an electronically registered lower pitch than a male and for her to be classified as having a high-pitched, shrill and whining voice while the male's higher pitch could be classified as pleasing and acceptable. However, research along these lines has not been undertaken; it would require an assumption that there was nothing particularly prestigious about male language use.

## Who does the talking ?

A firmly held conviction of our society is that women talk a lot. When Cheris Kramarae (Kramer, 1977) investigated what people thought were the characteristics of women's language she found that the common responses were that women 'talk a lot' about 'trivial topics' and that they indulge in 'gossip and gibberish' (p. 157). Supposedly, it is because of these talkative tendencies on the part of women that society requires a barrage of clichéd injunctions and warnings against woman talk.

There is a Scottish saying: 'Nothing is so unnatural as a talkative man or a quiet woman' (Swacker, 1975: 76) and because the members of society are so convinced that, unless contained, women talk too much, advice to women on this matter has been freely given. Even Sophocles wrote in *Ajax*: 'Silence gives the proper grace to women' (Kaplan, 1976: 28), while many contemporary books on etiquette which hand out advice to young women on how to be popular propagate the belief that the best and most attractive woman is a quiet one. 'I hate girls who can't stop talking' and 'I like girls who listen to me without interrupting and who pay attention' are the statements of young men in *The New Seventeen Book of Etiquette and Young Living* for the edification of young women. 'Any male is happy to be the source of information', states the editor sagely, for 'Everybody loves to hear praise, and boys in particular' (Haupt, 1970: 101–2).

Under these circumstances it is not surprising that investigators of sex differences in language should have begun by looking for the excessive talkativeness of women. However, here, perhaps in more than any other research area, findings were in complete contradiction with the stereotype of women's language. There has not been one study which provides evidence that women talk more than men, and there have been numerous studies which indicate that men talk more than women.

Whether the setting has been naturalistic or artificial, men have done more of the talking. Swacker (1975) had her thirty-four informants (seventeen of each sex) talk into a tape recorder, taking as much time as they needed, and men talked much, much, longer than women – usually until the tape was finished! Argyle *et al.* (1968), Strodtbeck *et al.* (1957) and Wood (1966) also designed studies to measure amount of talk and found that it was men who talked more.

In an analysis of television programmes, Jessie Bernard (1972) found that males talked more often than females, and in her analysis of husband/wife conversations Phyllis Chesler (1971) found that it was often impossible for women to talk when males were present – particularly if the males were their husbands! Chesler states that if women wish to talk then they must talk to each other for there is usually little or no opportunity for them to talk in the presence of men. 'Very rarely', states Chesler, 'do men listen silently to a group of women talking' (p. 179), whereas the reverse – women listening silently to a group of men talking – is a common occurrence in our culture.

How can we explain this contradiction? On the one hand we have a society which believes that women are the talkative sex and on the other hand we have overwhelming evidence that it is men who do the talking. How do we explain the continued existence of this belief? All of us, every member of our society, must have consistently been in contexts where men talk more and yet our belief that women are the talkative sex has not been questioned or undermined.

I do not think these contradictions are as 'real' as they first appear. I think there is a simple explanation for the way in which we have been 'conned'.

The concept of women as the talkative sex involves a comparison: they must talk too much against some sort of standard or yardstick and we have erroneously assumed that the measurement of women as talkers is in comparison to men. But this appears not to be the case. The talkativeness of women has been gauged in comparison not with men but with *silence*. Women have not been judged on the grounds of whether they talk more than men, but of whether they talk more than silent women. When silence is the desired state for women (and I suggest that it is in a patriarchal order, as do numerous other feminists) then any talk in which a woman engages can be too much. What an advantage for males in a patriarchal order!

In a male supremacist society where women are devalued, their language is devalued to such an extent that they are required to be silent. Within this framework it becomes 'logical' to have one rule for women's talk and another for men because it is the sex – and not just the talk – which is significant. Cheris Kramarae has summed this up when she suggested: 'Perhaps a talkative woman is one who does talk as much as a man' (Kramer, 1975: 47). It is possible to go even further and to suggest that when women are supposed to be quiet, a talkative woman is one who talks at all.

This area of research is extremely significant; it is also significant that, except by feminists, such research has not been pursued. Why is it that research on sex differences in language has concentrated upon finding the deficiencies in women's words, pronunciation and pitch – with so little success – whereas in this area of amount of talk, which promises to be so productive – has there been so little effort expended? The answer lies I think in the patriarchal order and the beliefs which are necessary for the maintenance of that order. It is important to substantiate women's linguistic deficiencies and it is necessary to preserve some of the myths upon which those deficiencies depend. While the focus is on examining segments of women's language for signs of inadequacy, research does not challenge those myths, for – regardless of outcome – the supposed deficiencies of women's language remains. That the deficiencies are not found can be explained by the suggestion that researchers have been looking in the wrong place. A new segment is chosen for attention but the assumption persists. This is not the case with studies on amount of talk. The excessive talkativeness of women is readily exposed as a myth with the result that many awkward questions are raised.

It is difficult to isolate interruptions from amount of talk for he who interrupts most (and I use *he* specifically) tends to do the most talking. According to the stereotype of women's language, females are supposed to nag, chatter, talk too much and listen too little, and are therefore the prime suspects on any measures of interruption. But research findings reveal just the opposite. In mixed-sex conversations it is primarily males who interrupt females.

In their study, Don Zimmerman and Candace West (1975) found that 98 per cent of interruptions in mixed sex conversation were made by males. In no case did they find that females thought this was 'out of order' or sufficient reason for protest; on the contrary, females tended to be silent after being interrupted by a male. Their conclusions are interesting: 'We are led to the conclusion that ... men deny equal status to women as conversational partners with respect to rights to full

utilization of their turns and support for the development of their topics'
(1975:125). They see this as another example of male dominance, as
men exercise control over the talk of women. Just as they have more
rights to the formulation of meaning in the language as a system, so it
seems that men have more rights when it comes to using that system.
Males have greater control of meaning and more control over talk.

Interruption is a mechanism by which (a) males can prevent females
from talking, and (b) they can gain the floor for themselves; it is
therefore a mechanism by which they engineer female silence. Whereas
it is normal practice for males to interrupt females there are penalties if
females try to (dare to?) interrupt males. There is a whole set of beliefs
which reinforce this asymmetry and ordain that it is not proper for a
woman to interrupt/contradict a male, particularly 'in public'. This
contributes to the construction and maintenance of male supremacy.
Because both sexes have given their consensus to the promotion of male
primacy, there is a sense in which women have 'aided and abetted' in
the provision of greater linguistic rights for males. If women were to
withdraw their consensus it would soon become clear just how fragile
some of those rights are.

Testing what happens when women no longer support male
dominance at this micro-level can prove to be quite 'entertaining'.

> 'I have tried it out on a few occasions and the result is always the
> same. When a man interrupts me on about five occasions, when
> there have been five times that he has prevented me from
> finishing what I want to say, I think that's about enough. So then
> I stop paying attention to him. He is only interrupting *me* so *he*
> can talk so I make myself "unavailable" as his audience. And
> men don't like it. They think I am being rude. But they are being
> rude when they interrupt me in the first place.'(2)

The findings of Pamela Fishman (1977) support this observation. It is
women, argues Fishman, who are supposed to be proficient at 'the art
of conversation'; this is consistent with the belief that they should not
talk too much, for it is not the conversation of women that they are
supposed to be able to develop, but that of men. It is up to a woman to
'draw him out', and 'women who sit silently while a conversation
flounders are seen as hostile and inept' (p. 101). Women are permitted
to introduce a number of topics which cater to men's interests, and
when men take these up, they often do so by interrupting and assuming
control (for further discussion, see pp. 49). But the woman who

doesn't provide enticing dishes to tempt a man's conversational appetite can be seen as rude and ungracious:

> 'Try interrupting a man. Try talking about what you want to talk about and for as long as it takes you to say it. It's seen as a hostile act. You are dominating and bitchy.'(3)

Men may engage in interruption of women with impunity but it seems that there are many penalties for women who interrupt men. Even being as 'neutral' as possible, offering neither support nor rebuff, can be seen as an unfriendly gesture by many men who in a patriarchal order are accustomed to conversational deference, who are used to having their topics taken up with interest by women, who are used to being given the floor — and undivided attention. To find themselves deprived of these 'rights' could conceivably cause them consternation and it is perfectly logical in such a context that they should 'blame' women for their discomfort.

Some people have pointed out that power is a determining factor in interaction and that it is common for anyone to be relatively quiet in the presence of superiors, as it is common for anyone's superiors to feel free to talk, and to interrupt (Coser, 1960; Goffman, 1972). In this case we may therefore just be observing the power differences between the sexes; as the 'superiors' men are free to do the talking and the interrupting when interacting with women.

More research is needed in this area: little has been done. It would be useful to know the extent to which women participate in the construction of this aspect of male superiority; it would be useful to know what happens when women cease to cooperate, when they opt to withdraw as the interested audience to males, or even when they begin to interrupt men. I do not think that there are groups of enthusiastic investigators eagerly waiting to conduct such research.

Implicit in much research in language and sex is the concept of sexually defined 'territory' and there are clear lines of demarcation between the feminine and masculine variety of language; for example, Trudgill (1975a, b) compared language and clothing and indicated that there were as many penalties — for males — in crossing the sex-lines on language as on clothing. Many researchers accept that there are penalties for men who 'talk like women', and for women who 'talk like men', which raises the question of who decrees these penalties, and who hands them out? Who enforces sex demarcation lines in language variety? Who ridicules a man who 'talks like a lady' or mocks a youth whose voice has not broken?

The belief that men and women talk in sex-specific ways (and on sex-specific topics) is dependent in part on the ability to enforce those divisions, and there is some evidence to suggest that this task is undertaken primarily by men.

In his work in a mining community in Britain, Klein (1971) contends that although both sexes may cross the divide, and both could be penalized, it was men who took the responsibility for reinforcing sexual divisions in language. Certain topics — for example, politics and sport — were defined by the men as their particular property, as were certain styles of talking, and women who ventured into their areas were rebuked or ridiculed. Likewise, any man who strayed into what the men considered was the woman's area was rebuked and ridiculed by his fellow men. Such behaviour can be quite severe punishment and from Klein's point of view it was almost invariably meted out by men.

Although such research is by no means conclusive it does point the way to possibilities for investigation. It can be seen that both sexes share the rules for talk, but the enforcement of these rules and the penalties for breaking them are imposed by one sex. In hypothesizing that males have more rights than females when it comes to talk, this is an area which looks promising; needless to say it is not an area that has been pursued.

It has been suggested that power differences are measured in the way in which 'conversational topics are raised, developed, changed and dropped' (Thorne and Henley, 1975:17) and the play of power can often be seen at work in mixed-sex conversations. In one discussion which I taped, this point was brought home clearly when I later listened to and analysed the tape.

Present at the discussion, which was a workshop on sexism and education in London, were thirty-two women and five men. Apart from the fact that the tape revealed that the men had talked for over 50 per cent of the time, it also revealed that what the men wanted to talk about — and the way in which they wanted to talk — was given precedence. Whereas many females wanted to discuss their own experience of sexism, the men wanted to talk in more general and 'abstract' terms. Women wanted to talk about what happened to them while, generally speaking, the men wanted to talk about sexism in the curriculum and sexism 'in the system'. One of the most noticeable features of this discussion — which I wasn't aware of at the time — was that it was men who determined what the topic would be. They did the interrupting and they insisted that the discussion get back to the point: *their* point.

There is no doubt in my mind that in this context at least (and I do not think it was an atypical one) it was the five males and not the thirty-two females who were defining the parameters of the talk. I suspect that neither the women nor the men were conscious of this. There was no overt hostility displayed towards the females who 'strayed from the point', but considerable pressure was exerted by the males – and accepted without comment by the females – to confine the discussion to the male definition of the topic.

Some of the comments which the men made were 'I don't think this sort of discussion leads anywhere', and 'I think it would be better if we devised strategies for dealing with sexism: we don't need to be convinced that it exists.'(4) No male gave any indication that he thought the female perspective was valid and I would say that the males were made 'uncomfortable' by the women's wish to talk about their personal experience of sexism in education.

This introduces the problem which males supposedly have with talking about the personal – a problem which is accepted by some males (Korda, 1975). It is often believed that males have difficulty in expressing emotion and disclosing their personal selves – partly as a product of their conditioning – and that they need some encouragement and assistance to begin to talk about their feelings and therefore to participate in the sort of discussion with which women are familiar. However, if males do begin to talk about their personal experience, it seems that they might well lose control of the conversation topic.

Dana Densmore (1971) claims that power often lies with those who do not disclose their vulnerabilities and that strategies such as denying the validity of a topic, refusing to talk on someone else's chosen topic, abstaining from self-revelation and withholding personal information, all contribute to the maintenance of power. Men who may wish to stay in control of conversation may quite accurately perceive that the disclosure of their emotions leads to a reduction in control, with the result that they may not find the prospect of self-revelation an enticing one. The behaviour of remaining 'aloof' while 'someone else discloses, facilitates dominance' (Jenkins and Kramer, 1978:80) and it is therefore possible that it is the desire to be dominant (which is not quite the same as socialized behaviour) which leads to the supposed male difficulty in dealing with the personal.

So while many males may be sympathetic to the issues of sexism, and be willing to discuss them, they bring with them the possibility of confining the discussion to their own terms (see also p. 84), with the result that females can, once again, be silenced on an issue which is significant to them and which evolves from their own personal experience.

Diana Leonard (1979) has claimed that the oppressed are in a better position to describe and express their oppression, but this factor can be overlooked, even by sympathetic males who are accustomed to defining what is worth talking about and what is not. At the discussion which I taped, the males – who had not shared the same experiences of oppression – did not question the legitimacy of their own interpretation and definition, and neither did the females. This illustrates the way in which both sexes accept that it is the right of males to decree reality and to monopolize talk.

Male control of conversational topic is not directly related to expenditure of effort, as Pamela Fishman (1977) has pointed out. She claims that women are required to do all the chores in mixed-sex conversation; they are required to perform all the invisible but necessary tasks if a conversation is to be kept functioning. Because of its parallels with housework, Fishman argues that women do the shitwork in conversation.

She listened to fifty-two hours of taped conversation between mixed sex couples who had agreed to tape recorders in their apartments, and her specific aim was to determine who controlled the topic. Her conclusion was that women made the conversational effort but men exercised control by taking up a topic (which women 'offered' and which interested them) and by proceeding to do the talking. It was because they did very little that they were instrumental in what would be talked about (p. 100). The following is my transcript from a social gathering, and I think it a good example of Fishman's thesis: it is 'the art of conversation' where male talk is being encouraged at the expense of female; where she is making the effort, 'drawing him out', until he chooses to take over and to 'hold the floor'.

Female:    Did he have the papers ready for you?
Male:       Mmm.
Female:    And were they all right ... was anything missing?
Male:       Not that I could see.
Female:    Well that must have been a relief, anyway ...
Female:    I suppose everything went well after that?

Male:      Almost.

Female:   Oh. Was there something else?

Male:      Yes, actually.

Female:   It wasn't X ... was it? ... He didn't let you down again? ...

Male:      I'd say he did.

Female:   He really is irresponsible, you know, you should get ...

Male:      I'm going to do something about it. It was just about the last straw today. How many times do you think that makes this week? ...(5)

By my reckoning the woman makes eight conversational gambits to which the man gives a perfunctory response. But he is tempted by the ninth, and he interrupts, and proceeds.

Females are constantly engaged in the struggle to get a response to their own remarks, argues Fishman. They do the support work. They restrict their own opportunities for expression by concentrating on the development of male topics. Women, says Fishman, are required to be 'linguistically available' to men; their own talk is not important. They are obliged to be the audience, the good listener, and to keep the conversation flowing (1977:101):

> There is a division of labor in conversation. Though the women generally do more work, the men usually control the conversations that couples have. Since the men's remarks develop into conversation more often than the women's, men end up defining what will be talked about and which aspects of reality are the most important.

Males, in the patriarchal order, are accorded 'superiority' by virtue of their sex; they have this 'superiority' consistently confirmed in interaction with females who abdicate in favour of males by restricting their own opportunities for expression, by deferring to male interests and definitions, and by concentrating on supporting male efforts. This behaviour has not just 'naturally' unfolded in women. There are penalties for those who do not learn the lesson, for as Fishman says: 'Women who consistently and successfully control interactions are criticized by men' and are likely to be called 'bitchy', 'domineering' or 'aggressive' (p. 101).

It is not sufficient that males should be seen to be in control: females are required to be seen willingly supporting that control.

To my knowledge there is no other research comparable with that of Fishman's, despite the obvious potential that such an area has to offer. Her research serves to expose part of the mythical nature of the stereotypes of female and male language and as such would appear to be not in the interests of maintaining the patriarchal order. But her findings, and those of some other feminists, suggest that while there are sex differences in language, they are not the 'typical' ones that many investigators have tried to isolate. They are not female deficiencies – as has so frequently been supposed.

## The verdict

This has not been a 'balanced' appraisal of language/sex research for I have given almost the same space to the discussion of sexist research as I have to feminist research and it would be a mistake to assume that this reflects the priorities of the research area as a whole. My division does not reflect the quantity of the work which has been undertaken for there are many studies I would classify as sexist and there are few that are feminist. When it comes to quality however it is a different matter.

The work which I consider sexist has been devoted primarily to pursuing the source of supposed female deficiency or else it has interpreted research findings in favour of males: sometimes it has done both. My objection to such research is not simply because it is sexist, but because it is poor research. Often poorly designed, based on untested assumptions, utilizing suspect methodologies, and based on the premise that the male way is the right way, it has added very little to our understanding about language and has more than once led us up 'blind alleys'. Feminist research, on the other hand, has invariably been the source of many new insights and has opened up new and challenging areas for future research.

To do this, feminists have found it necessary to slip outside the traditional linguistic boundaries. Of course, feminist research is not unbiased. The choice of what to believe or not to believe is not between 'biased' and 'objective' research: the issue is which set of biases takes more of the evidence into account. This is not to suggest that feminist research has the answers, only that it has opened up an area in which more, and more useful, answers might be found. Operating with a different set of assumptions and values – particularly about women – feminism is constructing different knowledge.

Within this feminist framework some of the traditional divisions between sexism and language, and sex differences in language, begin to fall away. It is the *silence* of women, in language and in the use of language, that has emerged when women are considered in the patriarchal order. Silence provides an integrative base for the two previously separated research areas: it indicates that they have more in common than they have to divide them.

Framing questions in terms of the silence of women leads to an examination of the language which excludes and denigrates them, and it also leads to an examination of their access to discourse. When the only language women have debases us and when we are also required to support male talk, it is not unlikely that we shall be relatively silent. When the only language men have affords them the opportunity to encode meanings and to control discourse, when they have made the language and decreed many of the conditions for its use, it is not unlikely that they will use it more and that they will use it more in their own interest; thus they assist in the maintenance of women's silence.

The primary focus of language/sex research should be broader – and braver – than it has been in the past. Research should begin to concern itself with the relative silence of over half the population. Language is a powerful human tool and we must begin to ask what role it plays in maintaining and perpetuating existing social structures, what contribution it makes to our hierarchically ordered classist, racist and sexist world view. When we begin to address ourselves to questions of this kind, it will be possible to shift towards locating inadequacies and deficiencies within the social structure and not within individual human beings.

*A priori* I do not accept the deficiency of women – or the concomitant supremacy of males: this is my bias. I find nothing in existing research on language and sex which leads me to modify that bias.

# · 2 ·

# Constructing Women's Silence

✳

How women came to experience this double penalty in terms of language is a matter for speculation, as are so many other theories of the origin of sexual inequality (Eichler, 1979), but there is a historical aspect to the silence of women which casts some light on their present position.

Historically, women have been excluded from the production of cultural forms, and language is, after all, a cultural form – and a most important one. In fairly crude terms this means that the language has been made by men and that they have used it for their own purposes. Because women have not been involved in the production of the legitimated language, they have been unable to give weight to their own symbolic meanings (S. Ardener, 1975), they have been unable to pass on a tradition of women's meanings of the world.

Both sexes have the capacity to generate meanings but women have not been in a position to have their meanings taken up and incorporated in those of the society. They have not been in the public arena, they have not been the 'culture'-makers with the result that any meanings which they may wish to encode, but which are different from or at odds with those that have been generated by men, have been tenuous and transitory: they have been cut off from the mainstream of meanings and therefore have frequently been lost.

Women have not been the influential philosophers, the orators or poets, the politicians or rhetoricians, the grammarians, the linguists or the educators, and they have not had the same opportunity to influence the language, to introduce new meanings where they will be taken up, to define the objects or events of the world. This is not to suggest that women have not philosophized, made speeches, written poetry, held theories about language, education or the world, but only to emphasize that the outlets for their talents have been confined. The meanings which they have generated and which may have diverged from those of men (partly as a product of different circumstances and experiences) have not always gained access to the public arena, have not always been central to the culture, and have not been transmitted to the next generation. In a way, each generation has been required to forge anew meanings which are specific to being female.

Elaine Showalter (1977) has made a comparable point about the literary tradition of women where – for numerous reasons – the women writers of one generation were frequently unknown to those of the next. The 'chain' was broken so that each generation had to begin afresh to create its meanings, unaware of what had gone before. Adrienne Rich (1979:11) has commented on this problem:

> The entire history of women's struggle for self determination has been muffled in silence over and over. One serious cultural obstacle encountered by any feminist writer is that each feminist work has tended to be received as if it emerged from nowhere: as if each of us had lived, thought and worked without any historical past or contextual present. This is one of the ways in which women's work and thinking has been made to seem sporadic, erratic, orphaned of any tradition of its own.

Just as the meanings of history and literature are lost, so too are the meanings of the language (to which history and literature are both confined). Women have 'made' just as much 'history' as men but it has not been codified and transmitted; women have probably done just as much writing as men but it has not been preserved; and women, no doubt, have generated as many meanings as men, but these have not survived. Where the meanings of women have been discontinuous with the male version of reality they have not been retained. Whereas we have inherited the accumulated meanings of male experience, the meanings of our female ancestors have frequently disappeared.

Meanings and names did not exist before human beings: we have supplied them, we have literally 'made them up'. But it has been a limited version that we have retained, for as Mary Daly (1973) asserts, it is males who have named the world. It is probably inevitable that those who perform naming should do so from their own point of view, taking themselves as the centre, the reference point, and naming all else in relation to themselves. Currently, this is what feminists are doing as they *rename* the world in relation to themselves, so it is not the process of naming itself which gives rise to protest, but the monopoly which males have had on this process. It is because they have excluded women from naming the world, from encoding their own experience, that feminists now find it necessary to rename.

The names which men have supplied have been biased, and they have been 'false' (Daly, 1973) because these partial names and their meanings have been insisted upon as the whole. Any differences, any alternative names which women may have wanted to supply, have been 'disallowed' with the result that women – and their experience – have frequently been made invisible. There is a 'loud silence' when one searches for the meanings of women in the language.

## The inaudibility of women

A contemporary example can serve as an illustration of this process. The society in which many of us have been reared has a legitimated meaning for *motherhood* which means feminine fulfilment, which represents something beautiful, that leaves women consumed and replete with joy.

I am not suggesting that motherhood does not or cannot have such a meaning, but that it is a partial meaning and it is false to portray this as the only meaning. For many women motherhood may have been an entirely different experience. Such women may have generated alternative – even conflicting – meanings (and names) in relation to motherhood but their meanings have been without authority or validity. Such meanings then, may not have been handed down, or if they were, would not have carried the same weight as the legitimated ones.

For those women for whom motherhood may have represented neither joy nor beauty, a substantial problem arises. There is no reference point for their experience, no way of making it seem real, with the result that they can be left feeling extremely inadequate, convinced that there is something wrong with themselves, because their meanings do not mesh with the accepted ones. This in itself can place even more pressure on them to be silent. They are not willingly going to advertise their own 'neurosis', and risk being labelled 'unnatural', so they may elect not to transmit their experience and their version of motherhood to the next generation. They may even withhold such information from their own daughters.

And so the chain is broken. The daughters may grow up never suspecting that there is any alternative to the meaning of beautiful and beatific motherhood, never having gained access to any contrary female version of the event.

Some women who have experienced motherhood in the past few years have spoken of the 'conspiracy of silence' which surrounds the event (Buchan, 1978). Despite prenatal classes, etc., many of them have felt unprepared, and at times have been critical of their mothers – and their woman friends who have experienced childbirth – for not being more frank and disclosing the alternative female reality.

> When it came to sex education my mother was excellent. And my friends and I have often talked about sexual/personal matters, so I was completely unprepared [for childbirth]. My mother said I would have to work hard, and my friend who had a baby a month or so before had just said it wasn't all that it was cracked up to be. I was so angry afterwards. I wanted to know *why* they hadn't told me, why they hadn't shared that experience and they said they hadn't wanted to frighten me. But I was much more frightened ... thinking something was going wrong ... than I would have been if they had talked about it. I've been told I am a social disaster now because I always tell women what it was like for *me* so they can have a more realistic picture of what to expect. People don't like that. It makes waves. There seems to be a conspiracy to stop women from getting information on what happens, on what it feels like ... to be out of control. A lot of men are horrified when you confront them with some of the facts. It disturbs their serene ideas of motherhood. They want to think of it as beautiful and they don't like you introducing contradictions. Conversation just falls apart when I tell them that the doctor sewed my arsehole back in the wrong place. You can't make anything beautiful out of that.(6)

This is not an unusual commentary upon motherhood. In her book, *Becoming a Mother*, Ann Oakley (1979:97) records the similar experiences of many women:

> I remember telling a girl in the shop who hasn't had a baby yet and who asked me. And I told her; I said it's very painful and she was really shocked. But I wish somebody had told me if I'd asked

them, because I said it really is painful, it's terrible in fact. No wonder women die in it. She went: my God, really? What kills you — the sheer pain?

There is no doubt that this woman is *renaming* motherhood in a way that is consistent with her experience. Her meaning may only be part of the totality of women's experience of motherhood but it is nonetheless a genuine meaning and one which has significantly been omitted from the legitimated meanings. That her meaning is not well known, that it has not permeated the acceptable meanings of the culture and been shared, is evidenced by the shock of the woman to whom she is talking, who has not encountered this particular name for childbirth before. With the growth of feminism there has been increased opportunity (with an increase in confidence for women and an increase in the likelihood of the validation of their meaning) for women to name experience in defiance of male meanings. When they do dare to name experience from their perspective many women state that they feel they were tricked by the old meaning (Oakley, 1979: 109):

Now I just recount it, I say that it was awful and that I'm disillusioned, but *then* — a couple of days afterwards — I felt I'd been *tricked*. Actually tricked by the health visitor, by the books I'd read — by the Gordon Bourne book, because he says the word 'pain' should *not* be applied to labour contractions. And somebody had said well it's not like it is in the films or something. And I thought well it's *exactly* like 'Gone with the Wind' — it's exactly like those old movies when they're all writhing about in agony; that's *exactly* what I was doing.

Although there are many new versions in which women have revealed new meanings of childbirth and have repudiated many of the old one-dimensional names of a monolithic experience of beauty and rapturous joy, there is still opposition to this renaming, sometimes by females within one's own family circle (Oakley, 1979: 109):

The whole mental thing; the whole physical bit; the lot in fact has been completely different. They all lied to me. I mean all those myths that it's like shelling peas — our family's never had any difficulty — *that* sort of thing has been shattered. Our family *has* had difficulty even if I'm the only one. These books; they should say; right, girls, it can either go well or badly. All that sort of silly nonsense, rubbish, forget it. Don't write things like that to people

because it did a power of *bad* for me. Everybody said you'll forget
terribly quickly what it's like, in a week's time you'll say oh it was
okay. That's supposed to be the thing about childbirth. But I've
been determined NOT to forget.

Here is someone who is deliberately resisting a return to the old name of
childbirth and who is insisting that the full meanings be allowed to exist.
But even as she argues for the diversity of names which encompass
women's experience, there are calls for the end of feminist-inspired
demeaning of motherhood (Leach, 1979). Those meanings which do
not support the patriarchal order are frequently seen as threatening,
and, of course, they are often seen this way by women and men alike,
for *both* sexes inhabit a male-decreed reality and make sense of the
world in terms of male meanings. If the new names provided by women
are not fostered and supported, then there is no reason to expect any
changes in this male monopolization of meaning. These new names will
be lost just as were those names which were undoubtedly generated by
some of our foremothers. This chain can also be broken.

It would be unreasonable to attach 'blame' to women who do not
'publicly' declare their alternative meanings of motherhood and who let
the partial, and false, meanings persist. They may be being protective:
they may also be being realistic. They may have chosen not to present
any alternative they have experienced because so great is the power of
the dominant reality to define the world that even those women who are
closest to them could reject their meanings and attribute them to
neurosis. A mother who speaks 'disparagingly' of childbirth – and that
is how it could be interpreted – to her daughter who is about to
experience it for the first time, could, at worst, be branded as
monstrous, and, at best, be labelled as embittered. Under such
circumstances one cannot 'blame' women who remain silent when their
own version of experience conflicts with legitimated reality; but,
likewise, one would want to urge them to break this silence.

It is through the silence of women that male knowledge of
motherhood – and of numerous other events – goes unchallenged. The
male version of reality can be perpetuated, and even strengthened,
because it remains unquestioned. (This would not be the case if more
women talked about the alternatives, as, for example, did the above
speakers.) It is quite possible that males may not even suspect that their
meanings of women, and women's experience, are only the partial
meanings of the spectator.

However, even if women do try to break the silence of their experience, there is no guarantee that their meanings will be considered 'real' or acceptable. While it is only individual women who challenge the false nature of male meanings, it is more likely that the woman will be dismissed than that the meaning of motherhood – for example – will be extended. There are many readily available devices for invalidating women's experience, so that women who do not experience the 'joys' of motherhood, as defined by males, may be the 'unfortunate' victims of a doctor/hospital/husband or even their own disturbed views: they are the 'exceptions' who can be treated sympathetically and understandingly, the object of pity rather than the genuine subject encoding experience.

There are numerous reasons for suspecting that many of the legitimated meanings of our culture are false and misrepresentative because they have been primarily constructed by men. Men may know something of motherhood – after all they comprise the majority of obstetricians – but they know only from their specific position as men, and only from the perspective of spectator. This must provide a limited view of the event, for the meanings of motherhood which men have provided are based on the way in which motherhood relates to them. It would not be at all surprising if motherhood meant something entirely different to those who were the participants. Adrienne Rich (1977) has demonstrated that there is a completely different set of meanings when motherhood is named by women.

But as with so many aspects of female experience which have been named by men, there are many 'obstacles' which can prevent the female meanings from surfacing. The female version has been blanketed (Delamont and Duffin, 1978) and made invisible or negative. This is one of the sources, and one of the manifestations of woman's identity as 'other' (de Beauvoir, 1972: 16). Men have not *supplied* meanings which undermine their power, diminish their prestige, or detract from their image. Intentionally or otherwise they have formulated a semantic rule which posits themselves as central and positive, as the norm, and they have classified the world from that reference point, constructing a symbolic system which represents patriarchal order. They have been engaged in this process for a long time and *we* have inherited their accumulated meanings which portray men positively while females – wherever they are taken into account – are portrayed negatively.

Both sexes have inherited these meanings and are required to accept them as the only reality, but they are the product of one sex's view of the world, and its own place within that world. It is to be expected that the partial and single view of reality which has been constructed by one sex is a 'better fit' with their own experience than it would be for the sex whose meanings have been omitted, who have been silenced.

Michael Young (1975) defines knowledge as 'available sets of meaning', and the knowledge which we have inherited has been constructed mostly by males in their attempt to provide meaning for their existence, with the result that the possibly vast repertoire of women's meanings – which could explain and order their view of the world – are missing from the language and from areas of codified experience such as history or art or political science. This is a dialectical process: women have been underrepresented in the language and therefore often underrepresented in the various bodies of knowledge that have been constructed. And while they are underrepresented in codified knowledge they continue to be underrepresented in the language itself. This is the silence (and invisibility) of women in patriarchal order. 'In a world where language and naming are power,' says Adrienne Rich (1979:204), 'silence is oppression, is violence'.

The silence of women has been a cumulative process. Conceptually and materially excluded from the production of knowledge, their meanings and explanations have been systematically blocked and their invisibility has been compounded. It is this 'non-existence' (Rowbotham, 1973b:37) of women in language/knowledge/culture that feminists are beginning to unravel and to remedy. Superficially, the process may appear simple – women have been left out and now we must put them back in – and in the early days of the current women's movement many thought that it would be relatively easy to reinstate women in codified meanings. But that has not been the case.

Women's meanings cannot just be added on. Little is gained by the production of more knowledge about women while it is confined to patriarchal definitions and while it is constructed according to patriarchal criteria. The historical silence of women is not broken by a proliferation of studies on maternal deprivation, an increase in information on the mental and physical 'sickness' of women, or greater efforts to uncover the source of women's language deficiency. It is not enough to recover the 'Great Women' of history for even the notion of greatness has its origin in patriarchal hierarchies and implies 'a desire to parallel the records of men's achievements' (Daly, 1978:24). If women are to have their own voice and not just to echo men, then new *cerebration*, a new way of knowing is required.

When modern feminists first began to be suspicious of the methods which had been used to construct knowledge, they were often cautiously critical. Reared in a culture which would have us believe in the absolute nature of 'objective facts', it was sometimes too much to comprehend in a short space of time the nature and extent of the hoax that had been perpetrated. Jessie Bernard (1973) courageously claimed that a masculist bias had been implanted in the very methods of inquiry, and Joan Roberts (1976) pointed out that the new 'scientific' judgments about women were simply asserting the old prejudices, but with more authority. The patriarchal criteria of credibility, when placed under feminist scrutiny, began to emerge as yet another set of male meanings, another male encoded dogma no more or less credible than its religious predecessor.

It was not just the knowledge, the encoded meanings, which we inherited that were unacceptable, it was also the rules for encoding that knowledge, for those rules would not serve feminist ends. Women needed to reconceptualize the objects and events of the world, to reorganize ways of making sense of the world, if they were not to engage in 'standard patriarchal scholarship, which merely re-searches and re-covers "women's history" ' (Daly, 1978:23) and leaves the patriarchal order, and the silence of women, undisturbed. From the outset the construction of feminist knowledge, the encoding of women's meanings, has been a direct challenge to the patriarchal order.

Women are renaming the world and are breaking out of their imposed silence. This is 'a sequence of extreme acts' which Mary Daly terms *metapatriarchal* and she states that she has chosen the term *meta* because it has multiple meanings. 'It incorporates the idea of "postpatriarchal", for it means occurring later,' she says, and 'It puts patriarchy in the past without denying that its walls/ruins and demons are still around us. Since *meta* also means "situated behind", it suggests that the direction of the journey which feminists are taking is into the background and away from the foreground of patriarchal meanings, and as another meaning of this prefix *meta* is "change in, transformation of", the term *metapatriarchal* seems an appropriate renaming (recycling) of the world for women' (Daly, 1978: 7).

But in trying to produce knowledge about women which is consistent with their experience, and not confined by patriarchal meanings, where do we start and how do we go about it? Is there anything of the patriarchal order we can take and use for ourselves, or must we begin anew?

Assuredly, there is no one, right answer to these problems – that being one of the first patriarchal pitfalls to be avoided – but beginning with the understanding that the *personal is political* feminists have begun exploring a new way of knowing[1] and their actions are not designed to support or maintain patriarchal order. It is interesting to examine some of the accusations which have been levelled at these 'alternative' feminist meanings for the basis of these charges exposes one of the fissures of patriarchal order.

When women do begin to work towards encoding their own meanings, they are merely doing what men have done for centuries: they are attempting to name the world from their own perspective. But their actions are not, of course, always viewed in this light. One of the major protests against women's meanings is on the grounds that they are false and biased. Classified as the 'subjective' (and emotional) knowledge of women and polarized against the 'objective' knowledge of men, there exists in patriarchal order a ready-made format for dismissing feminist meanings. But this assumes that the unequal division of subjectivity/objectivity is 'neutral' and valid – an assumption which is encouraged within the patriarchal order but one which cannot be accepted by feminists. Piercing through to the essence of this debate, Adrienne Rich (1979) summed it up succinctly when she stated that 'objectivity' is nothing other than male 'subjectivity'. The patriarchal order is the product of male subjectivity and it has been legitimated and made 'unquestionable' by conceptualizing it as 'objectivity'. She says (1979: 207):

> Feminism means finally that we renounce our obedience to our fathers and recognize that the world they have described is not the whole world. Masculine ideologies are the creation of masculine

---

1 Mary Daly (1978) has used the term *lucid cerebration* as a label for this new way of knowing. She defines it as 'the free play of intuition in our own space, giving rise to thinking that is vigorous, informed, multidimensional, independent, creative, tough' (p. 23). If I understand her correctly she uses the term *spinning* to represent 'the journey' which feminists are making and articulating and with her own usual 'vigorous, informed, multidimensional, independent, creative, tough' thinking she invests spinning with a wealth of women's meanings which makes it of superb value for women. *Spinning* is an excellent example in itself of the way the silence can be broken. She takes the word *spinster* with all its current derogatory meanings, reinvests it with its original meaning, that is 'a woman whose occupation is to spin', and retrieves it from patriarchal order by producing its meanings for women: 'There is no reason to limit the meaning of this rich and cosmic verb. A woman whose occupation is to spin participates in the whirling movement of creation' (p. 3). 'Spinsters can find our way back to reality by destroying the false perceptions of it inflicted upon us by the language', says Daly. 'We must learn to dis-spell the language of phallocracy' which keeps us under the spell of silence (p. 4).

subjectivity: they are neither objective, nor value free, nor exclusively 'human'. Feminism implies that we recognize fully the inadequacy for us, the distortion, of male created ideologies, and that we proceed to think, and act, out of that recognition.

The dichotomy objectivity/subjectivity is, in the words of many feminists, a masculine ideology and, for us, is partial and false. In the construction of feminist meanings, the distinction does not apply and feminists are seeking criteria of credibility at a *metapatriarchal* level. Under the patriarchal division, women could so easily be dismissed as 'non-data' (Daly, 1973); in the name of 'objectivity' females who did 'not behave as expected in experiments' and were therefore 'considered to have "skewed" the data' were 'rejected as subjects' (Tobias, 1978:89). Such rules for the construction of knowledge simply are not good enough for the construction of feminist meanings. It is precisely because so many distortions can occur in the pursuit of 'objectivity' that feminists have found it necessary to go further. In going further, feminists are challenging some of the fundamental premises of patriarchal order, they are challenging the ideologies which maintain that order, they are challenging one of the sources of male power.

While men have had a monopoly on the production of meaning it has not been inordinately difficult to sustain the belief that there is but one, single, reality. Mary Daly (1978) refers to this as *monodimensional* reality. With the enforced silence of women any possible alternatives have been preempted so that the single (and partial) male view of the world has usually been accepted by both sexes as the only view of the world. Within the confines of this single reality it has been plausible to accept the existence of a single 'truth', and an 'objective' way of proceeding towards it. From the perspective of male subjectivity it has not been unreasonable to accept the complete pattern of a single, ordered universe over which they exercise control using the concepts of truth and objectivity as guides. It is a neat pattern, and while there were no unbelievers, no heretics exposing its discrepancies, there were no reasons for doubting its authenticity.

But feminism has partly changed this. The very existence of feminist meanings — few and fragile though they may be — undermines the existence of monodimensional reality. The production of feminist meanings is incontestable evidence of the existence of more than one, single, reality: there must be at least two! Such evidence cannot be incorporated into monodimensional reality because to 'admit' the existence of an alternative is to dismantle/transform monodimensional reality. In the terms of monodimensional reality you cannot accept that there might be two or more realities and still retain the belief that there is only one. And if there are two or more realities then there is – at least – the possibility that there are two or more truths, and two or more ways of proceeding towards them!

So feminist meanings challenge patriarchal order at its core and one should expect that the efforts made to dismiss/discount/discredit those feminist meanings would be quite energetic. One should also expect that the patriarchal order could be capable of 'absorbing' these meanings and rendering them harmless.

I would not argue with anyone who asserted that feminist meanings/knowledge is *political*: it is about a redistribution of power, a reclaiming of the right to name, an end of silence, and is, therefore, a frankly political activity. But it is no less political than masculism or men's studies (the bulk of codified knowledge) have been. The meanings encoded under the rubric of psychology, or history, or even biology, for example, have also been political, although not necessarily frankly so. That these meanings have not been open to question, that they have been justified on the grounds of 'objectivity', is no longer a defence, for 'objectivity' – as it has been defined and appropriated by males – is just as much a political act as any feminists are currently engaged in. Procuring female silence, eliminating any alternative, any opposition, is a highly political act and any protests against feminism – on the grounds of its political nature – cannot be taken seriously.

Under patriarchal order, the rules for the construction of knowledge about females have been simple. Women have not counted except in so far as they relate to men. Their silence has been successfully engineered. This is the knowledge we have inherited and these are the accumulated meanings which we have to contest. They are not our meanings. We must begin to make our own but we must also recognize that we cannot forge a complete new set of meanings overnight. We are still circumscribed by patriarchal order and have taken only tentative steps towards our release. But we have made a huge leap in our discovery that these meanings are not our own, that they are *man*-made and *man*-governed. 'In order to create an alternative an oppressed group must at once shatter the self-reflecting world which encircles it', states Sheila Rowbotham, and at the same time it must 'project its own image onto history' (1973b: 27); this is what feminism is attempting to do as it encodes its metapatriarchal meanings. And as it engages in this process it changes the rules for making sense of the world, it transforms the rules by which patriarchal knowledge has been produced.

# The invisibility of women

The construction of feminist knowledge has exposed the inherent bias – there is a need for a new term which has more weight – in traditional, male monopolized knowledge. In the interests of credibility it is necessary that there should be a 'corrective' to this bias and feminism is one of the possible correctives (Howe, 1977:17). But the corrective is not confined to the meanings themselves for there must also be a corrective in terms of arriving at those meanings. Men's subjectivity is not enough: the subjectivity – the symbolic weight – of the other half of the population must also be taken into account.

This is where current feminism has started, with women trying to evolve their own meanings in a way that meets their own needs and matches their own experience. To do this it has been necessary to examine, to evaluate and to discard many of the traditional analytical tools which have been used in the construction of knowledge.

Having become aware of the silence of women, Joan Roberts (1976) began with the task of trying to find women's meanings in order that they might be included, but she states that after having searched for relevant facts and concepts she realized that 'neither facts nor concepts about females existed in scholarly areas'. What she did find was that ideas which presumably pertained to both sexes were actually based on the study of males and merely extended to females. She also found that male objectivity had produced 'a paucity of fact and a prevalence of opinion' when it came to women, and she was forced to conclude that 'the challenging and arduous task before us was to rethink the concepts inherited from men – about them, about us, and therefore about humanity' (1976:5).

Many feminists shared her conclusions. Whether the discipline was art (Nochlin, 1972), biology (Hubbard, 1979) history (Lewis, 1980) literature (Kolodny, 1980), language (Jenkins and Kramer, 1980), politics (Lovenduski, 1980), psychology (Walker, 1980) or sociology (Roberts, 1980), the task was to reconceptualize the way in which knowledge could be constructed so that women could be included. It was obvious that if women were to be simply grafted on to men's knowledge (and according to the same rules) then such meanings, even if initially *positive*, would soon be pejorated and become negative, as both Muriel Schulz and Julia Stanley have indicated (see p. 21).

It is in the rules for making meaning, for structuring the world, that the changes need to come. Again there are interconnections, for it would be a superficial and self-defeating exercise to attempt to change the meanings of women without changing the rules by which these meanings are constructed (or vice versa), and changes in one will be of assistance in changing the other. This is no monodimensional, linear reality but a multidimensional, non-linear, interrelated reality in which either/or, right/wrong subjectivity/objectivity are not useful distinctions.

One of the first steps which feminists took in constructing their meanings was to document the absence/silence of women, for – paradoxically perhaps – this was one means of making females visible. Feminist critiques of the disciplines emerged and many of them are now feminist classics, for example, Naomi Weisstein's 'Psychology constructs the female ...' (1971). The silence of women began to resound as documented record after documented record of female 'non-existence' began to emerge. Women began to reject the definitions which had confined and distorted them and they began to become aware of the void which existed where their own meanings could have been. There was, of course, shock. Many could not comprehend how they had been so monstrously misled.

I can remember how stunned I was when it began to dawn on me. I had been conned. I had swallowed it completely. I had genuinely believed that my education was valuable, that I had been presented with insights into the human condition and at first I was just paralysed when I began to understand that I had only ever been given insights into the male condition. And insights, well, that isn't the right word, is it? They weren't insights, they were deceptions ... lies. But then I got angry, I mean really angry. Two years of nineteenth-century history and not a mention of the woman question. I didn't even know women had fought for the vote. I went back to my lecturer and said, look, just look at this! There was more written about the woman question in the nineteenth century than there was about socialism. Why didn't you tell us that ... ?

He was very, very cool. He said it wasn't significant! Can you imagine ... it wasn't significant. Well I couldn't win against him, but I really wanted to know how it could have happened. Christ, the nineteenth century isn't that long ago. How could people forget? How could that sort of ... mammoth censoring take place and no one shout that it was unfair? How did they get away with it?(7)

It seems that it was not necessarily a matter of trying to 'get away with anything'. It has not been necessary explicitly to disguise or censor women's meanings for the rules for the construction of knowledge, the criteria for deciding what is relevant and what is not, what is data and what is not, are such that it is often unlikely that women will get into history – or sociology – for example. When women are 'taken care of' at the encoding level there is no need for males – malintentioned or otherwise – to erase them deliberately. They are conveniently made invisible from the outset.

It is possible to show how these encoding rules have operated through a variety of disciplines[2] but one discipline can serve as an example of how simple this process can be – when males have a monopoly on decreeing meaning. Partly because it has been diligently documented – and partly because the parameters are probably familiar – I have chosen to analyse sociology to illustrate the means by which the patriarchal order has engineered the silence of females in codified knowledge.

Jessie Bernard (1973) already had an established reputation as an academic in sociology before contemporary feminism made its criticisms felt and she therefore had some 'legitimated authority' (that is, male approval) when she began to expose some of the flaws in the construction of sociological knowledge. She stated without equivocation that sociology was a male science of society and that 'Practically all sociology to date has been a sociology of the male world' (p. 73). Bernard declared, and many agreed, that males had taken themselves as the reference point, assessed problems and determined priorities from their perspective, and then proceeded to conduct their research and construct their sociological knowledge on these most subjective and unquestioned premises. By such 'convenient' means females were

---

2 See Dale Spender (ed.), *Men's Studies Modified: the Impact of Feminism on the Academic Disciplines* (Pergamon, 1981) for a fuller coverage of the way women's meanings have been excluded from a variety of disciplines.

readily excluded from that codification of meanings for, to begin with, given the sexual division of labour in society (something which male sociologists generally 'took for granted'), the likelihood of female problems and priorities matching with those of males was fairly remote. Constructing knowledge on these male defined premises almost guaranteed that the experience of females would remain 'invisible' and consequently come to be regarded as 'unreal'. Where women did come into sociology it was frequently as they related to men and as their existence was problematic to men.

The codification of knowledge is a cumulative process and what may have been 'oversights' in the initial stages of a discipline can become huge gaps in meaning as the discipline 'progresses' without putting in what it first left out in the preliminary stages. The absence of women in sociological meanings becomes relatively greater as meanings about men and their world proliferate.

As with language, some can claim that sociology is not a 'male science' (as Bernard states) because there are women sociologists, but the weaknesses in this argument are the same as with language. The existence of women sociologists in no way refutes the contention that sociology is the 'property' of males: both sexes may share the rules and methods of sociology, both sexes may operate within its framework, but males have defined that framework and women were neither fairly represented in the initial construction of the meaning of sociology, nor are they fairly represented in the meanings which have flowed from the first endeavours.

By taking themselves as the norm, men have constructed a body of knowledge in which their own image is continually enhanced and strengthened (with predictable consequences for women). Ann Oakley (1974) has shown how the whole discipline of sociology has been constructed on sexist foundation stones which ensure the silence of women simply by eliminating them from serious consideration. Every discipline must have a paradigm, a model which decrees what is of that discipline and what is not, what is relevant, appropriate and useful, and these paradigms which are rigorously followed (and taught) were not handed down from some benign authority: men made them up. The paradigm which controls what becomes sociological knowledge has been made up by men – the fathers of sociology – so that women and their world do not rate. Women have been excluded 'from everything from the classification of subject areas and the definitions of topics and methods of empirical research to the construction of models and theories generally', states Oakley (p. 3). And her claim is not difficult to substantiate.

It is easy to locate the way in which women have been left out of the subject areas and the definitions of what constitutes a suitable topic, and not much more difficult to locate the way in which they have been excluded from methods of empirical research and been silenced in models and theories generally.

The world of women is defined out of the subject matter and the devaluation of women is thereby doubly enforced; their world did not count originally and sociology is testimony to the fact that their world does not count now. There are numerous examples of the way women and their concerns have been eliminated from consideration but one dramatic example is in the study of *power*. First of all the concept of power which is employed and deemed worthy of study is that which is relevant to men. We may have a vague notion that there is some power which women have – 'the power behind the throne', 'behind every great man there is a great woman', etc. – but these meanings have not found their way into sociology. It is power, as it applies to males, that has been studied and this does not just mean that we are 'forced' to know more about male types of power, more about 'the might is right' variety, it also means that the particular form of power which males utilize comes to be accepted as the only 'real' power, thereby banishing any meanings of women's power to the periphery of knowledge and reality. One of the tasks which feminist sociologists have set themselves is that of redefining power, of breaking outside this astigmatic, monodimensional definition of power so that it encompasses women's meanings. Because of the emphases provided by sociology, many are convinced that there is only one form of legitimate power and that it applies to males. Because of the role power has played in a hierarchical society, it also tends to be something which many feminists – understandably – find unacceptable. But power could have many different and even useful meanings if the experiences of women were to be taken into account.

There are other by-products of this utilization of the concept of power: it has led sociologists to focus on institutions through which power has been exercised – institutions such as the legal and political systems – and these are male dominated areas where women have been only involved 'tangentially'. As Ann Oakley says, 'the more sociology is concerned with such areas, the less it is, by definition, likely to include women within its frame of reference' (p. 4).

Another area where sociologists have been able to decree that women's experience is non-data, is that of work. The practice has been to define work as 'something which men do', again with the result that women's work is made 'invisible' while the superiority of the male life style is artificially strengthened. While both sexes share these definitions of work, accepting that the activities which males engage in are more important, while those that women engage in are inconsequential and insignificant, they stem from one sex's subjective view of the world.

Vast areas of female 'work' have been ignored to the extent that trying to include them in the male defined parameters of what constitutes work would be ridiculed. But given that 'work' is one means of attaining economic security, why should the arbitrary sexual division of labour be used to justify the legitimacy of male efforts and to dismiss female efforts in this respect? In a patriarchal society women may work at success with the same commitment as men, but it will take different forms. Being 'attractive' is not only one means of seeking economic security if one is female, it is also very hard *work*. The maintenance of an attractive figure, hairstyle, wardrobe, etc., can be no less arduous and time consuming a task than the maintenance of many a male career. Producing leisure for men can be no less demanding than producing for the GNP. If women's work were to be given equal status with men's work, and if women's meanings were allowed to emerge, entertaining, homemaking and child-rearing would no longer be dismissed and women would no longer reveal the absurdity of male definitions by stating 'I don't work. I'm only a housewife', as they rushed for twelve hours per day, seven days a week, to meet the demands which society imposes upon them but which it does not count.

As women have begun to shed some of the man-made meanings which have constrained their existence and reality, we have become aware of the radical changes which can occur when meanings are shifted. Feminists have been instrumental in establishing that housework, for example, is real work and should be valued as such, but perhaps for obvious reasons they have not been quite so prepared to assist in valuing beautifying and production of leisure for men, preferring to eliminate rather than to value these activities. Their insistence on these woman-centred meanings reveals the male bias in sociological definitions. Not only has the sociology of housework made its appearance as a 'corrective' to male bias in definitions of work but, as women's work has begun to be visible, even more woman-centred meanings are generated from this base. Instead of viewing 'working women' through the filter of what happens to their children, or what demands they make on their husbands (a most male-biased view) studies are now being done on the effects on women who are obliged to do a double-shift to do unpaid domestic work and paid work in the labour force. This is also an example of the way in which women's meanings cannot simply be added on to existing male meanings. By defining *housework* as work, women have extended the meaning of work itself: and by naming women's experience as the *double-shift* new light is cast on the work which men perform. From this new ordering of reality, new possibilities arise, so that women can now begin to define their production of leisure for male consumption as a demanding, time consuming, and unjust task. Men's meanings may accommodate or conflict with these new woman-centred names but they will not be quite the same again.

As the sociology of housework has been established as a legitimate if not a prestigious area of study, the dialectical process can again be observed at work. While on the one hand the existence of this new branch of sociology undisputedly provides females with greater representation in sociology, on the other hand it is also indisputable that it enjoys low status. Women are generating and encoding their meanings but, in a patriarchal order where they are still confined to negative semantic space, these meanings can be readily devalued. It simply is not enough to get women into the subject area of sociology: the status of women must change as well. But there would be no change in women's status while they remained outside the definitions of sociology.

Because, ironically, women can also become visible through the exposure of their invisibility, other gains have also been made in the topics of sociology. Angela MacRobbie and Jenny Garber (1975) revealed the absence of women in studies of 'youth culture' where sociologists by virtue of their male-as-norm definition of 'youth' have been almost exclusively concerned with males, with the result that the subculture of adolescent females has been relegated to the realm of non-existence. Women have also been omitted from 'deviancy theory', as Ann Oakley points out, and it is a mark of male short-sightedness that it has often been prostitution that has been considered female deviancy; it would be better classified as work, and its role inside, as well as outside, marriage investigated.

Susan Isles (1978) has shown that within criminology another double-standard has operated, one which classifies male offenders as criminals and female offenders as 'sick'. Even though this may have been advantageous for women in criminal terms – for a psychological test, a warning, and an injunction to return to the role of good wife and mother must be considered preferable to a prison sentence – it also illustrates the operation of sexism in the codification of knowledge. Like other aspects of women's behaviour, women's crime has not been treated seriously: it too has been made invisible. One consequence has been that even where women's criminal habits cannot be denied – shop-lifting being a case in point – little attention has been paid to it in sociological study.

When it comes to the theories which inform and structure sociology, the design is such that women can be included or minimized. Ann Oakley (1974) and Margrit Eichler (1979) have been among the many feminists who have demonstrated that stratification theories are based on males and cannot with any great degree of validity be transferred to women. Oakley claims (1974:9) that stratification theory which has been fundamental to sociology is based on three largely untested assumptions, which are:

(a) that the family is the main unit of stratification (an assumption which is becoming increasingly questionable. MS magazine reported in March 1978 that the nuclear family is now a minority unit in the USA and the Equal Opportunities Commission states in 1983 that 'Only 5 per cent of all households are made up of working husband, economically inactive wife, and two dependent children')

(b) that the status of the *male* in the family determines the social position of the family as a whole, and

(c) that it is rare for a woman to be able to gain a social position independently of the male to whom she is 'attached'.

Although numerous indices could be used for social stratification, occupation is a common one and it is the occupation of the male which usually determines the family's social position. Females become non-existent under such practices with their own achievements classified as irrelevant and non-data. It is not necessarily that they don't have occupations (or education, or skills), but what they have do not count. As Oakley points out, 'an occupationally based class categorization of married women would put many of them in a different class from their husbands' (p. 10). If women were to be included in the formulation of these theories which influence the construction of sociological knowledge many accepted 'truths' would become quite absurd; put simply, the incorporation of women into stratification theory, if such were possible, would not only mean the production of a great deal of new knowledge, it would also mean discarding much of the old.

The profile is much the same when it comes to women in the paid workforce. There are so few studies of women in the workplace and those that have been undertaken often reveal the masculist perspective which has spawned them because they are usually studies which facilitate the acceptance of women and paid work as problematic. Women and work are often studied from the standpoint of the way in which *their* work impinges upon *male* consciousness.

Embedded in the sociological rules for the construction of knowledge is a sex-differentiated definition of work which encourages sex-differentiated studies and conclusions. With such a definition it is possible logically to carry out a study of maternal deprivation under the rubric of 'women and work', while any notion of paternal deprivation, if it did arise, would appear as ludicrous or facetious. Ann Oakley has said that women have been asked – in the interests of constructing sociological truths – why it is that they work, because their working behaviour is seen as problematic, as something to be explained, according to the dictates of sociology. To ask a woman why she *does* work is akin to asking a male why he does *not* (1974:19), and the knowledge which proceeds from these sexist assumptions helps to construct, rather than challenge, sexist 'truths'.

Only a discipline which took sex differences in work for granted could fail to notice that there has never been a study of female redundancy in the workplace. Only a discipline which encoded exclusively male meanings could accept that females are non-workers and therefore cannot be genuinely redundant or unemployed, despite the number of dependants they may possess. The 'interesting' questions which have arisen for exploration in sociology in relation to women and work are why would they do it and what problems it causes, and one can begin to visualize how different sociological knowledge would look if these questions were seen to be equally 'interesting' when applied to males. While sociology continues to construct knowledge on the premise that women are not *real* workers, it is in no danger of helping to make women visible or autonomous. There is little risk that conventional sociological studies will encode women's experience of the workplace. It will provide no insights into women's meanings of paid work because it has evolved parameters which preclude it from even venturing into such an area. If sociologists had been concerned with an occupational sociology of women, then we would not have had to wait until 1978 for feminist studies of sexual harassment of women in the workforce. It has been part of the work experience of women for many generations, but it has not been 'worthy' of study.

Oakley also stated that women have been silenced when it comes to the methodology of sociology and, though not quite so well documented, her claim can still be substantiated. The methods which have been considered 'proper' for the construction of sociological knowledge also reveal the subtle debasement and dispersement of women's meanings. Jessie Bernard (1973) has said that men have asked the questions and have also ordained the methods of answering them and this has lead to a *machismo* element in research. Bernard argues, and few feminists would disagree, that within the male scheme of values it is important to have control and so the research procedures which have appealed to them, which have been more highly valued, are those in which they as scientists exert control. Bernard calls this *agentic* research and says that the 'scientist using this approach creates his own controlled reality. He can manipulate it. He is master. He has power ... He can play with a simulated reality like an Olympian god' (p. 23). It is not coincidental that the data yielded via the agentic approach has been called *hard data* and that it is accorded high prestige and greater authority and weight. The meanings which are the outcome of this approach are supposed to be more reliable, more 'objective' and less open to challenge.

Sociology could have employed other methods for constructing knowledge, but from the perspective of the dominant group alternatives did not seem so desirable. Bernard states that there is an alternative method, one which she has labelled the *communal* method, and it is an approach which is wary of employing controls precisely because they 'interfere' with the results and distort the meanings which can arise. If this approach had been used more in sociology, and if it had been considered valid, it is likely that whenever women were the object of study more of their meanings would have been able to surface because of the very absence of 'male' control. It was the communal approach which was used by Betty Friedan (1963) when she involved herself with the lives of women, imposed no controls, and simply tried to listen to what they had to say. She heard the *other* meanings which were shadowily hovering in women's lives and she significantly labelled them as 'a problem without a name'. Obviously these meanings had no name, for, from the perspective of males, the problem did not even exist.

Some of the meanings which women may be generating to explain their existence could literally be 'unthinkable' to many men, so male sociologists are not likely to plan for the emergence of such meanings in their research. By using the agentic method of research, however, they have further strengthened the barriers to the emergence of women's meanings. Whenever the meanings of women have made their presence felt, it has usually been under the rubric of 'soft data' and therefore more readily discounted. Built into the paradigm of sociology are many, many blocks to women's meanings: the patriarchal order has many tools for silencing women.

Feminist critiques have challenged the validity of many theories and practices, and not just of sociology, and this work has prompted a rethink across disciplines, especially in the social sciences and humanities. Feminists have not just asked why and how women have been ignored, but why, when 'studied at all they have been considered in a prejudiced way within male determined theories' (Mack, 1974:162). Whereas initially there may have been some puzzle about these questions, there is now a clear and simple explanation.

It is no simple matter to simply introduce women into sociology, for example, and this is partly because if women are going to be put in, men are going to be put out. And many members of the dominant group who still control sociology are not likely to respond enthusiastically to this new development, unless it is to resist it. Many 'reputations' have been made on sociology as it now stands, and those who have reputations sometimes have a vested interest in keeping the paradigm in its present form: they can see themselves as having the most to lose if the very substance of sociology is reconceptualized (Kuhn, 1972).

But it is not just academic reputations which could be lost if women were to be taken into account. Equality means nothing less than an end to the supremacy of one sex.

For generations women have been silenced in patriarchal order, unable to have their meanings encoded and accepted in the social repositories of knowledge. The process has been a cumulative one with silence built upon silence. When women's voices do penetrate, that same cumulative process can apply in reverse. Woman-centred meanings will multiply as the pattern of women's existence begins to emerge in both formal and informal contexts. There will be numerous spheres of female existence that will begin to come into focus, which will begin to become *real*. Women will gain confidence from this emerging reality and will make greater efforts in shaping it. As they do so, they will make a contribution towards changing society and its rules for making sense of the world. Sociology, and many other disciplines, will be transformed.

To do this, the newly formed and fragile women's meanings will need to be nurtured and sustained. From providing an alternative individual meaning for motherhood, to constructing a collective understanding of the domestic labour debate, women must take every opportunity to encode their own meanings, and to validate the meanings encoded by other women. Male-defined meanings are so pervasive in patriarchal order and alternative women-centred meanings are so few that the effort to encode and preserve the woman-centred meanings must be constant.

# · 3 ·

# The Dominant and the Muted

❋

In order to explain some of the evidence which he encountered in his anthropological studies, Edwin Ardener (1975) used the terms *dominant* and *muted*. Ardener himself perceived the bias in the rules for encoding knowledge in anthropology and his initial efforts were directed towards describing the silent/muted nature of women. He asked why it was that women, who theoretically comprised at least half the sample of the anthropologist, did not command half the attention. He convincingly established that females have not been studied to the same extent — or in the same way — as males, with the result that they are relatively invisible in anthropology. Ardener was extremely critical of anthropologists who claimed to have 'cracked the code' of a community, without reference to at least half the population. 'The fact is,' he declares, 'that no one could come back from an ethnographic study of "the X", having talked only *to* women, and *about* men, without professional comment and some self-doubt,' whereas 'the reverse can and does happen constantly' (E. Ardener, 1975:3).

In other words, Ardener had come across the silence of woman and suspected, initially, that the flaw was confined to anthropological methodology.

Ardener argued that the models — the meanings/theories/structures — which exist have been formulated by males and they have been validated by reference to other males. Stating it simply, men have made up the meanings for society and then have checked with other men to see if those meanings are accurate. Because this activity has been the prerogative of men, Ardener labelled men as the *dominant* group.

76

Women were the *muted* group because they were excluded from the formulation and validation of meaning and therefore denied the means to express themselves. Women were locked out, and, to Ardener, the problem was to find some means of access for them.

Coming from a different background, but encountering the same problem, Dorothy Smith (1978) reached similar conclusions. Her description of the role the two sexes play in the formulation of meaning fits well with Ardener's, for Smith says that 'women have been largely excluded from the work of producing the forms of thought and the images and symbols in which thought is expressed and ordered'. Smith agrees that these are the models of society and they have been produced by men and validated by men. 'There is a circle effect,' she says, and 'Men attend to and treat as significant only what men say. The circle of men whose writing and talk was significant to each other extends backwards in time as far as our records reach. What men were doing was relevant to men, was written by men about men for men. Men listened and listen to what one another said' (p. 281). Although Smith doesn't use the word muted to describe the condition of women under these arrangements, the term is not inconsistent with her meaning.

With the acceptance of the term *muted* to label the existence of women, the research distinctions between sexism in language and sex differences in language (as discussed in chapter 1) become increasingly meaningless. They are part of the same problem – the silence of women in patriarchal order. Women are muted because men are in control and the language, and the meanings, and the knowledge of women cannot be accounted for outside that male control. If women's meanings are to have unfettered impression, then it seems that men must cease to have control.

Inherent in this analysis of dominant/muted groups is the assumption that women and men will generate different meanings, that is, that there is more than one perceptual order, but that only the 'perceptions' of the dominant group, with their inherently partial nature, are encoded and transmitted. This does not necessarily resort to biological determinism – a criticism which has been made of Edwin Ardener – but neither does it exclude a biological dimension. The possibility of women and men generating different meanings can be conceptualized without recourse to biology as a form of monocausation (the product of a monodimensional reality). In speaking of the 'consciousness of women' – a concept that has parallels with the generation of meaning – Sheila Rowbotham (1973a) has stated that this is not to suggest 'that biology is destiny. I do not believe that women or men are determined by either anatomy or economics, though I think both contribute to a definition of what we can be, and what we have to struggle to go beyond' (p. x). Although there may be some criticisms of the model offered by Ardener (and of Mary Daly and Simone de Beauvoir and Adrienne Rich and Dorothy Smith, and the many others who have posited the existence of meanings that are specific to women), it would be unjustified to dismiss them on the grounds of biological determinism. All these theorists recognize that women and men are positioned differently in patriarchal order and this in itself makes it possible to speak of women and men as 'inhabiting different worlds' (Bernard, 1973), which give rise to sexually differentiated meanings and explanations of those worlds.

If the 'social' factors were to be removed, if (in the wildest fantasy), the patriarchal order were to be eliminated, then I have no way of knowing − and I suspect no one else has either − whether females and males would still inhabit different worlds and still call on different explanations. Nor do I need to know such details to accept the assumptions (and documentation) that men have controlled meaning and made women silent. It is my belief that if women were to gain a public voice, they would in many instances supply very different meanings from those which have been provided, and legitimated, by males.

## Male registers

Shirley Ardener (1975) has built upon the theoretical model outlined by Edwin Ardener and she has suggested that the silence of women is not undifferentiated but has several dimensions. According to Shirley Ardener, the male control of meaning extends to the *registers* of public discourse so that it is both the meaning and the *form* in which that meaning is expressed (in public discourse) that has been encoded by men and is controlled by men. It is for this reason, she says, that men feel more 'comfortable' with public discourse because it is their medium: they have evolved a register in keeping with their values.

Women may feel 'at home' with 'the art of conversation' but men may feel 'at home' with 'the art of rhetoric' or 'the art of persuasion' and perhaps there is no ready transfer between these 'arts' which the dominant group has devised. (Note that it is still in male interests to have women excel at the 'art of conversation' which is also designed to accommodate male needs.) It has already been suggested that men frequently neither know nor can operate the rules of the art of conversation (Pamela Fishman, 1977; see also discussion, p. 48) and it is possible, that, for many women the arts of rhetoric, oratory, persuasion – the arts in which leaders are made and followers are won – may be equally mysterious.

Shirley Ardener's observations have their origin in an anthropological perspective and I have tried to do a 'linguistic translation'. It seems to me that there is some similarity between her account of the public register and the explanations of feminists who have been concerned with *assertiveness training* for women – helping women to have a voice, sometimes in public. I have always been cautious of assertiveness training, and the assumptions upon which it has often rested, because frequently the premise has been that men are the successful speakers and that women need to learn to talk like men. It has attributed this success to linguistic factors and has not always considered the role played by sex.

I have thought it perfectly feasible that women could learn to speak *exactly* like men and yet still be evaluated as less successful – even hesitant and tentative – precisely because it is not always the language which determines the evaluation, but the sex. Assertiveness training programmes based upon the premise that all will be well when women can talk like men have seemed to me to be misguided because they have overlooked the crucial deciding factor, sex. Women will still be judged *as women* no matter how they speak, and no amount of talking the same as men will make them men, and subject to the same judgments.

But Shirley Ardener's speculations have cast new light on old beliefs. There can be little doubt that the dominant group have evolved registers which support their dominance and which might not be consistent with women's experience – be it experience imposed upon them or otherwise. First of all, visibility is a primary factor, for those who engage in public discourse are of necessity visible, and this is probably a more comfortable position for a male, used to visibility in language and culture, indeed, who frequently assumes visibility *a priori*, than it is for a female who is accustomed to being invisible.

The concept of leadership, and all its concomitant attributes, is also inextricably linked with *public* discourse. Those who hold the most sway, who are more influential, who are *dominant*, are those who are sufficiently forceful to carry others along with them. Sally Gearhart

(1979) has made some interesting points about this facet of public discourse and she has likened acts of persuasion to 'acts of violence', claiming that it is no less an assault on someone's existence to make them change their beliefs by oratory than it is by the sword. Both deny the autonomy of individuals. Gearhart sees persuasion, as it has been developed (in the political arena, the advertising arena, etc.), as an inherent part of patriarchal order in which there is a demand for the division between leaders and followers and where public discourse has evolved to meet this demand.

Gearhart's case is more speculative than documented but it is none the less worth considering. It is compatible with Shirley Ardener's thesis that the registers of public discourse have been encoded by males for their own ends and that women shall either be excluded, or made 'uncomfortable', or serve those ends if, and when, they do participate. If this is the case, then assertiveness-training programmes might well engage in some reevaluation, for assuming that it is possible to get women to talk in the same way as men in these male-defined registers, then rather than undermining the patriarchal order, such women could well be subscribing to it. Perhaps assertiveness-training programmes could be seeking a more suitable register, could be helping women encode new meanings in new forms which are more compatible with their experience and more subversive.

Although females and males have been raised with different liguistic expectations and have become skilled at different linguistic activities, there have at times been some females who have appeared to have been 'at home' with the register of public discourse. Once women were allowed to 'speak in public' – which is a relatively recent occurrence and indicates the blatant male control that has been exercised in the past where early feminists frequently had to have their speeches read by men – many of them became forceful public speakers. Bella Abzug is one, and Shauna Adix – a public speaker who is praised and respected in the National Women's Studies Association – another. Adix reports being 'at home' in public discourse and of experiencing none of the fears, doubts, distress, which many other feminists report when required to perform in this medium (Adix, 1979). And then of course, there is Margaret Thatcher, who proved by her own election to be more persuasive than the males themselves!

In general, however, most women seem to feel (and I suspect with good cause) that it is more difficult for a female to operate in male-defined public registers than it is for a male.

Part of it is confidence, of course. When you grow up female in this society, then you learn not to have confidence in yourself as a person. You have to overcome that, and men don't, or at least not in the same way. But even ... and if ... when you catch up on that, there is still a problem. I find it easier to talk to women informally. That's the way I want to do it. That's how you can listen and exchange, which is what I want to do when I talk ... Not just to speak *at*, to deliver a convincing monologue from a platform. Public speaking is a pretty one way process and I am against it in principle. It gives a lot of rights to the few who do the speaking and none to the many who have to listen.

So it's still a problem for me. Sometimes people tell me I'm good at it, and I get a bit confused ... being good at something you don't approve of, making yourself sick ... I get stomach nerves ... with everyone telling you it's necessary. Sometimes I think we won't get very far unless women are public speakers, and sometimes I think we won't get very far when they are. I wish ... I wish I could think of more egalitarian ways of talking *with* a lot of people.(8)

I do not think it too far fetched to suggest that this woman, and Shirley Ardener, are focusing on a similar, if not the same, phenomenon.


## Telling it slant

According to Shirley Ardener the meanings of women are *blocked* at many levels. Because the registers for public discourse (in both the written and spoken forms) have been encoded by men, Ardener argues that women must *monitor* their expressions in a way that men do not. In order to meet these linguistic demands which are not of their own making, and which may even conflict with demands of their own making, women are obliged to monitor, to transform their meanings so that they conform to male requirements. When the meanings of women are consigned to non-existence, when the registers for discourse are male decreed and controlled, women who wish to express themselves must translate their experience into the male code. They are then a *muted* group. Adrienne Rich (1979:208) has tried to articulate the distortions of this state of existence:

In denying the validity of women's experience, in pretending to stand for the 'human', masculine subjectivity tries to force us to name our truths in an alien language; to dilute them: we are constantly told that the 'real' problems, the ones worth working on, are those men have defined, that the problems we need to examine are trivial, unscholarly, nonexistent. We are urged to separate the 'personal' (our existence as women) from the 'scholarly' or 'professional' ... As Tillie Olsen puts it ... 'Not to be able to come to one's own truth, or not to use it in one's writing, even when telling the truth having to "tell it slant", robs one of drive, of conviction, limits potential stature ...' Everywhere, women working in the common world of men are denied that integrity of work and life which can only be found in an emotional and intellectual connectedness with ourselves and other women.

That there is a block between the generation of meaning and the expression of meaning for women is a premise which is shared by many feminists. It is the block which arises when it is necessary to 'tell it slant' so that it is expressed in the form of patriarchal order. Shirley Ardener goes so far as to say that 'because of the absence of a suitable code, and because of a necessary indirectness rather than spontaneity of expression, women, more often than may be the case with men, lack the facility to raise to conscious level their unconscious thoughts' (S. Ardener, 1975; ix). There is nowhere for women's meanings to go because 'the conceptual space in which they would lie is overrun by the dominant model of events generated by the dominant group' (p. xiv). This is a very similar concept to that of negative semantic space as outlined by Julia Stanley. Many women have tried to articulate positive meanings of female outside the 'private' realm and have found that there is no readily available conceptual space to accommodate them (see particularly Mary Daly (1973; 1978) and Penelope (Julia Stanley, 1977) and discussion on p. 21). They may begin to doubt the authenticity of those meanings, to 'lose conviction' as Tillie Olsen puts it, because self-generated meanings can become vague, shadowy and elusive when they have no outlet (see Berger and Luckmann, 1972) so their silence is reinforced at more than one level. Subversive meanings can also incur penalties. Even Copernicus, Galileo and Darwin discovered that there is not always encouragement and acceptance for those who try to introduce meanings for which there is no conceptual space in the social order, and it would be surprising if women – particularly as individuals – were to find their new meanings fostered and their efforts in generating them praised.

There are numerous devices which help to block the meanings of women, to inhibit them, to coerce silence, to make them muted.

Of course it is possible that some women may be unaware of their muted state, that they might have come to accept the definitions of the dominant group in their entirety, but this will not automatically stand as evidence that their meanings are consistent with those that have been encoded by men, that they do not have to transform and accommodate before they can express themselves in the register of the dominant group. It could be that any discrepancies that they experience are being resolved by even greater commitment to male-defined goals. It could be that *all* women feel this mismatch between their experience and encoded experience but whereas some may explore these discrepancies – such as Tillie Olsen, for example – others may deny them in their attempts to make sense of their world.

They may also just accept such discrepancies as part of 'the way the world works' and neither explore, nor deny them, but live with them. Having had no experience other than sensing a mismatch between their own meanings and encoded meanings, it is quite possible that women could assume that this is a universal feature of existence and common to all. If this was their understanding then they would consider it futile to attempt to overcome these difficulties.

But if these difficulties *are* peculiar to women, then this could have manifestations in their language use. If there are more *blocks* to female expression, as Shirley Ardener suggests, then the possibility of sex differences in language use arises – not because of the women, but because of the restrictions imposed by the language.

It could be that there are barriers to women's language use – at both the deep (semantic) and surface (register) level, and that there is an additional process that women must engage in. Edwin Ardener hypothesizes the existence of this 'extra' stage: Shirley Ardener refers to it as 'a necessary indirectness rather than spontaneity'. Tillie Olsen refers to it as 'telling it slant'. Many, many feminist writers who have tried to articulate the difficulties encountered in trying to encode feminist reality have also, directly and indirectly, referred to the phenomenon of being confined to the words of the dominant group, and of 'having to try to tell our truths in an alien language' (Rich, 1979: 203).

|       | Deep structure          |                      | Surface structure               |
|-------|-------------------------|----------------------|---------------------------------|
| Men   | Generation of meaning   | ——————————→          | Expression in male-defined register |
| Women | Generation of meaning   | ——→ TRANSFORMA-TION ——→ | Expression in male-defined register |

The concept of *hesitancy* takes on new dimensions in this context for when individuals are required to transform or monitor their language they are sometimes more hesitant: for example, trying to speak in a class register to which one is unaccustomed, trying to converse in standard English when one's 'first' language is another variant of English. Even people who are engaged in translating from one discrete language to another are sometimes more hesitant in their language use because there is not an uninterrupted process from thought to expression. It is feasible that such hesitancy could exist for women – they could be robbed of drive, conviction and stature when they have to 'tell it slant' as Tillie Olsen suggests – but it is a very different form of hesitancy from that which has been conventionally put forward as part of the stereotype of women's inferior language (see p. 23). It has its origin not in the deficiencies *of* women but in the deficiences *for* women of male-encoded registers.

## In a form acceptable to men

While men are the dominant group and women are muted there is a myriad of controls which help to engineer women's continued silence. It is not just that the language does not accommodate some of the meanings women may want to articulate, it is not just that the male-controlled registers may be an inappropriate form for the expression of women's meanings, there is also the problem posed by male sanctions. Shirley Ardener reminds us that unless the views of women are presented in a way that is acceptable to men, women 'will not be given a proper hearing' (p. ix).

There are probably few feminists who have attempted publicly to encode women's meanings and who have not been victims of male 'put-downs' which help to assure they will not be given a 'proper hearing'. There is a range of clichés that can be called upon to justify male dismissal of women's words, but they are usually variations on the theme of 'I think you have a case but why do you have to put it so vehemently/aggressively/irrationally/emotionally?' In this way, the dominant group can still retain control, it is still the female who is 'in the wrong' and must adjust. This can be a very convenient mechanism because the argument can be dismissed *without reference to the content*.

> Arguments about housework have turned out to be a no-win situation for me. It doesn't matter about my evidence. It doesn't matter that I can present him with a chart showing how many hours I work and how many he works. The issue is always about the way I tell him. He objects to me 'lecturing' or 'moaning' so he says. If we could *talk* about housework in a reasonable manner, he would listen. But he tells me I go about it in the wrong way. We may start off discussing housework but we end up discussing my weaknesses. I have even apologised at times, and do you know, I still end up doing the housework and he does virtually none.(9)

This is not a public context, but it helps to illustrate the way males can, and sometimes do, control women's meanings, by insisting that talk be conducted in a manner they find acceptable. For many reasons I think it likely that when women want to talk about 'alternative' meanings they will find that there is *no* acceptable way. Male dismissal may be in terms of their *style* but that is not the issue which is at stake, for there are times when the style is 'impeccably proper' but the dismissal remains.

> Female: You are assuming that the patriarchal world view is the only world view. I am assuming that it is not. I assume an alternative. I do not think either of us is more or less biased than the other.
>
> Male: But I suggest you lose credibility when you take up such a position ... Look, please don't mistake me. I'm all for women's rights. I think you have a very good case. Equal pay for equal work, etc. But I cannot take you seriously when you go on in this biased and ... emotional way.
>
> Female: The emotion is your contribution, and not my behaviour. I am perfectly calm. I am suggesting the possibility of an alternative world view, which is based, quite unapologetically, on rethinking what is valuable and useful ...

Male:    But your hatred of males is so ... so venomous. You
         are being so ... so aggressive, so unfeminine ...
         might I even suggest, so bitchy? You would do so
         much better if you presented your arguments in a
         different way. More low key, more persuasive ... less
         biased. Your attitude won't get you very far at the
         moment.

Female:  You mean I should talk sweetly, ask nicely, flatter
         and cajole?

Male:    That's it! That's exactly what I mean! _I'm_ trying to
         help, making a perfectly reasonable suggestion, and
         you – you just fly back at me like that!(10)

Of course, it was very considerate of the above male student to try and
help his female tutor out of her difficulties with presentation! From my
point of view, I could argue that it was the male who was being
'emotional' and 'biased', but such an issue did not arise in the
discussion. Despite the differences in status (teacher and student) this
male assumed from the outset that he was the greater authority on _style_
(which of course is justified in patriarchal order) and he indicates the
power of all males to define reality, to decree what is reasonable/
proper/worth while and appropriate/acceptable. This phenomenon can
be observed in most mixed sex conversations. It is another means of
blocking the emergence of female meanings.

There is a rationale behind the insistence of the dominant group that
women talk in a 'ladylike' way. As Robin Lakoff (1975) has pointed
out, when one talks like a lady, one isn't always taken seriously. Little
girls, she says (1975: 5–6) are required to learn to talk 'like a lady' and

> If the little girl learns her lesson well, she is not rewarded with
> unquestioned acceptance on the part of society: rather the
> acquisition of this special style of speech will later be an excuse
> others use to keep her in a demeaning position, to refuse to take
> her seriously as a human being. Because of the way she speaks,
> the little girl – now grown to womanhood – will be accused of
> being unable to speak precisely or to express herself forcefully.

Lakoff considers this a double bind: a woman is damned if she does not
talk 'like a lady', but she is damned if she does! To be counselled to be
more 'ladylike' – which is the substance of much of the advice given to
feminists – when it is the very concept of 'ladylike' that they oppose, is

indeed ironic. It is also advantageous for the dominant group because it coerces language towards male-defined terms and allows males to exercise control over women's language.

## The contradictions of a woman speaker

In the hundreds of mixed-sex conversations that I have taped there are virtually no instances in which the females – at least to begin with – do not accept the male prerogative to legislate on language, and thereby to control and block women's meanings and enforce their *muted* nature. There are numerous examples of the power which males have to define reality, to decree what the point is, to discipline women's language (see p. 142 for further discussion). It is relatively easy to substantiate the thesis that when women do not speak in terms that are acceptable to men, they do not get a proper hearing; in fact, it would sometimes be easy to substantiate that they get no hearing at all. Women are 'queried', they are interrupted, their opinions are discounted and their contributions devalued in virtually all of the mixed-sex conversations that I have taped. And there is little doubt in my mind that females have traditionally reacted to this by retreating into silence. Systematically rejected, denied the confidence to express and affirm the validity of their own experience, any human being would, I suspect, employ similar 'protective' strategies and reinforce their own muted position.

For those who occupy a muted position in society, there is frequently an inherent contradiction in being a speaker. That being muted is not a feature of sex, but of power, can be readily illustrated.

Recently I attended a conference where some of the women were very critical of the men in terms of their strategies for control of the discussion. Protests were registered on the grounds that the women did not get as many opportunities to speak, that when they did speak they were frequently interrupted (by men), that they were not listened to with equal attention (or that they were not listened to at all). The general level of noise in the room seemed to increase when a woman was talking and the talk of women was treated as an opportunity/excuse for men and women to exchange information; this did not happen to the same degree when it was a man who held the floor.

Whether or not these criticisms were valid (I suspect that they were) was not solely what interested me. I became fascinated by the male reaction to the charges that they were 'talking too much', that they were talking on the basis of unjustifiable premises (that is, that women did not count as much as men) and that they were talking without attempting to appreciate any reality other than their own. (These are the charges which are constantly levelled at women, needless to say.)

Some of the males responded by leaving. Some objected, and some even attempted to trivialize the criticisms, attributing it to over-sensitive women and categorizing it as 'a fuss about nothing'. But of those who were left who took the criticisms seriously and who were concerned with modifying their behaviour, there were some difficulties.

Male 1 :        It's almost as if I can't do anything ... I can't say anything ... it's going to be wrong ...

Male 2 :        It makes talking very problematic ... I have to think every time before I speak ... I've got to try not to offend any of you [women] ...

Male 1 :        Even if I don't *intend* to dominate the discussion I can see how you would interpret it that way. Anything I say can be 'taken down and used in evidence against me'. I've suddenly become very self-conscious about what I'm saying now ...

Male 3 :        If there's going to be a problem every time I open my mouth, just because I'm a man, I don't see how we can have meaningful discussions. It puts a lot of pressure on us [men] to be quiet ... and I can't see that that's fair ... I don't call that equality ... You women have the upper hand and everything we say is going to be in question.

Female 1 :      But that's exactly what we have been saying. *You* make it a problem for us to talk just because we are female. You put a lot of pressure on us to be quiet. You're just beginning to experience what is for us a permanent condition of existence. Don't you understand it's *always* a problem for us to be women and to speak ...

(general commotion and confusion)(11)

The males present still would not accept the women's version of the difficulties associated with talking. One woman explained in what I thought to be a very coherent and cogent manner that whenever women spoke, it was always in the context of being women and that there could even be surprise expressed that women had something sensible/intelligent to say. 'Whenever I speak and don't seem to be making my point, like now,' she said, 'I always have to ask myself whether its because I'm a woman! No man wonders if things aren't going over well, because he is a man!'(12) If some males did accept what the women were saying, they were not the vocal ones. Most of the comments made by the men centred on the injustice, for them, of talk being a problem, for them. This raises an interesting consideration.

Obviously, women cannot have equal access to discourse and at the same time leave the rules for male access to discourse undisturbed. The difficulties experienced by these men indicate that there is quite a gap between *their* definition of equality and the *women's* perception of it. I think this lies partly in the male — or more precisely these males' understandings — of equality, as being 'women performing in the same way as men' without any modification in the way in which men themselves talk.

The men who spoke did not seem to wish to divest themselves of any control, to share power, to 'take turns', to participate in listening as well as talking. Any problem which was created for them by women's entry to discourse was seen as unfair. They seemed to want to retain their control, while agreeing in principle that women should have greater access to discourse. There are inherent weaknesses in this approach for, if followed to its logical conclusion, all would be talkers and no one would be *listeners* (for further discussion of this trend see p. 121).

The crucial issue here is that if women cease to be muted, men cease to be dominant and to some males this may seem unfair because it represents a *loss* of rights. Clearly it is the elimination of dominant and muted groups which feminism seeks — for reversal, with males merely becoming the muted group, although a good consciousness-raising activity, would not be a satisfactory end. It is necessary that there be modifications in male language behaviour as well as female.

That there is often an inherent contradiction in being a woman speaker (who speaks to men) is I think undeniable. It is the contradiction of being muted and a speaker and it will be resolved when women are no longer muted. But I think it is to be expected that many males will resist the deconstruction of women's position precisely because it brings with it the deconstruction of their dominant position. Perhaps for males who genuinely wish to see women have greater access to discourse, *this* represents a double bind.

## Dominance and tunnel vision

It is a fundamental tenet of the Ardener model of dominant/muted groups that conflicts in meaning are resolved in favour of the dominant: in this interactive process it is such resolution in their favour which helps to construct their dominance. Despite the steps which women are taking to end their muted existence, we are still muted. We are not 'outside' this structuring and we should therefore be reflexive, applying the theory of dominant/muted groups to ourselves. We should expect that we have a disposition to find in favour of males, that we should think it 'logical' to interpret the world in a sexist way: for example, to agree that it is unjust when talking becomes a problem for males. Because I am aware that this has been the way the world works and that I cannot, quickly and completely, sever myself from the order in which I was reared, I find myself questioning any decision I make which 'finds in favour of males'. I am suspicious when I reach a conclusion that males may have a 'better case', and this is not simply paranoia. There are substantial reasons for hypothesizing in this dichotomous world, that it is more likely to be males who are in the wrong.

In my research on language one factor which I have often observed is that while women may appreciate the parameters of male reality, men frequently cannot appreciate the dimensions of female reality. Women 'see more' and I think this is explicable in terms of the dominant/muted structure.

Women live under the reality of the dominant group. They are required to 'know' it, to operate within it and to defer to its definitions. For this reason I do not find it surprising that women more readily appreciate the reality of men, for in patriarchal order male reality has usually been posited as the *only* reality. For males, however, the situation is somewhat different.

Men have generated the reality, which women are required to share, and they do not usually have reason to believe that their reality is questionable. This is not just because they can dismiss any alternative meanings which women may offer as 'unreal' (or crazy and neurotic) but because women may also collude in preserving the male illusions. Women can remain silent when it comes to recognizing the inadequacies and the distortions of male definitions of the world and, as such, Sheila Rowbotham (1973a) has called them 'accomplices'. Women may protect males from the false nature of their meanings and thereby reinforce male 'blindness'.

There are occasions when, theoretically at least, it is within women's capacity to enlighten men as to the inaccuracies of some of their definitions, but for numerous (understandable) reasons, women often do not exercise that power. Instead they help to preserve male definitions, to 'hide' contrary evidence and to perpetuate the circumscribed vision of many males.

> Of course your father doesn't *know* you and of course it's my *fault*. I didn't let him find out. He would have been so shocked. He has an image of a pure, sweet, little girl and I've done everything to keep it that way. I haven't told him what you are doing, where you are living ... or who you are living with either for that matter ... I *tell* him what's in your letters, I don't give them to him to *read*. And I censor and embellish. And he thinks you are *that* image. It would just destroy him if he found out any differently. And it makes my life easier. I would be the one to bear the brunt of it if he found out you weren't his delightful, innocent daughter.(13)

From some of the discussions I have taped it seems that this practice of protecting males from the inadequacies of their own definitions is widespread. One woman reported that at a gathering of ten couples who had adult children, each woman was aware of 'irregularities' in their children's lives, while no male was so aware. One male did not even know that his son was divorced because he would have found it difficult to cope with this evidence in the face of his definition of marriage as permanent and desirable.(14) If these wives were going to such lengths to preserve the male meanings, it is obvious that their husbands would have little reason to suspect that there was more than the meanings *they* generated to be taken into account.

It is this 'masquerade' that women are often engaged in which has been explored by Susan Koppelman Cornillon (1972). She chooses *femininity* as an example and she indicates that although it may constitute a concept which both sexes share, it has been generated by one sex and therefore has very different meanings for the two sexes, although males may be aware of only one. Says Cornillon (1972: 113): 'in a male culture, the idea of the feminine is expressed, defined and perceived by the male as a *condition* of being female, while for the female it is seen as an *addition* to one's femaleness and a status to be achieved.' This is an example of the subtle but significant difference between the sexes whereby the dominant group is limited to its own definition, while the muted group understands that definition – and much else besides. Concrete examples can help to illustrate the operation of the constraints upon male understanding.

Under the male definition of femininity there is the notion of female 'hairlessness'. The feminine woman has no facial hair, no hair on arms or legs or under arms, and women who wish to conform to this definition of femininity will constantly present themselves to males without a hint of hair. Because of this, many males could be forgiven for assuming that their definition is perfectly valid and accurate as they are confronted with *no* contrary evidence. But women's reality is not so monodimensional: they are aware that the male definition is not accurate but they will contribute towards preserving the male illusion.

In my youth I went to great lengths to preserve this illusion, quite convinced that it would be *my* failure (and not just a failure of male definitions) if I did not conform to the definition. Not only did I, and most of my friends, remove the incriminating hair, we also went to great lengths to conceal our activities. There was guilt associated in being caught in the act of shaving – even in leaving the razor where it could be detected – because it would have helped to expose the illusory nature of ourselves as feminine.

We knew that such hair grew and in this respect we were ahead of many males. Individually, I imagine we all agonized over it and felt that we were deficient, and we were all exceedingly careful to remove it as often as 'necessary'. In such circumstances it is easy in retrospect to testify to the validity of Cornillon's claim. We strived to be feminine. It was an elusive status which we worked hard to achieve: it was an *addition* to our femaleness. But to a male who never encountered the hairy evidence, it would have been plausible to assume that feminine women were without body hair and that this was a condition of their femininity and not an addition, a product of their efforts to conform to male definitions.

Women may have been silent but their silence cannot always be construed as agreement, or as an absence of contrary information. In the context in which women have perceived the falseness of male meanings, even though they have not spoken of them, women are still in possession of 'more of the facts'. The illusions of the dominant group may have been sustained but women have not necessarily been the *victims* of these illusions in the same way as men. Where they have been victims it has been because they have interpreted their failure to meet male standards as their own personal inadequacy, rather than questioning the inadequacy of the standards themselves.

This is where consciousness-raising groups (CR) have made a significant contribution for it has often been within such groups that women have made the discovery of which Cornillon speaks. They have realized the limitations imposed by monodimensional male reality. They have recognized the enormous discrepancy between the evidence they have in their possession and the evidence which men have access to. Within CR groups women have come to realize that there is at least a dual reality, with some evidence which supports the male version, but a great deal which does not. But CR groups do not constitute a *public* arena – women are not talking to men – and while the women who have participated in them may have come to appreciate the multiple nature of reality, many males have had no such privilege. Males may still be locked into their own reality without even being aware of the existence of evidence which does not endorse it.

Because I think the definitions of many males false and limited, I am suspicious of resolving any conflict of meaning in favour of males. I have yet to be convinced that many of them are in the position of having a wide range of evidence to draw upon. It is in this sense that I believe women have potential power because their experience as a muted group has given them access to a broader range of meanings, which they can begin to use. It is also why I believe it would be unsatisfactory for women to become the *dominant* group: it fosters the growth of false meaning. Marginality can be productive.

CR groups have constituted one of the first steps towards realizing this potential power. It is where women have started to deconstruct their muted condition and to utilize their extended, and fuller, meanings. The process is not always easy and many women have even found it painful to form the new connections that are necessary, but once formed, the silence of women begins to be broken. They move towards a metapatriarchal reality.

I recall one CR session where such a *change* took place. One member of the group, O, was very upset and when encouraged to talk, diagnosed the origin of her distress as lack of sleep. At first this was accepted but then there was a puzzle as to why she was missing so much sleep. Her job did not make demands on her that would interfere with her sleep, she had been married only a short time and she had no children. Initially it was assumed that she was suffering from insomnia, but it emerged that this was not the case.

It was her efforts to be feminine which were causing her loss of sleep.

O's new husband thought curly hair was feminine: he also thought hair rollers were decidedly unfeminine. Endowed as she was with perversely straight hair, this presented O with a problem which she proceeded to 'solve' in nothing less than an incredible way.

Each night she had gone to bed at the same time as her husband and, unknown to him, had set her alarm clock for one and a half hours later. When her alarm rang (secreted under her pillow) she would get up and put rollers in her hair. Returning to bed she would then reset her alarm clock for one hour before they got up in the morning. Then she would remove the rollers when it rang (and hide them) and be ready to greet him in the morning – with curly hair! Sometimes, she said, she lay awake almost all night waiting for the alarm to ring. The only sleep she got was the hour before they got up in the morning, after she had removed the rollers.(15)

Her husband believed she had curly hair and was very feminine: why should he not? She had gone to almost unendurable lengths to sustain that belief. Whereas he was familiar with only one reality, she, however, was familiar with at least two. Before this CR session, O did experience a dual reality but had no way of interpreting it in her favour. After the CR session she was able to make very different use of this knowledge. This is where women can begin to deconstruct their muted condition and to take advantage of the 'contradictions' which are part of their daily lives.

Prior to the CR session, O explained these 'contradictions' in terms of her own inadequacy. That this is a common way for women to resolve contradictions and to interpret the world is also taken up by Cornillon. When faced with the 'gap' between their own experience and the male version of reality women have reconciled the difference in terms of their own deficiency.

According to Cornillon, most females interpret their failure to correspond to the meanings of the dominant group as a failure to be 'normal' and this is accompanied by a sense of shame which prompts them to try even harder to achieve the terms of male reality. Women, says Cornillon, 'never "blow" their own or each other's "cover stories" of "normal femininity" ' (p. 114). They maintain the pretence of femininity for the benefit of males, while individually being aware that it is a pretence.

What CR has done has been to show the collective nature of women's experience. It has provided the support for women to 'blow the cover of normal femininity' and to expose its deceptive and false nature. And of course many males are totally unprepared for this 'alternative' meaning which shakes the foundations of their reality.

> I get lots of advice, you know, people telling me I'm 'letting myself go'. But I'm a female and I reckon whatever I am, I'm feminine. I don't have to *do* anything to be feminine. It's a shock my husband can't take. As far as he is concerned, I've just gone crazy. He keeps his ideas of 'prettiness' and I just move further away from them. He says he can't understand why I wilfully want to be unfeminine – you know, why I wilfully won't shave my legs, go to the hairdresser, diet – a whole pile of things I've *stopped* doing. He thinks I should see a psychiatrist ... I think *he* should.(16)

Instead of denying the contradictions many women are now exploring them, and this is not the typical behaviour of a muted group. But whereas many women are perceiving the distortions which they have been required to engage in, many males refuse to accept that there have been distortions. There is no way of determining how this conflict will be resolved but if traditional patterns predominate it will most assuredly be resolved in favour of males. Males enjoy numerous 'advantages'.

In the pre-CR days when Betty Friedan (1963) conducted her research, she found that individual women were experiencing the gulf between male meanings of women's existence (as the happy, fulfilled mother-in-the-suburbs) and their own meanings. And they were 'explaining' this gulf in terms of their own inadequacy. Friedan called this 'the problem that has no name' because these women's meanings 'did not fit into the same categories as the problems which had already been given names' (by males) (Rowbotham, 1973a: 5). But the problem has been named in CR groups and with this naming women have begun to break the silence. Women are beginning to name the problem as one of male control of society but, unfortunately, because they have not had access to the same range of experiences as women, many men are not in a position to hear, or to understand, what it is that women are saying.

Once women understood that it was not their *personal* problem, they were able to begin to impose new patterns on their experience, able to begin to define reality as it fitted them. They were able to begin to re-evaluate women's experience from the perspective of women. Although only a beginning, it is a task which a muted group does not engage in.

I suspect that females have long known that the dominant reality is arbitrary and not *the* reality, but it was only with the advent of the recent feminist movement – and CR groups – that they have been able to turn this understanding to profitable account. It puts them in a better position than many males who believe that there is only one reality. For it is not just that women can 'see more', it is also that they are more experienced in accommodating apparent contradictions. They are often more flexible and have more complex awareness of meaning as they have learnt to juggle the dominant reality with their own. They have had to develop these skills. Their existence at times has depended on being able to make compatibility out of contradiction, on being able to 'communicate'.

That there has been a breakdown in communication between the sexes is a problem which appears in much current literature and which is sometimes explained in terms of the vastly different interests of the two sexes (Komarovsky, 1962). But such an explanation doesn't go far enough; it omits too much evidence. It is more than a difference in interest which divides the sexes: it is also a difference in the perception of reality.

It is a popular cliché that men are frequently unable to understand what women are talking about, as if in some way this is the fault of women. I think it perfectly plausible that men may not understand at times what women are talking about, but I think it more likely that the limitation lies with the men and with their *tunnel vision*.

Males who have accepted the definitive nature of the dominant reality are unlikely to be familiar with any other focus. Whereas multidimensional reality may be a daily lived experience for many women, it may be nothing less than an absurd, and abstract, concept to many men. Whereas women may have become skilled in handling the complex and contradictory meanings which are an inherent part of multidimensional reality, men may have been confined to the skills which are necessary for functioning in a monodimensional reality, skills in defining what is real and what is not, what is right and wrong, relevant and irrelevant, appropriate and inappropriate: namely the skills of tunnel vision, of eliminating and dividing according to the principles of linear progression.

It is this patriarchal pattern of thought, this tunnel vision, which Joan Roberts has tried to conceptualize. She suggests that within patriarchal order we have been locked into thought patterns which are based on the premises that there is only one reality, that it is monodimensional and proceeds on predictable and systematic lines, that it is linear, and based on simple cause-effect relationships. Roberts suggests that this is an inadequate – and mistaken – view of the way the world works. There is too much that cannot be 'explained' in this framework; there are too many contradictions for the framework to stand. What we have confidently called *logic* and believe to be 'uncontaminated' by human values, may indeed be culture-specific, arbitrary and inappropriate. We may need to change our ideas of what constitutes logic if we are to come closer to making sense of the world.

In other words, tunnel vision may be an inadequate means of illuminating the world we have constructed and we may be in dire need of modifications, or new vision, if we are to explain productively the apparent 'absurdities' of the world we inhabit. Roberts asks (1976:46):

> what if the masculist world view which has depended on a logic of time lines is erroneous? What if the most fundamental error is the search for monocausation? What if the world is really a field of interconnecting events arranged in patterns of multiple meaning? What if the search for simplistic 'orderliness' is itself the common problem ...?

It is not difficult to explain why the dominant group has not entertained such a view of the world and why it has evolved its monodimensional linear view: the dominant view of the world is a world which is eminently *controllable*. The view which Roberts posits offers no such possibility of control. But if there is some substance to Roberts's thesis, then it is not too much to suggest that women, more than men, may be in a good position to cope with this possibility. They have often had considerable practice and preparation.

Such tunnel vision is not confined to esoteric institutions where 'academic' knowledge is constructed – though it may thrive there – but has its manifestations in everyday life. I think it is at the core of the rejection of women's meanings as unreal or crazy. Because of the limitations imposed on the dominant group – limitations of their own making – it is likely to be a genuine statement when men declare, in resigned or mystified fashion, that they do not know what women mean. The penalties of the division of dominant/muted have not necessarily been confined to the muted group. Women may have been deprived of the full use of their voice, but men may have denied themselves the full use of their vision.

There is however another factor which must be taken into

consideration. It may not just be that members of the dominant group
cannot appreciate any reality other than their own: it may also be that
they do not want to. The implications of the possibility of multiple
reality could be extremely threatening, partly because it exposes the
illusory nature of male supremacist reality. Joan Roberts has said
(1976:19):

> Because of female exclusion from thought systems, the hardest
> thing for a man to know IS what a woman wants. But it is harder
> still for him to listen and to accept her thoughts because they are
> certain to shake the foundations of his beliefs.

It is quite possible that many men will not want to hear what women
have to say precisely because the dominant reality will be challenged
when women speak. Within the framework of monodimensional reality
the dominant group cannot continue to accept their view of the world as
the only view and at the same time accept that women can construct an
alternative reality. If women's meanings are to be taken into account
then men's will need to be transformed and there are perhaps many
men who do not see this as an improvement.

It is understandable that the contemplation of the legitimacy of
women's meanings might be too threatening for many males who could
find themselves faced with an identity crisis. If they are not the superior
sex, who are they? The balance of power shifts – slightly!

Entertaining the possibility of multiple realities from the standpoint
of tunnel vision could be more disorienting than entertaining its
possibility from the multidimensional female perspective. Whereas for
the dominant group it could amount to a *disintegration* of their world,
for the muted group it could amount to a *confirmation* of their world.

Elaine Showalter has said that 'women have the best seat in the
house' and this is not a sentimental evaluation of women but a well
substantiated assertion. Women do see more from where they sit, and
as their reality becomes less readily deniable, they are in a better
position to talk about what they see. This is an exciting process because
some of the things which women are talking about have not often been
described and encoded in public discourse before. At the moment one
of their particular strengths is that they have an audience – of women –
and this is significant. (See p. 125 for further discussion of the role and
the value of single-sex talk.)

The distinctions between dominant/muted have been blurred when
the muted group no longer looks exclusively to the dominant group for

confirmation, that is, when women consider other women a serious audience. Women, particularly in CR groups, are concerned with talking to each other and in doing so are freeing themselves from some of the conditions which have produced their silence.

For the dominant meanings of society even to be open to question represents a shift in power because males may find themselves in a position of having to defend their meanings as women's challenge grows. This is a radical change from an order in which their meanings were taken for granted, and where it was assumed without question by both the dominant and muted group members that male meanings constituted *the* incontestable reality.

Although it has often been obvious that women have suffered disadvantage by virtue of their membership of the muted group, what has often not been appreciated is that males too have suffered disadvantage.

Jean Baker Miller (1976) has also explored the significance of the dominant/muted nature of social organizations under patriarchy and she is convinced that the tunnel vision of males, which has its origin in this division and the need to exercise control, leads to far more serious consequences than just a breakdown in communication between the sexes. To preserve their supremacy, males have been required to develop an order which encompasses that supremacy. They have been obliged to promulgate the belief that there is only one reality and that it is their position to decree what it is. They have put themselves forward as the superior sex because they are the ones with access to the right answers: in order to sustain their position they have been obliged to deny that which they cannot explain. To maintain their control, the dominant group must be seen as superior, so within patriarchal order – which they have created – males are by definition precluded from being 'wrong'.[1] This has necessitated the assignment to women of those areas

1 It is a fundamental tenet of patriarchal order that women are 'wrong' and the semantic rules continually affirm this tenet. Sheila Rowbotham (1973a) has commented on this: 'Every time a woman describes to a man any experience which is specific to her as a woman she confronts his recognition of his own experience as normal. More than this, his experience of how he sees the "norm" is reinforced by the dominant ideology which tells both him and the woman that he is right' (p. 35). Rowbotham is also acknowledging and taking up a point made by Simone de Beauvoir, who said (1972: 15): 'A man is in the right in being a man: it is the woman who is in the wrong'. I think both these writers are referring to the semantic base of our language which classifies the male as positive, and the female not just as negative but as minus. Thus women occupy the zone of negative semantic space, they are unable to decree their own reality, hence they are 'wrong'. This represents the ability of the patriarchal order to position males and females and to ensure the reproduction of that order: where women are classified as wrong, their meanings and existence can be dismissed.

which cannot be controlled, where things go 'wrong', where the elements are inexplicable, undesirable, or capricious.

According to Miller, males have been forced to forgo much of their *human* experience precisely because it is difficult to impose order on such experience. Much of their existence goes 'unacknowledged, unexplored, and denied' because it does not conform to the prescribed patterns of order. For males to be right, to be the norm, women under a dichotomous and hierarchical order must be wrong, must be deviant. This has made women 'the "carriers" of society for certain aspects of total human experience – *those aspects that remain unsolved*' (Miller, 1976:22–3; my emphasis). What men cannot explain within the patriarchal order they have established, they have classified with women, with minus male, thereby reinforcing their own supremacy and the definition of woman as 'other'.

To Miller this is not just unfortunate, it is tragic, for the dominant group which holds the power is disconnected from fundamental human experience. Yet it is the group which legislates on human experience, which defines reality. Much of 'current literature, philosophy and social commentary focuses on the lack of human connection in all our institutions', she says, yet such a lack of connection is to be expected in our society where men have defined and organized the world on the basis of their own limited – and false – perspective. We should not be surprised that we are unable to organize technology towards human ends when human ends have never been part of the pattern of male experience and aspiration. To *appear* as the superior sex, males have classified themselves as the culture-makers and have artificially and specifically divorced themselves from human ends. Human ends have not figured prominently in male meanings because they tend to be disordered, chaotic, inexplicable and beyond control. It is human ends which have traditionally been assigned to women, states Miller, 'indeed women's lives have been principally occupied by them' (p. 24). That which is beyond male control has been classified with women and there is a vast repository of minus male meaning created, which while under ostensible male control can be contained, but which gives rise to male fear when that control is threatened (1976:24):

When women have raised questions that reflect their concerns, the issues have been pushed aside and labelled trivial matters. In fact, now as in the past, they are anything but trivial; rather they are the highly charged, unsolved problems of the dominant culture as a whole and they are loaded with dreaded associations. The charge of triviality is more likely massively defensive, for the questions threaten the return of what has been warded off, denied and sealed away – under the label 'female'.

Miller's thesis is that males have allocated to women that which is outside their control and which they fear, *because* it is outside their control. Within that imposed patriarchal framework it is the task of women to produce order out of the chaos of human experience, and in the process women become more closely identified with chaos in the minds of the dominant group. *Woman* has become synonymous with chaos, but, by controlling women, the illusion of overall male control remains intact.

Within Miller's conceptualization of the problem it is easy to discern why it has been a male priority to keep women quiet. The expression of women threatens to unlock the doors and to unleash all those mysterious, illogical and disordered aspects of human experience which challenge the appearance and the actuality of male supremacy and control. In this context, the need for women's silence in patriarchal order should not be underestimated. It is a prerequisite for male supremacy and without it the whole order could crumble.

It may not have been intentional that when they were dividing the world males took for themselves the categories which they could establish as productive. It may not have been deliberate design that they appropriated strength, reason, logic, objectivity, etc., for themselves and then proceeded to invest these characteristics with positive value while allocating weakness, irrationality, emotion and subjectivity to females, defining these as negative in value. But regardless of intent, we have inherited man-made categories of masculinity and femininity and we are beginning to perceive that those divisions with the supposed supremacy of the masculine are neither desirable nor inevitable. Feminists wish to dispense with these mutilating categories.

These categories which are complex constructions represent the virtual obsession of the dominant group with dichotomies and hierarchies, for these are fundamental premises in an order based on the supremacy of one group over another. Within patriarchal order it is necessary that humanity be divided and made unequal, but, complex as this construction has been, it contains fissures. It depends upon the muted group voluntarily subscribing to these categories. John Stuart Mill observed that it was not sufficient for women to be slaves, they must be *willing* slaves, for the maintenance of patriarchal order depends upon the consensus of women. It depends upon women playing their part as a muted group, voluntarily suppressing the evidence that exposes the false and arbitrary nature of man-made categories and the reality which is built on those categories.

This is a dialectic process. There will not necessarily be any redistribution of male defined power – legal, political, educational, etc. – simply because women cease to be silent, but neither will there be a redistribution of power if women remain silent. As women cease to be muted, male supremacy becomes problematic; as it becomes problematic, women receive more encouragement to break their silence.

With their tunnel vision of monodimensional reality, the dominant group has placed itself in a position where the 'feedback' it gets is likely to reinforce the belief that it is right, that its meanings are appropriate. Like rulers surrounded by sycophants, this is not always a strong position from which to make judgments. The information which is forthcoming from the 'accomplices', the 'willing slaves', is not always reliable and can be misleading. It is not just that much may be unknown, but that it is unknown that it is unknown. Males have been, and can still be, deceived.

It is paradoxical that part of the mechanism for ensuring the continued silence of women lies within women's control. They can cease to collude, they can abandon their role as willing slaves. The categories of masculine/feminine, dominant/muted, positive/negative – and all those hierarchical dichotomies fundamental to patriarchal order – can begin to be subverted when women start to encode their own meanings, because the dominant group is *dependent* on these categories for their continued, unaltered existence.


## Pluralism

Most women within the women's movement are developing their skills at handling more than one reality. The pluralism of the movement is itself both a source and a manifestation of the ability to function in a multidimensional frame of reference. There are numerous 'truths' available within feminism and it is falling into male defined (and false) patterns to try and insist that only one is correct. Accepting the validity of multidimensional reality predisposes women to accept multiple meanings and explanations without feeling that something is fundamentally wrong. Women within the movement are increasingly capable of coping with the illogicality of traditional logic and with the ostensible irrationality of holding contrary beliefs to be 'true'.

The concept of multidimensional reality is necessary for it allows sufficient flexibility to accommodate the concept of equality. Multiple reality is a necessary condition for the acceptance of the experience of *all* individuals as equally valuable and viable. Only within a multidimensional framework is it possible for the analysis and explanation of everyone to avoid the pitfalls of being rejected, of being classified as wrong.

For example, some women may feel that it is a patriarchal imposition to allocate child-rearing exclusively to women, while others may feel it is a patriarchal imposition to prise women away from child-rearing and to force them into the market-place. Within monodimensional patriarchal order 'equality' is not possible: one analysis must be right and the other wrong, one must be superior and the other inferior. Within multidimensional reality both views can be accommodated as equally true for those individuals. There is no right/wrong but equal value.

It *is* difficult to make sense of it, because it's not the conventional way but you have to begin to understand that we are all using the same *process* and we reach different conclusions, and I think they are only superficially different by the way. We reach different conclusions because we have had 'superficially' different experiences ...

One example is contraception. You know how a lot of people get upset because the pill was developed for women? Right? There are a lot of women who argue that it's the sexism of the medical profession that developed a pill for women and not for men. And they're right. But it could have been awful if there was a pill for *men*, and not for women because reproduction would be in the hands of men. One of my friends would have had another child against her will I'm sure if it had been men who had the pill because her bloke wanted a son – mind you they had two daughters – and she didn't want any more kids. We talked about it. He would have had an 'accident', I'm sure. And she would have had to face, you know, an abortion or a pregnancy. One or the other. But *she* took the pill, and there weren't any accidents. Vasectomy and sterilization is a bit like that as well.

Of course it's sexist when doctors encourage women to be sterilized, but it would also be sexist if they encouraged men to have vasectomies ... Would you trust a guy who told you he had a vasectomy? Would you want to take your own precautions as well?

You can't just say – you know, you're right and you're wrong. They're both 'right'. A woman who says a pill for women is sexist has got just as much reason to hold that opinion; there are as many reasons for thinking that as a woman who says a pill for men is sexist. So they've both got to be right and we have to learn to live with the fact that there's more than *one* answer.(17)

As women have found out, there can be no equality when one is right (the male) and the other is wrong (the female). Right and wrong are the foundation stones of hierarchical meanings and such dichotomies are not at all useful for feminism which is trying to structure non-hierarchical social organization.

This valuing of all contributions equally should not be confused with the male defined meaning of *tolerance*. Tolerance can only be exercised by those who are in power and it is often nothing but another means of protecting that power. Tolerance does not eradicate the distinction between right and wrong, it simply makes being in the wrong slightly less offensive. It is not tolerance which characterizes the women who are handling the inherent contradictions of existence within feminism (we do not wish to be placed upon the pedestal and saddled with yet another 'virtue') but a reconceptualization, a new classification of the objects and events of the world. Out of the understanding that the personal is political has grown the realization that the explanations of others are appropriate for their circumstances equally well as one's own.

It is from the basis of multidimensional reality that women are generating their new meanings (Mary Daly, 1978, being an excellent example), and as they evolve new ways of classifying the world they move further from their strictly muted state. That this change is occurring is demonstrable – and not just through reference to some superb feminist writers who are evolving sets of new woman-centred meanings. It has caused me some 'consternation' while I have been conducting my research. In some cases women were moving so quickly away from their muted state that in typical 'academic' style I was concerned that I would not be able to document sufficiently some of the examples of women's language which I was seeking.

For example, the thirty-two females who were present at one educational conference which I taped initially provided data on women as a muted group, but after the tape of the first session was played to them (in which the five males present dominated and controlled the discussion), it would not have been strictly accurate to classify these women as a muted group for they had begun to move from that position. Having perceived the extent of their own silence – and the extent to which it had been 'self-imposed' – they consciously changed certain aspects of their language behaviour. Many women members of that original group are now insisting on equal access to talk, and are trying to encode new meanings and new registers within which to conduct their talk.[2]

Individual women who cease to be willingly silent will not of themselves change the power structure, but neither will that occur while women are silent and while they permit the dominant group to continue unchecked in legislating the meanings of society. Women have only just begun to encode and legitimate their meanings and it is unlikely that their efforts are going to be facilitated by the dominant group. There are many tunnel vision members of the dominant group who wield considerable power and who can be relied upon to make every effort to retain that power which allows them to block women at almost every facet of their endeavour. But that is only one truth: in a multidimensional reality there is another and that is that women have begun to deconstruct their muted state and show few signs of discontinuing their efforts.

2 I have had reports from some of the women who were present at that conference and who have gone on to tape mixed-sex discussions in their own workplaces. Their results have been consistent. They have found men talk more, interrupt more and control the topics of conversation, and they have demonstrated these findings to other women who have also been incensed and who have also determined to change this pattern.

# · 4 ·

# Woman Talk:
# the Legitimate Fear

❋

Underlying both research studies and the cultural attitudes concerned with woman talk (sometimes, unfortunately, one and the same thing) is the belief that woman talk is dangerous. When a society is structured so that it permits male primacy and produces male dominance, it is quite reasonable to classify woman talk as dangerous because the whole fabric of that social structure could be undermined if the expression of the subordinates were allowed free voice. Because woman talk is dangerous and a threat to patriarchal order numerous means have been developed to preempt it. The extent and complexity of male control of woman talk helps to reveal the powerful role that talk plays in the construction and maintenance of the social order.

One obvious means of preventing the talk of women is by intimidation. The threat to patriarchal order which is posed by woman talk is countered by a threat to women who are presumptuous enough to attempt to talk. There are numerous social injunctions against woman talk and there is method – not madness – behind the apparent contradiction that women, who demonstrably do not talk as much as men, are consistently culturally rebuked for talking too much. But so serious is the threat posed by woman talk, little can be left to chance and there are therefore more than social injunctions available to ensure that woman talk does not become a problem for male primacy and dominance.

Intimidation also makes its presence felt in the way which the talk of women is discredited. In case women do circumvent the restrictions and begin to talk, patriarchal order can defend itself by the wholesale discounting of what it is that women have to say. Few individuals in our society have difficulty in listing what is wrong with woman talk (Kramer, 1977) and why it is not to be trusted, and there is no shortage of derogatory terms available to assist them in outlining its negative features. It is not surprising to find that there are no terms for man talk that are equivalent to *chatter, natter, prattle, nag, bitch, whine* and, of course, *gossip*, and I am not so naive as to assume that this is because men do not engage in these activities. It is because when they do it is called something different, something more flattering and more appropriate to their place in the world. This double standard is of great value in the maintenance of patriarchal order. No matter what women may say it fosters the conviction that you cannot trust the words of a woman and that it is permissible to *dismiss* anything she might say. By such means does the dominant group exert control over woman talk.

## A place for talk

Blatant intimidation, however, can be provocative: it can be *visible* and therefore open to dispute and even to the possibility of rejection. It is safer to employ it as a last and not as a first resort. One simple – and slightly more subtle means – of curtailing the dangerous talk of women is to restrict their opportunities for talk. This can be readily accomplished when women are in the presence of males – where they can exert direct control – but it becomes a more difficult task in their absence. However a 'solution' has also been found for this problem.

Jo Freeman (1975) has noted that there are very few places in which women can come together and talk and it would be a mistake to assume that this is an interesting but incidental feature of our social arrangements. Traditionally, for women there have been no comparable locations to the pub which can encourage woman talk; there have been no opportunities for talk like those provided by football or the union meeting. Because women have been without the space and the place to talk they have been deprived of access to discourse *with each other* (they have even been encouraged to accept that talking to each other does not count), as well as deprived of access to discourse in the presence of men.

Why is it that one of the most salient features of our social organization has been the *isolation* of women? From our urban and suburban 'planning' to modern architectural home design it is possible to discern the pattern of isolating women from one another, and I suspect this isolation, this deliberate obstacle to communication between women, has been necessary for the continued unchallenged existence of patriarchal order. When women come together and talk they have the opportunity to 'compare' notes, collectively to 'see' the limitations of patriarchal reality, and what they say – and do – can be subversive of that reality.

The hypothesis that one fundamental aim of our present social structures is to keep women quiet – and thereby keep them 'in their place' – is one which appears reasonable and supportable. Women experience reduced opportunites to talk either by being directly controlled by males in mixed-sex discourse or by being indirectly controlled by males who have systematically denied them places – and opportunities – to conduct single-sex talk. It is when these controls prove insufficient that intimidation can be called upon in its more explicit forms. In mixed-sex *and* single-sex conversation women must face the constant allegation (external or internal) that they talk too much, while any talk which is confined to women can then also be discredited. The choices are to be silent, or if not, then to be classified as talking too much or talking without any authority.

This is more than convenient: it is essential.

## Consciousness-raising as subversion

The revolutionary nature of CR can be seen in this context and it is not coincidence that CR groups have played a major contributing role in the growth and inspiration of the women's movement. When women first began to experience the need to talk to each other they were usually obliged to meet in each other's homes for there was nowhere else – no public place – for them to go (Cassell, 1977). And the males who objected to – who were even frightened by – this radical change had good grounds for their anxiety. They were justified in thinking woman talk was dangerous and a threat to their existence.

Many women have commented on the conflict that their attendance at such meetings caused. 'This bonding between women evoked resentment, hostility, or ridicule from husbands and lovers,' states Joan Cassell, 'who appeared to perceive women in groups as a threat. (The most positive male reaction reported was an uneasy and often reiterated, "What do you *talk* about with them?")' (1977:50). That men were threatened by this development is the testimony of many, many women in the movement.

> 'Every time I went to a CR group, there was a hassle ... well, really, it was more than a hassle you know. I didn't understand at the time that he was really frightened. I used to just think he was being difficult ... you know, just plain nasty, that he didn't want me to go out ... but did we have some fights? He tried to make me promise that I would *never* talk about him. He would get so ... so angry. He didn't want his private life "paraded in public" he said. And when I wouldn't promise, of course I *couldn't* promise not to talk about him, he was, well, uncontrollable ... I didn't realize the significance of it all at the time, you know. If I did talk about him ... warts and all, you know ... how could he keep his image of superiority? He thought he was being exposed ... that his superiority would be seen as a fraud ... [laughter] And he was right, of course. That *was* what it was all about' [laughter].(18)

Although many people were aware of the conflict which arose between some men and women when women chose to get together to talk, few of them, seem to have been quite as astute as the above woman in discerning the probable basis of this conflict. Sometimes very different 'rationalizations' have been offered.

Gene Marine (1972), for example, has written *A Male Guide to Women's Liberation* which is designed to explain the women's movement to males who might find themselves, involuntarily or otherwise, associated with it. He attempts to reassure males who are living with women who are attending CR sessions and he feels obliged to make some very soothing remarks – about woman talk. 'There is one uneasy question', says Marine, 'to which every husband and boyfriend wants the answer ... he wants to know: Does she talk about me?' (Marine, 1972:182).

Marine answers 'yes'. He cannot eliminate this fear but he does try and minimize it. He informs his readers that women will most definitely talk about the men they live with, but with goodwill and tolerance, on the part of the male, this difficulty can be overcome. The closest Marine comes to identifying the crucial factors in this woman talk is when he advises males to 'stop gnawing at the pedestal of your own ego' (p. 182), and tries to convince them that it is not so terrible to have some of one's weaknesses exposed. He suggests that men would be better served by concentrating their energies on building better relationships with their new, liberated women, than anguishing over events over which they have no control.

## Undermining male control

Males are not generally used to being without control and this could be just as traumatizing to some as the actual subject matter being discussed. Anxiety may stem from what women might say but it may also stem from the realization that men no longer *control* what women might say in CR.

> 'Just about every woman I know who lives with a male has problems. They want to know what you are doing, where you are going, what time you will be home, what you are going to talk about ... you know, every little detail they can. As if knowing it all is somehow going to bring it all under their control. They feel pretty insecure at times. My guy thinks there is some sort of conspiracy going on and that he is going to lose. He is vague about it, but that's really what it is. I find I have to put a lot of energy into convincing him. That's why, I think that's why, women are finding it easier to form relationships with other women, because, well women aren't threatened in the same way by the independence of other women as men are. Most of the men I know want women to be accountable, otherwise they think they don't know ... where they stand. They can't control things if they don't know that.'(19)

Knowing there are conversations entirely beyond one's control is not a new experience for women, they have often been 'talked about' and with little or no opportunity for redress. The days when a woman's 'reputation' was at the mercy of the men in the pub are not so far removed for us to have forgotten how we were controlled by the talk of men. That however was not *gossip* or *bitching*, nor was it *treacherous*. But it is not a puzzle to decide why these labels can be applied to woman talk, even when it does not have the same malicious intent.

> 'He always acted so hurt ... how could I talk about *him* to other women? I was being so unfair. You know, I must admit at times that the old guilt feelings on my part did come flooding in ... I

thought, well, maybe, perhaps it wasn't really the right thing to do. He said it was treacherous, completely unforgivable. Nothing was sacred if I was going to talk to *other women* – he used to say, he would call it "gossiping to those bitches about our relationship", they were his actual words. But I heard him say horrendous things about other women. Women he *had* slept with. Not that that's an excuse ... but I don't need an excuse, or that's what I keep telling myself. But it's the double standard. For all I knew he could have talked like that about me ... Actually, when we separated, he said it wouldn't have happened if I hadn't been so stupid digging up all the things that were wrong. He thought it was *my* fault because I started, that no relationship could survive that sort of scrutiny and discussion. Start gossiping about private matters and it all tumbles down around you. It was my ... disloyalty to him that, well, that he thinks caused our break-up.'(20)

When women begin to talk to each other as they have done in CR, the *image* of supremacy of individual males is at risk. The stripping away of one male facade of superiority is not sufficient to threaten patriarchal order, but when multitudes of males are 'exposed' patriarchal order is at least temporarily at risk. Given the pervasiveness of that patriarchal order, I have no doubts that the forces are regrouping and already that new strategies to quieten women are evolving. The way in which attempts have been made to discount – to ridicule, or trivialize – the words of many women in the women's movement are all too familiar. The image of the 'women's libber' as neurotic, disturbed, embittered, and, significantly, 'unable to get a man' is but another example of the forms of intimidation that are employed against women who speak out. They should be silent, and if they are not, there is a price they must pay. Their words – and their selves – can be dismissed.

## Woman-to-woman talk

One feature of woman talk that I think is proving to be unsusceptible to patriarchal control is the way women are valuing each other as talkers and listeners. This was not and is not intended. Many of the traditional devices that have controlled woman talk depend on women not taking each other seriously as speakers. This has seduced women into seeking the talk of men as the genuine talk of society; it has made them look to males for approval and confirmation. And of course that is a powerful position for males to be in because they could always exercise the option to withhold such approval and confirmation. By seeking reinforcement from other women, women have pre-empted this form of control and they are unlikely to be intimidated by the well-worn cliché that they cannot 'get a man', because they no longer think women are 'second best'. Besides, the burden of communication is lifted from women in this woman-to-woman context. Shirley Ardener (1975) has stated that between dominant/muted groups, the onus is on the muted group 'to form rickety or cumbersome links' (p. xiv) with the dominant group. When these divisions no longer apply, as in the case of all woman groups, the onus is on all – or none – to forge the links, and once more patriarchal order can be undermined when women find this an exhilarating experience – and when they decide that they will not in future accept the 'burden' of establishing conversation with males.

'My valuing of women was quite dramatic really. I can remember it all, because it was a precise incident. It was in Australia and there was a bucks' night, you know, all the men off together the night before the wedding? Well, it was a sort of political decision, a bit of one-upmanship, and the women decided to get together too. The wives. Oh Lord. I was a bit apprehensive about it. I wasn't that keen on an all-female evening. But I wasn't going to wait at home ... for him to come home drunk, as was the usual thing from bucks' nights. So there I was with a group of women. We were all self-conscious to start with. I think, well, most of us anyway had come for the same reasons, the same thing as I had. And we were all a bit suspended. It wasn't real without men. Just a fill in. But it didn't stay that way. We got talking. I suppose it was my first CR session, but I didn't even know the word then. And it was great, I mean it was just great. I hadn't felt so alive, so stimulated for years ... And I remember thinking at one stage, all those men, you know all of them off getting themselves hopelessly pissed. And I had actually thought I was missing something. Well, I mean, I don't think I've sought men's company since that day, well at least, not Australians. That's when I started to value women. It just got to be such a hassle trying to reach those same "highs" with men, well, well I guess I stopped trying. All the stimulating, interesting, intellectual conversations I have are with women.'(21)

It is not difficult to gather this sort of testimony from women. It is varied, but it contains many common elements. Talking about woman talk, particularly about CR groups, is a common and often positively rated topic within the movement. Most women can refer to an exhilarating, satisfying talk experience which is associated with feminism. Because I think the continued talk of women is a necessary condition for the transformation of the patriarchal order, I am sometimes concerned about the belief – be the foundation for it real or imagined – that CR groups are on the decline. I am of course aware that it would be useful for patriarchal purposes if women were to believe that CR groups were no longer necessary and so I am prepared to entertain the possibility that this might be yet another trap which women could fall into if they were to give credence to the belief. But if indeed there is a decline in the acceptance of the centrality of CR groups among women themselves, I am also prepared to entertain the possibility that woman talk has succumbed to successful patriarchal strategies designed to guarantee their silence. While women are talking – to each other and often about men – I feel more comfortable and am convinced that there is some threat to the patriarchal order.

I am convinced that it is difficult to maintain the divisions between dominant and muted while women talk, and it seems that many males also share this conviction. There are still communities where women remain completely muted, where the patriarchal order is preserved unchallenged and where males intend to keep it this way, specifically by denying women the opportunity to talk – particularly about them. Ann Whitehead (1976) has studied one such community in Herefordshire.

In this community extensive control is exercised over talk. The pub is the centre for talk and it is almost exclusively a male preserve, so the meanings of women are not allowed to surface in this context. Whitehead states that in the pub a great deal of 'verbal duelling' goes on among the males, and that male supremacy, and male dominance in their own homes, is fundamental to this 'verbal duelling'. But in order to present themselves as dominant, as 'master of their own home', the men must prevent the women from talking to each other and exposing the discrepancy between the necessary male image and the 'humiliating' male actuality. And it seems that the men are extremely successful in keeping their wives isolated from, and unable to talk to, each other.

Whitehead says that there are few places that women can get together to talk, and men exercise 'an intermediate form of control ... to prevent young women ever being in groups, and to prevent the development of solidary relations of support' (p. 199). Their strategies pay dividends, and she adds that (1976:199)

> husbands appear to make bargains which often include that their wives should see less or nothing of their girlfriends. These links are a threat in that they represent a *most dangerous channel of communication*. If the wives tell each other about their marriages, this information may be passed onto a husband. Where the first husband is also a drinking companion of the second, this information may be used in pub disclosures.

And what is disclosed is that the superiority of the male comes from a belief and not from their behaviour. Male supremacy is a carefully cultivated cultural construct that makes it seem 'reasonable' that males should be the dominant group. If these beliefs are exposed as fraudulent then the rationale for the existence of the dominant group is threatened, and this is equally as applicable to males as it is to females. Males too must work to retain the reality they have constructed and in which their dominant position appears justified. This reality is too fragile for 'lapses', even among men, to be allowed. It must be constantly reinforced and this is only possible by the suppression of women's meanings. So frequently are women in a position to reveal the false nature of the claims of the dominant group that there must be ways of procuring their silence.

There are, however, other communities where woman talk has broken the bounds of control. Although in their work, concerned with the relationship of language and reality, Berger and Luckmann (1972) can – unintentionally – reveal the way in which sexist language produces sexist reality, when they state self-assuredly that they know woman talk is irrelevant to them as men (p. 60), there is a growing number of men who would not share this belief.

## Politics and woman talk

Less than ten years ago it was acceptable for the sexes to be segregated at social gatherings and certain assumptions were made about the nature and value of the talk which took place within these segregated groups. There are grounds for hypothesizing that males exerted considerable indirect control over woman talk in this context because the talk of women was not perceived as a threat: it was trivial but harmless. Even in the absence of males, women could be relied upon to reproduce the dominant definitions of the world and to subscribe to the dominant reality. It was possible for males to engage in their 'serious' talk without feeling uneasy about the woman talk that was taking place out of earshot; they were not uncomfortable as women spoke about such topics as homemaking and child-rearing, for example. But in many communities today, this has changed. Women can no longer be 'trusted' to engage in trivial – and innocent – talk. The topics may remain the same (home chores, child-rearing) but frequently males are no longer at ease, and, it would seem, no longer able to exercise indirect control. Woman talk has emerged as extremely *relevant* for them.

'We often had arguments after we had been out somewhere, mixing with friends, when I had been talking to other women. I would start to see things, I mean, things I hadn't seen before. I remember being staggered once by a friend's description of the difficulties that she and her husband were having, after she wouldn't do all those life-support things. You know, after, she stopped. Well, I *was* doing those things. Exactly the same things, and, I was spending my time cleaning up after him, shopping, cooking, the washing, ironing, the lot you know. And I had so much more free time when he was away on one of his trips ... one of his frequent trips. Because I was so much better organized. Well, there wasn't nearly as much work when he wasn't around. I started to think that I worked so he could have leisure, I produced his leisure ... and that wasn't fair. And that wasn't going to continue ...

I tried talking to him about it, of course, but that didn't work. You know he could just not hear the things I was saying. He was convinced I was emotional, and, well impressionable. Just being influenced by women – unreasonable women mind you – who didn't have the same understandings *we* had. I think I could say that, that he absolutely refused to see what I was talking about. He explained it away as "other influences". And right in the middle of our discussion – you wouldn't call it that really – he asked me when my period was due. I remember that. I was furious. That sort of, would have explained, my "unreasonable" behaviour. But I had just finished. Anyhow, at least, that's what I said. So then it was about the unhappiness of all the women I talked to. Really. He used to go on about it was because they had poor relationships, that was why those issues became important, he said. Didn't I like doing things for him? That's what *love* was, and he liked doing things for me. He reckoned that if I was going to get so upset, you know, when we went out. Well then, we wouldn't go out any more.'(22)

It is interesting to note that *he* decides *she* won't have further contact with these 'unfortunate' women because it is disturbing *his* way of life. He uses many of the devices of the dominant reality to discredit her meanings. Deprived of indirect control over her talk with other women he attempts to reassert himself through direct control: he will restrict her opportunities for talking to them. In the above relationship the woman indicates that her husband 'had never been dictatorial about whom I should and should not see ... until I questioned the injustice of our workloads'(22), and then he became most insistent that she should have no further contact with these women who were 'influencing' her, even though, in the main, they were the same women she had known, and talked to, before she had questioned the sexual division of labour. The major change was in her unwillingness to reproduce, without question, the male meanings which ordered existence.

It can be demonstrated that modifications in male control of talk have occurred in the last decade and whereas women *were* genuinely and completely muted, they are now moving away from that position. While women reproduced the male limits of their world, they constituted little threat to patriarchal order, but now that they are beginning to encode their own definitions they are unmasking the patriarchal ideology which has defined and confined their world. Ideologies do not have the same power to organize behaviour when they are unmasked (Burns, 1973).

The change has not been in the topics talked about, but in the way those topics are structured, in the perspective from which they are viewed. When women began to make sense of the world with themselves as central, housework, for example, emerged in a new light.

'Most new discoveries are suddenly-seen things that were always there', says Susanne Langer (1976: 8), and women are making the new discovery that their existence and their talk have been circumscribed by male control; they are rejecting those male defined parameters and are suddenly seeing their existence afresh. 'A new idea is a light that illuminates presences which simply had no form for us before the light fell on them', she adds. Women's experience is now being illuminated by women themselves.

Many males have found themselves confronted with the demand that they participate in life-support tasks, for example, and although this in itself may have been traumatizing – and the significance of the demand should not be underestimated – this was only one area of change. They were also confronted with women whom they no longer 'controlled', women who were no longer playing according to predictable, patriarchal rules, women who could no longer be relied upon to know their place and to smoothly fit into the patriarchal schemata. It would be difficult to determine which was the greater source of anxiety for men.

The dominant group has good reason to believe that 'things could get out of hand' if these subversive activities of some of the muted group go unchecked.

'He really hated me going off to women's meetings. We fought constantly ... He said that I should talk to *him* if I had problems. He used to say how unfair I was because *he* wouldn't go out, without me. That was true, too, if you don't count going to work. But then he got more tense, and, well, things became very difficult. Finally he said, well, he said it was finished if I didn't stop. He just couldn't take it any more. What could I do? ... I didn't have anywhere else to go, so I stopped. I stopped going. I miss them, though. He's pleased. But it's not true that I can talk to him about the same things. I can't. It just isn't the same. When I try, and I did a bit, he just thinks I'm being unreasonable. He says I haven't got enough to occupy me. I'm on a course now ... maybe it will get better.'(23)

There is no guarantee that woman talk will continue: in fact, the odds are probably against it. When it becomes too threatening there are just so many sanctions available that can restore order:

'I am dependent on him. It's as simple as that. He can call the tune. I have to think of the kids ... if he says you don't go to those bitching sessions, I don't go. And he was right, it was causing us problems. I was, honestly, sometimes pretty discontented after them. I try to put it behind me now. I couldn't have kept going to the sessions, that is, I couldn't go on with them and stay in the same relationship. He would have had to change, and he didn't want to. He didn't see why he should. I think I can see his point. He had planned his life and I was, well, just upsetting the plans. So, that was it.'(24)

Once again these women are subscribing to the dominant reality, not through choice, but necessity. Though their reasons for abandoning woman talk might be regrettable, they are none the less realistic. While the dominant group controls the resources of society, particularly the economic ones, many women literally cannot afford to continue to participate in CR activities. And members of the dominant group are 'within their rights', within the patriarchal order, in utilizing those resources to their own ends. Politics is the name of this game.

The talk which women engage in today is often even seen as 'political' by males (McWilliams, 1974). The personal *is* political and women are involved in serious politics when they begin to talk about their personal experience from their own perspective. When women no longer merely reproduce the definitions of themselves as ordained by the dominant group – as passive consumers, as subordinates required to impose order and cleanliness on chaos and dirt (Miller, 1976) – then there is nothing less than a redistribution of one form of power taking place.

This redistribution challenges patriarchal order at two levels. At one level it challenges the assumptions of male supremacy because if women will not be subordinate it is difficult for men to appear superior. At another level the redistribution challenges the dominant reality for some individual males who find themselves living in conditions of intimacy with women who are constructing different definitions of reality. Their response may take the form of increased adherence to tunnel vision in the attempt to 'ignore' the alternatives with which they are being presented, they may begin to 'lay down the law' and directly remove women from the source of inspiration for these new meanings, or they may begin to move towards understanding and appreciating women's meanings. But all these responses may promote insecurity. When directly confronted with woman-centred meanings, many men show signs of considerable discomfort as they perceive that events are moving beyond their control; as some women gain confidence, understandably but not inevitably, some men become unsure.

'You might say that he wasn't at all subtle. I began to see that I had these choices, you see, that there were options open to me. I tried to talk about them, you know I really made an effort. I began to think it was all right for me to work, and not to be a housewife ... I was excited, and I wanted to explain, and to communicate. But that wasn't any good and ... he just got more

and more confused, and ... he just did. And he got upset. He said
I wasn't sticking to the bargain. I mean I didn't know what
bargain he was talking about and I said so. I said I didn't
remember making any bargain. But that was when he said it went
without saying that we had made a bargain, that everybody did,
and he thought I wanted to have children, and that, well, that I
had misled him. I'd been sort of ... deceitful.

   It was very difficult. It all changed, our relationship did. The
basis changed. He had always been the sort of initiator, in a way,
and I had reacted. Now he didn't know what to do, then, not
when I started saying what *I* wanted. Of course, you know, I tried
to make it more equal, like equal decisions, but it didn't work. It
was like he didn't know what to do if he wasn't the centre. He
couldn't really deal with anything unless he was in the driving
seat. Things were becoming more clear for me and more confused
for him. We could both see that ... But he believed it was my
fault. That it would go away ... you know, if I could just be the
girl he married.'(25)

Directly and indirectly women reveal through their own comments
the significance of their talk in patriarchal order. Because of this, I
become disturbed by comments such as the following: 'CR was
necessary in the early days of the movement, but there's not so much
need for it anymore. It's often just a waste of time, and frankly, well, it
can just stop you from doing positive things to change society.'(26)
Autonomy or absorption? Or a bit of both?

   Reality is constructed and sustained primarily through talk (see
chapter 5, and also Berger and Luckmann, 1972). Those who control
the talk are also able to control reality. There can be no doubt that
within CR groups women have been moving towards acquiring control
over their own talk, have been beginning to construct a metapatriarchal
reality and have been circumventing some of the restrictions habitually
imposed upon muted groups. But if that reality is to be maintained it
needs constant re-creation, it needs reinforcement, it needs to be
confirmed, and it is doubtful whether existence in a sexist society
affords sufficient confirmation. For some of the women who have
'withdrawn' from CR groups, the alternative reality which was
sufficient to generate practical changes in their daily lives (usually
referred to as difficulties or aberrations) faded, and no longer provided
an impetus for change after they withdrew. Without the reality

engendered and confirmed in CR, there is no pressing need for personal changes. Dominant definitions can be more readily accommodated.

It could be that CR groups have evolved new forms and that it is no longer essential to designate a specific time and place for the purpose of constructing a feminist reality. But when I see the vast, complex means that are available for confirming patriarchal order – which, despite all this, is still fragile – and the few, simple means that are available for confirming feminist order – which is so much more fragile – I retain my suspicions about this line of reasoning.

'When the women's movement began, CR ... had to be an *explicit* activity, didn't it? But that's not the case today, is it? CR is going on just about everywhere women gather, don't you think? It isn't a *separate* activity anymore, or at least, I don't think so. It's going on *all* the time, you know. It's CR when I have lunch with my friends, and it's CR when we talk in the pub, or at meetings or at work. Don't you think so? Don't you think it would be artificial to go back to meeting just to raise consciousness? I do. I think I'm raising my consciousness all the time. I think it's part of my daily life, don't you? Isn't it something you are doing every day?'(27)

I hope so. But is that enough?

## Are males the right models?

An analysis of woman talk and its role in society must remain fairly speculative because, not surprisingly, it is not a topic that has been pursued vigorously in the research community. Little or no reliable work has been done on the talk of women. Where research has been conducted on small group discussion, there are recent publications which make no reference to CR groups and, although such groups are primarily associated with woman talk, one book which does include an entry on CR confines discussion to the role CR has played in groups of the male Left (Jenkins and Kramer, 1978:80).

The absence of woman talk in the extensive and growing area of communication studies is also apparent and where women have been included the results are more often than not tinged with the customary sexist bias. The operation of the dominant group can be detected as men set up models (about women) and then check with other men for validation, thereby continuing to construct the muted nature of women. From their review of the literature Lee Jenkins and Cheris Kramarae (1978:78–9) contend that

> men have defined the games that women are supposed to play by men's rules and judged women's behavior accordingly. That is, men make up the theory and the test situations based on their experience and evaluate the women by their standards. The fact that women often behave differently in same sex groups, then, seems like an interesting curiosity rather than an indication of different modes of conduct ...

If women have not conformed to male models they have generally been ignored – they become non-data as Mary Daly explains – excluded, or measured in terms of their deficiency. For this reason what little research there is on single sex talk is often unsatisfactory.

There is also another major bias in research, yet, interestingly, it is one that has rarely been commented upon. Communication is a two-way process. It requires at least a 'talker' (sender) and a 'listener' (receiver) but the almost exclusive emphasis in research has been on talking. Little research has been done on listening as an aspect of interaction and this imbalance requires some explanation.

Is it coincidence that listening is something which women do more than men, something which is less 'visible', and which has therefore (mistakenly) been associated with passivity? Is it coincidence that women are often considered to be the 'better' listeners, providing the understanding and sympathetic ear, being more inclined to 'hear someone out'? Is there any connection between the devaluation of women and the devaluation of listening?

I suspect that there might be. I suspect that women may be more familiar with and more appreciative of the 'art of listening' (which is perhaps a more appropriate description than the 'art of conversation') and perhaps even more skilled at it. It would seem reasonable to assume that, from the perspective of the dominant group, listening may well be a skill which can be overlooked.

> 'Doesn't it make you furious sometimes the way men won't listen? Eh? There are times when I think they can't! They get so preoccupied with what they are going to say next, so concerned with getting their opinion in, nothing else matters. You know I don't even think it impinges. It's such a relief to talk to women

sometimes. They do *listen*, they weigh what you are saying. They aren't just waiting for an opening to hear their own voices. I get so pissed off trying to talk *with* men when they only know how to talk *at* you.'(28)

This is not just the experience of one woman – although it is one of the most forcefully expressed – for it seems that women in general do not feel that men listen to them attentively. A common 'complaint' I have encountered is that when women make suggestions they are frequently not 'taken up' but when men make the same suggestions, sometimes only minutes later, they are treated seriously; they are taken up, and they are frequently considered to be productive, if not brilliant, suggestions. What is going on in these situations? What dynamics are at work?

'I ask myself if it's because I'm a woman. Maybe, it's being a woman that disqualifies you, so they don't hear what you say. But that, well that's not enough to explain it all. Because five minutes later, less than five minutes sometimes, a man comes up with the same thing. And everyone says, how fantastic. Now has he "stolen" my idea? Has he heard it? Do you know what I mean? When I said it, well, there wasn't any response, like nothing ever happened when I said it. I want to know whether he heard me and waited for his opportunity or whether, well, you know whether it was his original idea. Didn't anyone hear me the first time or didn't it count? Does it have to come from a man? It all just makes me so furious.'(29)

There are no answers to these questions, but the problem seems to have been widely experienced by women. In this discussion, seven of the other eight women present all knew what the speaker was talking about and all seemed equally perplexed. They did not know whether their ideas were being 'stolen' or whether men genuinely believed that the ideas they were putting forward and which had previously been offered by women were their own original contributions. However, there was consensus that women were not able to always make the same contribution as males in discussions (in this case, mainly staff meetings) and that it was not because women did not have something to contribute, but because their words were not heeded.

Other issues have also emerged when women have spoken about sex differences in listening. One of the most interesting explanations I have taped is about the relationship between women's listening skills and their apparent intuition.

> 'Women aren't blessed with intuition. They just listen in a way that men don't, right? You know when I first joined [the staff] I was pretty intimidated, if the truth be known. Sort of didn't say a word, or anything. I was too frightened to open my mouth, you know, scared I would say something stupid. So I just shut up. Didn't say a word. [laughter] And you know what I found when I listened? All those little nuances, all those little things, underlying things that give you the complete picture. I knew who was *in* and who was *out*. The politics of it all ... it was all there to see ... But when you start talking, now that's different. When I started talking, you don't get that kind of information. You're too concerned about getting into it, saying your piece at the next opportunity. You're going over in your head, rehearsing what you're going to say. You don't hear any of the undertones 'cos you're too busy thinking about yourself and what you are going to say ...
>
> When you're *just* listening, you pick up all kinds of information. And when you *act* on it, you know, that's when people say how *intuitive* you are! Hell! It just so happens it's usually women doing the listening. That's all. When you're in charge, when you've got to dominate the meeting, well that's usually men, and they aren't listening. They don't know what sources of information they are missing. It's not intuition at all, is it? Women just "hear" things and see things; men don't.'(30)

Though unusual, this is none the less a plausible explanation and one which would be interesting to follow up in research. In present circumstances, however, such an eventuality seems unlikely.

What we do need to analyse is what sort of assumptions are operating when the research problems which are posed in interaction studies concentrate disproportionately on *talk*? Is this an index of our value system, and if so, what does it signify, particularly in relation to the sexual divisions in society? It could be that research on *listening* could reveal some of women's strengths (and perhaps some of men's 'weaknesses') and that in doing this reversal the evidence which emerges might not support patriarchal order. Such research could also possibly serve to enlighten us about sexual differentiation in interaction, and could, therefore, lead to changes. If listening were shown to be as important and as complex as talking, if it were shown to be equally valuable, there would be repercussions in all our social institutions. Educational theory, for example, along with political practices might be transformed by such an understanding. And the balance of power between the sexes might be disturbed.

Only because listening has been devalued could some research findings have 'emerged'. For example, listening would need to have been classified as non-existent, as non-data, in order for some of the results on verbal fluency to have been constructed. Fluency has frequently been measured in terms of *monologuing*, and not as a product of interaction, as Louise Cherry (1975) has pointed out. Given that very few of us engage in the practice of talking aloud to ourselves (monologuing), because of the tendency to classify such behaviour as evidence of mental disturbance, it is doubtful whether a measure of monologuing constitutes fluency, in a naturalistic setting. Apart from other reasons for discrediting some of these studies which have sometimes suggested that girls are more skilled at this monologuing (fluency) than boys, the total disregard of the role played by listening constitutes sufficient cause for being critical of such research. (And in the context of the ostensibly greater fluency of girls in the early years, why is it that this 'skill' mysteriously disappears at adolescence? Does this fluency conveniently metamorphose into gossip, which can be discounted when girls get to an age where they could count as members of society?)

Research, and the truths constructed by research, is a social product which feeds back to us the biases we first started with. We would be wise to take this into account in our study of mixed-sex interaction patterns. Perhaps because we have begun with the initial bias that the way males do things is the right way, and perhaps because males do the talking, we have constructed knowledge which embodies talk as *the* valuable trait in interaction. If different biases were fed into the research process we could receive different feedback. Merely in the interests of a 'corrective' – the term which Florence Howe (1977) has used for Women's Studies – it would be interesting to assume that the male way was not the right way, and that it was not desirable for women to model their interaction patterns upon males. Given this initial assumption, we could begin to receive feedback that talk is not always the superior and efficacious tool we have been led to believe, and that listening is a constructive and creative form of behaviour. Under such circumstances, it would not be males who were the models for interaction; neither would we be able to characterize males as the dominant group – for it is doubtful whether they could exercise control over listening comparable to the control they have exercised over talk.

## Single-sex talk: why women prefer to talk to women

Just as there is little research to guide us on the part played by listening in discourse, so is there little to guide us on the nature of sex-segregated talk. Despite the widespread belief that men talk differently in the presence of women – 'not in front of the ladies' (Lakoff, 1975) – and that women talk differently in the absence of men, there are virtually no studies which systematically explore the differences or similarities of single-sex talk.

Some work, however, has been done on the response to single-sex talk. Elizabeth Aries (1976) has found that women prefer to talk to other women – this does not preclude their acceptance of the patriarchal standard, for they may still value the talk of males more even while retaining their preference for female talk – and before examining the unique single-sex activity of CR (Jenkins and Kramer, 1978), it is worth considering women's preference for talk with other women.

First of all, given the sexual divisions of our society it is reasonable to expect that women could share interests with other women – about their work – which they may not always share with men. This might be a contributing factor in their preference for same-sex talk. But there may also be more compelling reasons for their choice. Mirra Komarovsky (1962) has found that sometimes women cannot get their husbands to talk to them at all and this would seem to be a good enough reason for finding talk with males unsatisfactory. Phyllis Chesler (1971) and Joan Cassell (1977) are, however, a little more specific when they claim that women cannot get their husbands to talk on topics the women wish to pursue, in a manner which they find acceptable. This finding is quite consistent with some of those presented in other chapters which suggest that males are more likely to define the topic of conversation for women, and if this is the case then a communication context in which women were more free to choose the topics for themselves would indeed seem to be preferable. (One can ask the questions about the significance of the phraseology that women 'cannot get their husbands to talk' for this would also seem to reinforce the belief that it is the responsibility of women to elicit the talk of men, despite the over-whelming evidence that, in all social contexts tested, including those

of extended interaction between husbands and wives, men talk more.)
Talking to males may appear 'hard work' for many women, hence the
preference for single-sex female talk.

> 'There are so many things you have to be conscious of when you
> talk to men. And they are not there when you talk to the girls. I
> don't have to flatter any of my [women] friends for example. It's
> much more sincere. I don't keep thinking, will they think me
> silly. When I'm talking to my [women] friends I don't keep
> asking myself what they want to hear, and then try and say it. I
> don't really ask what will make them feel good and then say it ...
> but I don't say things that upset them, it's not that. It just doesn't
> arise. I just talk. I'm sure we all do. I think it's just easier.'(31)

The conventional explanation that it is the 'gulf of interest' between
the sexes (Komarovsky, 1962) which makes talk between females and
males problematic at times appears inadequate. The preference of
women for talk with women is based on more than shared interests.
Perhaps men and women do not want to talk about the same things, or
in the same way, with the result that they cannot always serve as
satisfactory audiences for each other – or at least, this may be the case
in Herefordshire (Whitehead, 1976) – but there are other factors which
also must be taken into account.

The work undertaken by Elizabeth Aries (1976) provides some
insights. Over a period of time she observed single-sex and mixed-sex
talk and she concluded that, for women, single-sex talk offered some
concrete advantages. Aries states that whereas 'mixed sex groups seem
to benefit men more by allowing them more variation in interpretational
style' (not to mention the benefit of having a dutiful audience), for
women, mixed-sex talk 'brings more restrictions in style' (p. 15).
Stated fairly crudely, that women should prefer to talk to other women
is understandable given that they are curbed, constrained and even
silenced when they talk to men.

Aries found that when women talked to men they experienced a
reduction in their overall talking time, a restriction in the range of topics
they could talk about as they attempted to cater for men's interests, and
restrictions in their style as they attempted to speak in a manner which
was acceptable to men. These limitations do not seem to apply when
women talk to women.

There may, however, be more factors which contribute to their
preference for all-female talk. There has been the suggestion, and it has

some support, that in single-sex groups women are more likely to use cooperative verbal strategies (Aries, 1976) while men are likely to use competitive ones (Mitchell-Kernan, 1973) and when the two sexes interact it is not 'the women's way' (Cassell, 1977) which prevails. The competitive, 'one-upmanship' style of much male talk has been categorized by Whitehead who says of the males in the pub in Herefordshire where male 'verbal duelling' took place, that 'no statement went unchallenged' and that talk consisted of 'long, competitive exchanges' (1976: 191). Elizabeth Aries also contends that whereas there is *rotation* of the speaker in female single-sex groups – a more co-operative and egalitarian structure for talk – a stable *hierarchy* establishes itself in male single-sex groups, where someone becomes dominant and retains that position until there is a successful challenge. Then the hierarchical order is rearranged. It is possible that males are used to 'competing for the floor' while females are used to 'having their turn', and when these two styles are brought together the opportunities for males are extended while those for females are reduced.

In discussion it seems that women are more generally interested in a 'fair outcome' while men are more generally interested in 'establishing the winner' (Baird, 1976; Stoll and McFarlane, 1973). In mixed-sex talk this conflict of interest would no doubt be resolved in favour of males. Given all these factors which work against women in mixed-sex talk, their preference for single-sex talk is nothing less than sensible.

In single-sex groups, Aries found that men were more likely to talk about themselves, more likely to tell stories which emphasized aggressiveness and superiority, while women talked less about themselves and more about human relationships; this suggests that there is a fundamental difference in style between the sexes. This difference in style is more likely to find accommodation for women in same sex groups for, when in the presence of men, it is *they* who must give way, being placed in the position of a muted group, where they are unable to procure the space for the development of their own topics in a manner which is consistent with their own experience.

The advantages of single-sex talk have been summed up by one woman who claimed that 'there was no need to argue about whether or not the problems we felt were real' (Susan, 1970, 239) when men were not present. The result is that women can pursue topics that are of concern to them, in a manner which they find appropriate, without risk of the penalties which can be imposed by the dominant group in the patriarchal order.

The difficulties which can be encountered by women when they attempt to talk to men have sometimes been the subject of discussion among women themselves – and not just in the 'agony columns' of popular magazines. At an educational conference where women were addressing the problem of what to do with male speakers who dominated the talk even while they assured women of their opposition to sexism, it was decided that the patriarchal order was so pervasive it was almost impossible to change it.

'We are all living in a society where women are oppressed and where roles are defined. When you do get men and women together in a group you find that the roles are taken on almost subconsciously. You find for example that there are five men and they apparently speak for more than 50 per cent of the time even though there were thirty women. People just fall into the roles. They just listen to the man.'(32)

How to overcome these problems was the basis of a discussion in which the majority of women were of the opinion that the only solution was to *exclude* men. This, however, was not acceptable to one woman, who felt that men must be included and that women should become more adept at dominating the discussion. Basically, because this argument assumes that women should become more skilled in the strategies which men employ, I am not inclined to support it as a solution.

Perhaps instead of being concerned with making women talk more like men, it would be more productive to modify our male-as-norm line of reasoning and work towards helping men to listen more like women, because it seems to me that at the core of women's co-operative strategies for talking is a respect for, and competence in, listening. If co-operation (which implies being a willing listener as well as a willing talker) rather than competition and domination were to be highly valued in discussion, if 'talk' were seen as an opportunity for understanding the views of others and not just for airing one's own, we would witness profound changes which would not just be confined to mixed-sex talk. Many hierarchical structures, which currently permit and promote the talk of the few and the enforced listening of many, would be undermined.

In single-sex groups women value both talking and listening, and this is a strength. This is why they do not interrupt to the same extent as males, why there is not the same competition to gain the floor, to establish a stable hierarchy, to be dominant. This is why co-operation is possible in female single-sex groups. Perhaps it is why women have this extra sense, 'intuition', attributed to them. Perhaps this is also why CR groups exploded inexplicably among women in the late 1960s (Carden, 1974) and why CR has never achieved the same popularity among men. CR is consistent with women's ways of experiencing and structuring the world.

## Consciousness-raising: a woman-centred meaning

Whether the women's movement was the impetus for CR, whether CR was the impetus for the women's movement, or whether they were one and the same phenomenon, are questions which cannot be satisfactorily answered, but that CR was an integral part of the modern feminist movement and that it met the needs of women is beyond doubt. No one can state categorically when CR groups emerged, but many were flourishing by 1968 (Carden, 1974) and most who have investigated the origins of CR groups agree that they were 'spontaneous' formations which swept across America (Freeman, 1975) and other westernized countries. They were – and perhaps still are – widespread, with Joan Cassell stating that by the spring of 1972, for example, that 'every block in Manhattan had at least one consciousness–raising group' (Cassell, 1977: 34). If consciousnsess-raising is now defined as part of the daily lives of feminists which occurs whenever they meet, then it is even more widespread today.

Although there are now many definitions and explanations of CR, I suspect that they have been applied in retrospect and with the assistance of hindsight. Jo Freeman has stated that they were 'structures created specifically for altering the participants' perceptions and conceptions of themselves and society at large' (1975: 118), but I doubt whether many of the members of some of those initial groups would have been so conscious about the purpose of consciousness-raising and would have provided such a coherent and categorical statement. Rather, I think women found they were engaged in CR activities and that they worked: the 'explanations' for them came later. It is possible today to see that there was a precedent for these activities (even though it wasn't quite the same) in the 'Speak Bitterness' meetings organized by Mao Tse-tung during the late 1940s in North China (Dreifus, 1973: 2–5), but it was not as if women knew of this dynamic process and *emulated* it – they *rediscovered* part of it for themselves. 'Speaking Bitterness' was *imposed* and CR groups were *created*, and this also represents a fundamental difference between the two processes for there was no one instructing women to attend such meetings.

Offering explanations *after* the event, Cassell (1977 : 16) has defined the process of consciousness raising as one in which

> Consciousness is by definition a subjective state. Raised consciousness can refer to becoming conscious of something which one did not formerly perceive, of raising something from the unconscious to the conscious mind, to heightened consciousness of oneself on a state of affairs: to an altered consciousness − to 'having your head in a different place.'

To this I would add that CR is a process which helps to transform the muted condition of women. It is through this process that women begin to perceive the dimensions of the dominant reality, the existence of the dominant group's definition of them, and the false nature of all those meanings. Cassell states that CR is central to the contemporary feminist movement for it 'refers to such a transformation whereby the individual "switches worlds" ' (1977 : 18), and that this switch is one of moving from reproducing the world of the dominant reality to producing the world of the feminist reality. Women are 'converted', she states − and we should be mindful of the similarities and necessary differences between feminist 'conversion' and religious conversion − and once converted a woman 'inhabits a transformed world in which her identity, biography, beliefs and behavior have changed radically. She has become a feminist. She defines herself as a member of a group composed of women' (p. 19). She begins to see and understand what she has in common with other women and she uses that shared experience to generate and encode meanings which illuminate and define her experience positively. Instead of being a recipient of meaning she becomes a producer and as such begins to deconstruct her muted state.

The process has been an exhilarating one for many women. It is simultaneously exciting and wearing, fulfilling and frustrating. But having glimpsed the potential of women-centred meanings, it seems that it is difficult to revert to the unquestioned acceptance of the dominant definitions of the world, particularly if that glimpse can be repeated at regular intervals. The discrepancies have been disclosed, and even if not acted upon (as, for example, in the case of women who have been obliged to withdraw from CR groups at their husbands 'requests'), the *knowledge* of the existence of their false nature will not readily disappear. 'Even those who "drop out" ', says Freeman, 'carry the ideas with them and pass them on to their friends' (1975: 118).

It is no coincidence that while the initial processes by which new members come to understand the meanings of society is called *socialization*, the introduction to alternative meanings as encoded in feminism is called *resocialization* (Freeman, 1975). It is a form of starting afresh to organize and make sense of the objects and events of the world, this time with one's head in another place! Those objects and events of the world may be materially the same but resocialization ensures that they are perceived differently. It necessitates imposing a new order upon the world, the formulation of new categories and relationships between them. For feminists it means abandoning the semantic base of patriarchal order and redefining women so that they are not automatically the negative pole, so that they are not 'naturally' wrong, deficient, deviant, 'other' or victim. Once women begin to change these definitions upon which patriarchal order is based and by which it is made meaningful, they also begin to move outside their muted condition.

But how does this new classification system evolve? Where traditionally stratification has been used as a way of interpreting the world, it could be expected that the new definitions would come from the 'experts'. Working within the patriarchal framework it would appear 'logical' to turn to those who have 'authority' and who therefore are accorded more rights in determining reality. There are examples of new sets of meanings being formulated in this way and 'handed down' to the followers: from Freud to Joseph Smith (the Mormon prophet), there are instances of a new reality being encoded by an authority and accepted by those who adopt it.

Such a practice, however, would be self-defeating for feminism because it would perpetuate dominant/muted structures and create inequality, albeit *within* 'a group called women'. This would hardly represent an improvement and would be of little assistance in achieving the goal of equality. In order for stratification to be eliminated – including the stratification of dominant/muted groups – it is necessary that all those who inhabit this new reality should be participants in its construction; they must be producers and not consumers. Whether by accident or design, there can be no doubt that CR groups have facilitated the eradication of stratification and have provided an opportunity for those who are living within a system of feminist order to construct that order for themselves.

Equality is a fundamental tenet of feminism and CR groups have been structured so that they are a manifestation of this tenet, so that equality is not just theory but also practice. I do not think that finding a structure which fostered equality represented an overwhelming challenge for feminists, despite the hierarchical premises of patriarchal order, for women also had another tradition (although one neither acknowledged nor given credence) and that was the tradition of *co-operative* talk. Because of this, equality was not necessarily an artificial or external goal but was itself a product of their own generation of meaning. It 'matched' with the other woman-centred meanings they were attempting to encode.

Obviously, as they had been socialized into inequality within the patriarchal order, there were difficulties in making and using equality as an explicit structure and, because of this, some groups produced guidelines designed to facilitate equality of talk. Lee Jenkins and Cheris Kramarae have recognized that 'having rules for such groups seems in some ways paradoxical since the groups are designed to provide a new freedom for the women involved' (Jenkins and Kramer, 1978: 70) but, again, it is also worth remembering that these rules or guidelines were created *after* the event. They were produced by women who had experienced CR without having the assistance of guidelines themselves, and they were trying to give other women the benefit of their experience. There were women engaged in CR and participating in the process of constructing a new, autonomous reality, before such guidelines appeared.

What I find intriguing is that, from the outset, most women insisted that CR groups be confined to women. With the benefit of hindsight it seems clear that equality would probably have remained an elusive ideal if men had been included. Perhaps women were using their intuition when they determined on the necessity of women only meetings, but their position has certainly been vindicated. With the assistance of some research on male control of discourse – research which did not emerge until after the emergence of CR groups – it appears likely that there would have been stratification if men had been present. Their greater rights to discourse, acknowledged by both dominant and muted groups, would no doubt have precluded the evolution of a new reality compatible with female experience. In the face of the accusation that their problems were not real, that they were neither serious nor significant, women might not have had the confidence, the presumption – or even the opportunity – to persist with the generation and formulation of their own meanings. Old meanings could have reasserted themselves and men, and women, could have succumbed to the temptation of having men tell women 'how it really is'.

## When all are leaders ...

To some critics of the CR process, equality remains still an ideal. Sometimes this criticism is justified. Socialization takes many years and inculcates many meanings at the deepest levels, and resocialization cannot be accomplished overnight. (Its *potential* can possibly be glimpsed in a very short space of time, a phenomenon which Jessie Bernard (1975) has termed the 'click' phenomenon because it occurs so quickly and transforms so much as the basis for the new reality 'clicks' into place.) But despite the validity of the criticism, there is a need for caution because there is a danger of using the meanings of the dominant group to interpret the behaviour of feminist groups and this can be misleading.

The structure of CR groups has had to be forged on an equilibrium between the old and the new meanings. New meanings still have to be meaningful and sometimes this requires links with old meanings. Against the criticism that CR groups are not equal must be placed the criticism that when all members are 'equal' there is a 'tyranny of structurelessness' (Freeman, 1975). Both criticisms have some substance. It is within this context that I think many women's groups have found an equilibrium, though it could well be transitory.

If CR groups are organized without hierarchical structures there is the possibility of chaos; if organized with hierarchical structures there is the possibility of intimidation. Neither is desirable and it appears a compromise has been made. Leaders there are, but they are leaders with a difference; their task is to assist others to lead.

Women have a tradition of rotating speakers and this has been developed within CR groups. Joan Cassell has observed that while at any given time there might be a 'leader' within a CR group, it is not necessarily a stable situation. The leader changes. But this is not the only difference, because leaders within feminist groups are often seen to be using their role to 'abolish leadership' (Cassell, 1977). The so-called leaders in CR groups frequently use their position to help others lead and this distinguishes them markedly from leaders within patriarchal order. The existence of any leader is dependent upon the existence of followers, and if and when all women are – at some time – leaders, there can be no convenient category of faithful followers. The term leader then becomes meaningless within multidimensional reality, which acknowledges a multiplicity of leaders and abolishes the stable category of followers.

So while I can understand that there may be some women who seek to become permanent leaders, who seek to be *dominant* and to perpetuate the hierarchies inherent in patriarchal order, and while I can appreciate that ten people cannot simultaneously be leaders while the term retains some of its patriarchal force, I think that there is sufficient evidence to suggest that women have often transformed the dominant group's definition of leader. Although the term may remain the same, it has been invested with metapatriarchal force (Mary Daly calls this *recycling* words) within feminism, and can be used to represent a different phenomenon.

CR groups aim to dispense with leaders, not to foster the development of the few at the expense of the many and thereby create another (female) stratification system. They aim to explore the personal, not to minimize it and treat it as intrusive as so many leaders must do if they are to preserve 'ordered' and 'controllable' structures (see discussion, p. 47). They aim for the exchange of meaning and not for the transmission of the meaning from one individual or group of individuals to another – a necessary feature of 'giving orders' and being in control !

CR groups have had to develop processes which can appear contradictory within the framework of man-made meanings. They have had to 'discourage competition, aggression, and the establishment of a status-hierarchy, while encouraging trust, co-operation, collective consciousness, yet independency on the part of members' (Jenkins and Kramer, 1978:69). They have had to find ways of helping women feel that they are at the same time both individuals and members of a group; although there are many instances where they have not been completely successful (Cassell, 1977), there are also many where they have been successful, partly through the recognition of the *multiplicity* of the meanings of women. Women have been able to listen to each other and to accommodate what they have heard without necessarily feeling obliged to make others share exactly the same analysis as they do.

Even if I wished to, I could not determine which came first, the generation of women's meanings or the process of CR. I do not know if it is because of the particular but muted consciousness of women that CR became such a dynamic and powerful tool, or whether it was because women possessed such a dynamic.powerful tool they were able to encode their own meanings. To pursue this line of reasoning is to be confined to the linear, cause–effect, monodimensional reality which has its own inherent limitations, and I find it makes sense to utilize the concept of multidimensional reality and to assume the interconnected nature of women's meanings and CR. I can account for them in terms of having developed together and in conjunction with one another.

Within the egalitarian context of CR groups women have found the means for participation in the encoding of new meanings. They have experienced a growth in self-esteem – a predictable outcome of ridding themselves of the negative definitions of their existence which the dominant group has provided – a growth in competence, and in confidence, which in turn generates yet more new meanings. I do not think there would have been the same outcome had men been involved.

Not only would men, by definition, have brought with them the stratification that accompanies the juxtaposition of female/male; not only would they have brought their own patterns of order, the necessity for formal organization and hierarchy (see Cathy Roberts and Elaine Millar, 1978, for the study of one such 'breakdown' when men tried to impose their hierarchies on a mixed-sex group working for abortion reform); not only would they have brought their own meanings about their own supremacy – they could also have brought with them divisions among women themselves.

After having discussed with a group of ardent feminists the way in which women frequently defer to men in mixed-sex talk, I was assured by those present that although this may have been true in the past, it was no longer the case. To put it simply, I did not believe them, partly because I was constantly discovering, to my own dismay, that while I *believed* that I did not give more attention to men than women in mixed-sex talk, that I did not turn to them for guidance, defer to their opinions, seek confirmation from them, or favour them at the expense of women, the tapes which I studied told a different story. My own analysis of my own behaviour revealed that I operated the divisions of dominant/muted in mixed-sex talk.

Blatantly I had declared that I preferred talking to women. Confidently I claimed women 'made more sense'. But in the presence of men I 'unconsciously' reproduced the meanings I consciously deplored. If I had accepted the opinions of those feminists who claimed that they did not engage in the practice of promoting male supremacy, I would have been obliged – in true patriarchal fashion – to assume that I was deficient, and so when the opportunity arose to tape some of my sisters in mixed-sex talk, I took it.

My suspicions were confirmed. We *all* were more 'polite' to the males, we all allowed males to be the centre of attention and to determine the parameters of the talk, even though we felt free to disagree with them within those parameters. We paid less attention to each other and I do not think it unfair to say we *competed* for the attention of males – an obvious consequence of their control – and permitted them to define our unequal status. If males are in control, then women *must* get male acknowledgment and attention in order to talk and this can be divisive among women.

Summing up the traditional methods which women have been required to use in order to operate in the world, Letty Cottin Pogrebin has stated (1972:78):

> Men compete for rewards and achievements. We compete for men. Men vie for worldly approval and status. We vie for husbands. Men measure themselves against [their] standards of excellence and an established level of performance. We measure ourselves against one another.

This competition among women has been more by design than accident, and though feminism has outrightly repudiated the inevitability and desirability of such practices, perhaps remnants linger on, particularly while males are in control and we are forced to compete for their acknowledgment and approval. We still have one foot in patriarchal order and should not minimize the effects – or the dangers – of our position.

The extent to which competition and divisiveness among women is engendered by the presence of men is open to debate, but in the absence of men who can be the source of approval/approbation/affirmation, the likelihood of this occurrence is reduced. There is evidence which suggests that women talk and work co-operatively in single-sex groups and that this co-operation is jeopardized within mixed-sex groups.

To me CR groups, be they formally or informally arrived at, are crucial to feminism because they are both the source and the means of constructing the new and necessary feminist reality. They are unique and specific *woman talk*. There is a need for women to communicate with men and to attempt to raise men's consciousness, but not on men's terms. *Explaining* to men is not the same activity as *encoding* a feminist reality. Because these activities are inherently different I think a new name should be given to 'mixed-sex consciousness-raising' and this is an example of the need for women to devise new names to describe the world from *their* perspective.

Woman talk which has been disallowed and disavowed by the patriarchal order is one of the most powerful means of subverting and transforming that order. Because of this, the dominant group can be relied upon to hinder the growth and development of woman talk. I think women should resist these pressures to the utmost and that patriarchal myth should be made feminist reality. Women should become the talkative sex.

# · 5 ·

# Language and Reality: Who Made the World?

✳

'The objects and events of the world do not present themselves to us ready classified', states James Britton (1975). 'The categories into which they are divided are the categories into which *we divide them*' (p. 23). My question which arises from this statement is not whether it is an accurate assessment, for I readily accept that language is a powerful determinant of reality, but who is the WE to whom James Britton refers? Who are these people who 'make the world' and what are the principles behind their division, organization and classification?

Although not explicitly stated, Britton is referring to males. It is men who have made the world which women must inhabit, and if women are to begin to make their own world, it is necessary that they understand some of the ways in which such *creation* is accomplished. This means exploring the relationship of language and reality.

Susanne Langer (1976) has pointed out that human beings are symbolizing creatures (it is, perhaps, our capacity to symbolize that differentiates us from other species), and we are constantly engaged in the process of producing symbols as a means of categorizing and organizing our world. But it would be foolish to have complete faith in the system of order we have constructed because it is, from the outset, imperfect, only ever serving as an approximation. Yet it seems that we are foolish: we do 'trust' the world order we have created with our symbols and we frequently allow these representations to beguile us into accepting some of the most bizarre rules for making sense of the world. It is our capacity to symbolize and the use (or misuse) we make of the symbols we construct that constitutes the area of language, thought and reality.

It is because we can be seduced by language that a debate has been waged for many years on the relationship of language, thought and reality. On the one hand there is considerable evidence that not all human beings are led to the same view of the world by the same physical evidence and on the other hand is the explanation – namely the Sapir–Whorf hypothesis – that this is because of language. It is language which determines the limits of our world, which constructs our reality.

One of the tantalizing questions which has confronted everyone from philosophers to politicians is the extent to which human beings can 'grasp things as they really are'; yet in many ways this is an absurd question that could arise only in a monodimensional reality which subscribed to the concept of their being only *one* way that 'things' can be. Even if there were only one way, it is unlikely that as human beings we would be able to grasp that 'pure', 'objective' form, for all we have available is symbols, which have their own inherent limitations, and these symbols and representations are already circumscribed by the limitations of our own language.

Language is *not* neutral. It is not merely a vehicle which carries ideas. It is itself a shaper of ideas, it is the programme for mental activity (Whorf, 1976). In this context it is nothing short of ludicrous to conceive of human beings as capable of grasping things as they really are, of being impartial recorders of their world. For they themselves, or some of them, at least, have created or constructed that world and they have reflected themselves within it.

Human beings cannot impartially describe the universe because in order to describe it they must first have a classification system. But, paradoxically, once they have that classification system, once they have a language, *they can see only certain arbitrary things.*

Such an understanding is not confined to linguistics. The sciences of physiology and biology have also helped to substantiate – sometimes inadvertently – the false nature of impartiality or objectivity. Evidence gathered from these disciplines demonstrates that we ourselves come into the process of organizing and describing the universe. Unfortunately for those advocates of the human capacity to 'grasp things as they really are' there is one basic flaw in their argument – they have failed to take into account that the brain can neither see nor hear:

To speak metaphorically, the brain is quite blind and deaf, it has no direct contact with light or sound, but instead has to acquire all its information about the state of the outside world in the form of pulses of bio-electrical activity pumped along bundles of nerve fibres from the external surface of the body, its interface with the environment (F. Smith, 1971:82).

The brain too, has to interpret: it too can only deal in symbols and never know the 'real' thing. And the programme for encoding and decoding those symbols, for translating and calculating, is set up by the language which we possess. What we *see* in the world around us depends in a large part on the principles we have encoded in our language:

> each of us has *to learn to see*. The growth of every human being is a slow process of learning 'the rules of seeing', without which we could not in any ordinary sense see the world around us. There is no reality of familiar shapes, colours and sounds to which we merely open our eyes. The information that we receive through our senses from the material world around us has to be interpreted according to certain human rules, before what we ordinarily call 'reality' forms (Williams, 1975:33).

When one principle that has been encoded in our language (and thought) is that of sexism, the implications for 'reality' can readily be seen. So too can the implications for 'objectivity', because 'scientific method' has been frequently accepted as being 'above' fallible human processes and, because its truths have been paraded as incontestable, many individuals have had little confidence in their own experience when this has clashed with prevailing scientific 'truths'.

It is not just feminists who have come to challenge some of the accepted notions about the impartiality of science and who have focused on the relationship of language, thought and reality – although there are distinctive and additional features of the feminist approach which I will discuss later. There is new interest in such areas as the philosophy or sociology of science in which the question of 'objectivity' is being taken up, and where old answers are being viewed as inadequate and false (Chalmers, 1978; Kuhn, 1972). That science is a dogma, just as were the feudal, clerical and market dogmas which preceded it, that is open to query and to challenge (Young, 1975:3), is not a traditional evaluation of scientific method, but it is an evaluation that is becoming increasingly more popular. That reason, objectivity, and empiricism have been used to justify 'science' in a way that revelation, divine inspiration and mythology have been used to justify 'religion', is a factor which has not been explored: yet the parallels exist. It has been just as heretical or crazy to challenge one dogma as it was in the past to challenge the other.

But this is changing. Alan Chalmers (1978), for example, tackles some of the misapprehensions that are held about science and scientific method, whereby the naming of something as 'science' has implied 'some kind of merit, or special kind of reliability' (p. xiii). He too, takes up some of the issues of language, thought and reality when he readily demonstrates (partly by use of a diagram, p. 22) that not all human beings – scientists included – are led to the same view of the world by the same physical evidence, for what observers see when they view an object or event 'is not determined solely by the images on their retinas but depends also on the experience, knowledge, expectations and general inner state of the observer' (p. 24) which, as Chalmers illustrates, may very often be culturally specific and which I would argue is largely determined by language, which is the means of ordering and structuring experiences, knowledge, expectations and inner states.

Chalmers is intent on discrediting the premise that science *begins* with observation and he convincingly points out that this is a fallacy: contrary to the belief of the 'purity' of empiricism, he indicates that 'theory precedes observation' (p. 27) and the types of theories which are culturally available play a substantial role in determining what the observers – empirical scientists among them – can *see*.

When there are a sexist language and sexist theories culturally available, the observation of reality is also likely to be sexist. It is by this means that sexism can be perpetuated and reinforced as new objects and events, new data, have sexist interpretations projected upon them. Science is no more free of this bias than any other explanatory activity.

It is this recognition that human beings are part of the process of constructing reality and knowledge which has led Dwight Bolinger (1975) to 'reinterpret' our past and to assert that our history can validly be viewed *not* as the progressive intuiting of nature but as exteriorizing a way of looking at things as they are circumscribed by our language. Once certain categories are constructed within the language, we proceed to organize the world according to those categories. We even fail to see evidence which is not consistent with those categories.

This makes language a paradox for human beings: it is both a creative and an inhibiting vehicle. On the one hand it offers immense freedom for it allows us to 'create' the world we live in; that so many different cultures have created so many different 'worlds' is testimony to this enormous and varied capacity (Berger and Luckmann, 1972, have categorized this aspect of language as 'world openness' p. 69). But on the other hand we are restricted by that creation, limited to its confines, and, it appears, we resist, fear and dread any modifications to the structures we have initially created, even though they are 'arbitrary', approximate ones. It is this which constitutes a language *trap*.

It could be said that out of nowhere we invented sexism, we created the arbitrary and approximate categories of male-as-norm and female as deviant. A most original, imaginative creation. But, having constructed these categories in our language and thought patterns, we have now been trapped for we are most reluctant to organize the world any other — less arbitrary or imperfect — way. Indeed, it could even be argued that the trap which we have made is so pervasive that we cannot envisage a world constructed on any other lines.

It is, however, at this point that feminist insights into language, thought and reality, are differentiated. While it could be said that we invented sexism from out of nowhere and utilized the principle in encoding reality, I doubt that feminists would make such a statement. While it could be argued that it was mere accident that 'objectivity' and the 'scientific method' came to acquire their meritorious[1] status and while such a discussion could occur without reference to gender, I also doubt whether feminists would completely accept such an explanation. The distinctive and additional feature of feminist analysis of language, thought and reality is that feminists assert that we did *not* create these categories or the means of legitimating them. To return to James Britton's statement at the beginning of this chapter, I would reiterate that it has been the dominant group — in this case, males — who have created the world, invented the categories, constructed sexism and its justification and developed a language trap which is in their interest.

Given that language is such an influential force in shaping our world, it is obvious that those who have the power to make the symbols and their meanings are in a privileged and highly advantageous position. They have, at least, the potential to order the world to suit their own ends, the potential to construct a language, a reality, a body of knowledge in which they are the central figures, the potential to

[1] At this point I consulted *The Concise Oxford English Dictionary* to find out if the word I wanted was meritorious or meretricious. Obviously it is meritorious: meretricious (the closest entry to my feeling for meritricious) is defined as 'of, befitting a harlot'. Now where does that one come from!

legitimate their own primacy and to create a system of beliefs which is beyond challenge (so that their superiority is 'natural' and 'objectively' tested). The group which has the power to ordain the structure of language, thought and reality has the potential to create a world in which they are the central figures, while those who are not of their group are peripheral and therefore may be exploited.

In the patriarchal order this potential has been realized.

Males, as the dominant group, have produced language, thought and reality. Historically it has been the structures, the categories and the meanings which have been invented by males – though not of course by *all* males – and they have then been validated by reference to other males. In this process women have played little or no part. It has been male subjectivity which has been the source of those meanings, including the meaning that their own subjectivity is objectivity. Says Dorothy Smith: 'women have largely been excluded from the work of producing forms of thought and the images and symbols in which thought is expressed and realised', and feminists would state unequivocally that this has been no accident. She indicates how historically males have talked to males and thereby encoded (false) principles in language, thought and reality (1978:281–2):

> This is how a tradition is formed. A way of thinking develops in this discourse through the medium of the printed word as well as in speech. It has questions, solutions, themes, styles, standards, ways of looking at the world. These are formed as the circle of those present builds on the work of the past. From these circles women have been excluded ... throughout this period in which ideologies become of increasing importance first as a mode of thinking, legitimating and sanctioning a social order, and then as integral in the organisation of society, women have been deprived of the means to participate in creating forms of thought relevant or adequate to express their own experience or to define and raise social consciousness about their situation and concerns. They have never controlled the material or social means to the making of a tradition among themselves or to acting as equals in the ongoing discourse of intellectuals.

This provides a broad outline of the way in which women have been excluded from the production of language, thought and reality. It shows how they have been omitted from the circles in which such forms are produced, and often of course, omitted from consideration by the members of the circle. It explains why it is possible for women today to generate meanings which are at variance with the patriarchal order and patriarchal tradition. Our foremothers may have generated similar meanings to our own but as a muted group without access to the production of legitimated language their meanings may also have remained invisible.

It is not just the macro-view which Smith puts forward which helps to establish that women have been silent — not just in language, but in thought and reality as well. The micro-view also provides insights into the manner in which patriarchal order has been created. It is possible to find specific examples which illustrate the way in which the dominant group put the principle of sexism into the language: and, as has been indicated, once it is in, it goes on compounding as it is projected on to new objects and events. Once *in*, it is very difficult to get it *out*.

## The circumstantial evidence

The evidence for the relationship between sexism and language, and males, has been largely circumstantial: there *is* sexism in the language, it *does* enhance the position of males, and males *have* had control over the production of cultural forms. It therefore seems credible to assume that males have encoded sexism into the language to consolidate their claims of male supremacy. While personally convinced of the legitimacy of this argument, I have also recognized the desirability of being able to provide concrete examples of the process at work. Actually to document the introduction by males of some aspect of sexism into the language, to indicate the way in which males systematically proceeded to embed some form of sexism into language, thought and reality would be to put the discussion of sexism and language on a very different plane. Because I could see the advantages of being able to provide specific instances of male 'intervention', I was more than ready to begin such a search: the problem was, where does one begin?

Although it is not possible to go back to the beginning (earlier than any written records), it is possible to start with sexist examples and to work backwards in the hope of finding records which could pinpoint the introduction by males of specific sexist usages, structures or meanings. The language as it exists today can become the starting point for investigation and using the language itself as a source of evidence is not without precedence. Anthropologists, for example, have long known the value of language structure in 'cracking the code' of another society even if they have not adopted a comparable approach to their own. Whereas the almost inaccessible meanings of other cultures have sometimes been revealed by clues provided by the language structure, few efforts have been made to locate or interpret any clues which might reveal some of the 'hidden' meanings of our own. That there is no Hebrew word in the old testament for *Goddess*, for example, provides a clue to the meaning of a deity in those times – at least, among those who were engaged in the task of writing (Stone, 1977: 7), but that there is no word in the English language for a strong female (this is discussed more fully in the next chapter) does not seem to have been a factor which has interested many language scholars who wish to know more about our rules for making sense of the world.

Undoubtedly our own meanings are partially hidden from us and it is difficult to have access to them. We may use the English language our whole lives without ever noticing the distortions and omissions; we may never become aware that there is no symbol for women's strength. But although it is not always easy to get outside this language trap, to get outside the limitations of one's own language, it is not impossible. There are clues, if one is prepared to look for them.

Whereas the semantic base of the language is intangible and sometimes difficult to 'catch', the structure of the language is more concrete and more readily traced. When I became interested in locating examples of the male introduction of sexism, I had no preferences for either semantics or structure. While I traced the *meanings* of many different words I could not find more than circumstantial evidence that they were the product of male efforts (dictionary-makers, of course, being primarily male), but in tracing some of the *structures* of the language I was able to find numerous decrees, written down by males, which were directed towards ensuring male primacy within the language. Thanks to the zealous efforts of the prescriptive grammarians, there are accounts of males introducing sexism into the language.

There were also some perceptive writers who were offering clues about the language and who were indicating possible directions for research. In 1971, commenting on the social significance of our language structure, Richard Gilman said that (1971:40–55)

the nature of most languages tells us more about the hierarchical structure of male-female relationships than all the physical horror stories that could be compiled ... that our language employs the words *man* and *mankind* as terms for the whole human race demonstrates that male dominance, the IDEA of masculine superiority is perennial, institutional, and rooted at the deepest level of our historical experience.

With clues such as these offered by Gilman and with language structure appearing to afford far more opportunities for locating male intervention, I began to investigate the use of *man* and *he* for evidence of male effort in the introduction to the language.

To me, it seemed perfectly clear that the use of *man* and *he* as terms to denote a male, but on occasion to encompass a female, was an example of a sexist linguistic structure. Initially I saw it as a convenient means for making women invisible, for *blanketing* them under a male term. I also saw it as a means of creating difficulties for women because representing them with a male symbol on some occasions made this particular linguistic structure ambiguous for them. They were required to ascertain to whom this symbol referred, whereas no such problem existed for males who can never be ambiguous in such structures. If males are present, then males are named, but women are sometimes included in that male name. In order to know the meaning of a particular utterance, such as 'man must work in order to eat', women had to have additional information to determine whether they were included. No man needs to seek further information to establish whether men are included in a reference such as 'love is important for women', for if men were intended to be encompassed the statement would be 'love is important for men'! The use of *man* and *he* to refer also to a woman only creates difficulties for women – which is probably why linguists have never seriously addressed this problem.

Those understandings of the sexist nature of *man* and *he* now seem, in retrospect, to be very elementary and very crude. But that was the point at which I started. I began by trying to cultivate the position of an outsider and by asking myself questions about the significance of *man* and *he* in the English language. What are the implications of a society which has a language based on the premise that the world is male unless proven otherwise? What is the result of eliminating the symbol of woman from the language? What are the effects of making a common linguistic structure ambiguous for half the population?

Such questions are still not considered reasonable by some people who remain convinced that either the use of *man* and *he* to encompass women is insignificant and that any attempts to analyse such usage are 'making mountains out of molehills', or that this is mere linguistic accident (Morgan, 1972) and something we have to put up with; or both! But the introduction of the special use of *man* and *he* − of *he/man* language as Wendy Martyna (1978) so aptly puts it − was neither insignificant nor accidental and once encoded in the language it had many repercussions for thought and reality.

## *He/man* **language**

The rationalization that 'man embraces woman' is a relatively recent one in the history of our language. It was a practice that was virtually unknown in the fifteenth century. The first record we appear to have is that of a Mr Wilson in 1553 who insisted that it was more *natural* to place the man *before* the woman, as for example in male and female, husband and wife, brother and sister, son and daughter. Implicit in his insistence that males take precedence is the belief that males 'come first' in the natural order, and this is one of the first examples of a male arguing for not just the superiority of males but that this superiority should be reflected in the structure of the language.

Thomas Wilson was writing for an almost exclusively male audience, and an upper-class or educated male audience at that. Those who were going to read his words of wisdom − and to confirm or refute them − were men who were interested in grammar and rhetoric. Judging from the success of this particular ploy, it appears that Mr Wilson's audience appreciated the 'logic' of this particular rationale, and accepted it.

If females had been familiar with this decree − which seems unlikely, given that females of all classes were systematically denied access to education − they might have protested that the so-called natural order posited by Mr Wilson did not appear so unquestionably natural to them. But women were not included in the production of grammatical rules and their views on the logic of this usage go unrecorded. Their muted state is reproduced.

The records of 1646 reveal that the concept of the natural precedence of males having encountered no opposition − from males − has actually gained ground. According to one scholarly grammarian, Joshua Poole, it was not only natural that the male should take 'pride of place' it was also *proper* because, in his line of reasoning, the male gender was the *worthier* gender. He seems to have offered little evidence for his claim, but his male colleagues do not appear to have disputed it.

The seal was set on male superiority, however, when in 1746 John Kirkby formulated his 'Eighty Eight Grammatical Rules'. These rules, the product of Mr Kirkby's own imagination, contained one that indicated the esteem in which he held females: Rule Number Twenty One stated that the male gender was *more comprehensive* than the female.

This represents a significant departure from the simple proposition that males are more important. It is a move towards the concept that male is the universal category, that male is the norm. The *Oxford English Dictionary* defines *comprehensive* as 'including much', so Mr Kirkby was arguing that man included much more than woman because man was more comprehensive and this, according to Mr Kirkby's reasoning, should be encoded within the languages for all to comply with. As he could not have been arguing that there were more men than women, he must have been using some criteria other than number for his evidence of the more comprehensive nature of man. One is left with the conclusion that Mr Kirkby believed that each man represented much more than each woman and that it was legitimate to encode this personal belief in the structure of the language and to formulate a grammatical rule which would put the users of the language in the 'wrong' if they did not adhere to this belief.

That each man included much more than each woman was a personal opinion that Mr Kirkby was entitled to hold. It was his generation of meaning and it reflects his own perspective on the world and his assessment of his own place within that world. The activity which he was engaging in is one which human beings engage in constantly every day of their lives as they attempt to project meaning into their existence. But Mr Kirkby was a member of the dominant group and had the opportunity – experienced by few – of making his subjective meanings the decreed reality.

He handed down Rule Number Twenty One to a male world of grammarians who were not averse to sharing his assumptions about the centrality of the male and who were not reluctant to insist that 'non-males' – or, as it has become in Mr Kirkby's rule, 'minus males' – also share these assumptions. There is an example of one sex encoding the language to enhance its own image while the other sex is obliged to use this language which diminishes, or conflicts with its image.

Rule Number Twenty One is one man's bias, verified by the bias of other men, and imposed upon women. They did not participate in its production, they do not benefit from its use. It was a sexist principle encoded in the language by males and which today exerts a considerable influence over thought and reality by preserving the categories of male and minus male.

During Mr Kirkby's time, most people did not modify their language use to accommodate his rule. Although he wrote for such a select audience, even many males remained oblivious to his rule. It may have served to reinforce hierarchical distinctions among those who 'knew' that the use of *he/man* included women on the 'grammatically objective grounds' that *he/man* was more comprehensive, but it was not taken up avidly by the whole population. But the rule was there, it had been recorded, and it was extremely useful for the nineteenth-century grammarians who vehemently took it up and insisted on rigid adherence to this rule in the name of grammatical correctness – another invention of the dominant group which legitimates their prejudice!

Before the zealous practices of the nineteenth-century prescriptive grammarians, the common usage was to use *they* for sex-indeterminable references. It still is common usage, even though 'grammatically incorrect': for example, it is not uncommon to say 'Anyone can play if *they* learn' or 'Everyone has *their* rights'. Then – and now – when the sex of a person is unknown, speakers may use *they*, rather than the supposedly correct *he* in their reference.

To the grammarians, however, this was incorrect and intolerable. When the sex is unknown the speaker should use *he* – because it is the more comprehensive term. It is also, of course, the term which makes males visible, and this is not just a coincidence.

Users of a language are, however, sometimes reluctant to make changes which are decreed from above (see also p. 153 for women's reaction), and it is interesting to note just how much effort has been expended on trying to coerce speakers into using *he/man* as generic terms. As Ann Bodine (1975) has noted, using *they* as a singular is still alive and well, 'despite almost two centuries of vigorous attempts to analyze and regulate it out of existence' on the ostensible grounds that it is incorrect. And what agencies the dominant group has been able to mobilize in this task! Bodine goes on to say that the survival of *they* as a singular 'is all the more remarkable considering the weight of virtually the entire educational and publishing establishment has been behind the attempt to eradicate it' (p. 131). One is led to ask who it is who is resisting this correctness?

But the history of *he/man* does not end here. It has not just been the educational and publishing establishment that has worked towards establishing its primacy. The male grammarians who were incensed with the 'misuse' of *they*, were instrumental in securing the 1850 Act of Parliament which legally insisted that *he* stood for *she* (Bodine, 1975)!

The introduction and legitimation of *he/man* was the result of deliberate policy and was consciously intended to promote the primacy of the male as a category. If there are people today who are unaware of the significance of *he/man*, I do not think that some of the male grammarians who promoted its use were quite so unaware. The tradition of men talking to men, of men appealing to like-thinking men for validation of their opinions and prejudices, is one which can be traced in the writings of grammarians, and one which continues today. There is still a closed circle. We have inherited men's grammatical rules, and as Julia Stanley says (1975:3):

> these 'fixed and arbitrary rules' date from the first attempts to write English grammars in the sixteenth century and the usage that is still perpetuated in modern textbooks merely reflects the long tradition of male presumption and arrogance ... When a contemporary writer L. E. Sissman says that the sentence *'Everyone* knows *he* has to decide for *himself'* is both 'innocuous' and 'correct', he is merely appealing for authority to the men who have gone before him.

We cannot appeal to the women who have gone before. As a muted group we have no record of their thoughts – or of their objections – on this topic.

As the dominant group, males were in the position to encode forms which enhanced their status, to provide the justification for those forms, and to legitimate those forms. At no stage of this process were females in a position to promote alternatives, or even to disagree. To my knowledge there has never been an influential female grammarian and there were certainly no female Members of Parliament to vote against the 1850 Act. The production of this linguistic form – and the effects it has had on thought and reality – has been in the hands of males.

It is worth remembering this when encountering the resistance to changes which feminists are seeking. Currently, when they are trying to eliminate this practice of using *man* to symbolize *woman*, they often meet the objection that they are 'tampering' with the language. If one accepts that the language is the property of males then this objection is no doubt valid. But if the objection is based on the understanding that the language is pure and unadulterated then it is not at all valid. Feminists are simply doing what males have done in the past: they are trying to produce their *own* linguistic forms which do not diminish them. In this case it requires the removal of an 'artificial' and unjustifiable rule, invented by some male grammarians and sanctioned by other males, in the interest of promoting their own primacy. Feminists are trying to remove the 'tamperings' of males who have gone before.

## Think male for man!

The task of finding males in the act of structuring sexism into the language has been only partially completed by documenting the introduction of sexism into the structure of the language. In order to appreciate the full significance of this act it is necessary to look at the effects that *he/man* has had upon thought and reality.

*Man* (and *he*) is in constant use as a term which supposedly includes females, and one of the outcomes of this practice has been to plant *man* uppermost in our minds. There is quite a lot of evidence which suggests that people think *male* when they use the term *man* and one of the best illustrations that I have come across of this process at work is that provided by Elaine Morgan. Because she makes the point so well, I will quote her case in full (1972:2–3):

> I have considerable admiration for scientists in general and for evolutionists and ethologists in particular, and though I think they have sometimes gone astray, it has not been purely through prejudice. Partly it is due to sheer semantic accident, the fact that man is an ambiguous term. It means the species: it also means the male of the species. If you write a book about man or conceive a theory about man you cannot avoid using the word. You cannot avoid using a pronoun as a substitute for the word, and you will use the pronoun *he* as a simple matter of linguistic convenience. But before you are halfway through the first chapter a mental image of this evolving creature begins to form in your mind. It will be a male image and he will be the hero of the story; everything and everyone else in the story will relate to him ... A very high proportion of ... thinking ... is androcentric (male centered) in the same way as pre-Copernican thinking was

geocentric. It's just as hard for man to break the habit of thinking of himself as central to the species as it was to break the habit of thinking of himself as central to the universe. He sees himself quite unconsciously as the main line of evolution with a female satellite revolving around him as the moon revolves around the earth ...

The longer I went on reading his own books about himself, the more I longed to find a volume that would begin: 'When the first ancestor of the human race descended from the trees, she had not yet developed the mighty brain that was to distinguish her so sharply from other species'.

Here Elaine Morgan has begun to explore the relationship of sexist language to thought and reality and the fact that many people get a shock, a clash of images when they encounter her last sentence, is a measure of the extent to which we have been encouraged to think and to see male, by the use of the term *man*. And what Morgan has understood, many others have documented empirically.

Alleen Pace Nilsen (1973) found that young children thought that *man* meant male people in sentences such as 'man needs food'. As Elaine Morgan hypothesized, Linda Harrison found that science students – at least – thought male when discussing the evolution of man; they had little appreciation of the female contribution even when explicitly taught it (1975): J. Schneider and Sally Hacker (1973) found that college students also thought male when confronted with such titles as Political Man and Urban Man. Unless students are unrepresentative of our society – an unlikely possibility – there seems to be considerable empirical evidence to suggest that the use of the symbol *man* is accompanied, not surprisingly, by an image of male.

The relationship of language, thought and reality is more complex than a one-to-one correspondence of symbol and image, but this does serve as a starting point from which to ask questions. If both sexes have an image of male when they use the term *man*, does this have different repercussions for females who are excluded from the imagery than it does for males who are included? Are females – or males – even aware that females are excluded? And what effect does this male imagery have on our 'rules of seeing'? Do we project male images on to the objects and events of the world, are we 'trapped' into seeing male when without the particular blinkers provided by our language we might discern female images in the world we inhabit?

The answers to some of these questions are still a matter for conjecture. The answers to others are more readily available.

By promoting the use of the symbol *man* at the expense of *woman* it is clear that the visibility and primacy of males is supported. We learn to see the male as the worthier, more comprehensive and superior sex and we divide and organize the world along these lines. And, according to Linda Harrison and Wendy Martyna – who went slightly further in their research than other investigators who were exploring the links between male symbols and images – females understand that they are not represented in *he/man* usage; both Harrison and Martyna found that males used *man* more often than females and Martyna attempted to discover the basis for this choice.

When Wendy Martyna asked people in her sample what they thought of when they used the symbol *man*, the males stated that they thought of themselves. This was not the case for females. The females said they did not think of themselves, they did not use the term in relation to themselves, hence they used *he/man* less frequently than males. There is irony in the acknowledgment of females that they only used the terms *he/man* at all because they had been taught that it was grammatically correct! From this, Martyna concludes that 'Males may be generating a sex specific use of *he*, one based on male imagery, while females are generating a truly generic *he*, one based on grammatical standards of correctness' (Martyna, 1978). How convenient if this is the case!

The findings of Harrison and Martyna also raise another interesting possibility. When women use *he/man*, they do so because they perceive it – erroneously – as being grammatically correct. But they use these symbols much less frequently than males. Perhaps when they choose not to use it, women are the 'offenders' who are using *they* 'incorrectly'; perhaps it has been women who have resisted in part the prescriptive grammarians' injunctions and have kept *they* alive and well, precisely because they can use it without conjuring up male images and so do not feel excluded by the term.

The hypothesis of Wendy Martyna, that men use *he/man* because it includes them and women attempt to avoid using it because it excludes them, brings together the two research areas of sexism and language and sex differences in language use. It supports the Ardener model of dominant/muted groups, indicating the way in which males can construct language so that it provides positive reinforcement of their own identity while requiring females to accommodate and transform those usages. It demonstrates the 'necessary indirectness' of expression for females. That there may be a mismatch between the models of the world which females generate and the surface structure which males control is a contention not without support in the light of Martyna's findings.

When the symbol *he/man* disposes us to think male, women who are required to use those symbols are required to think again. This is an extra activity, one which males are not called upon to perform. As members of the dominant group, having ascertained that their male identity is constant, males are not required to modify their understandings: they are never referred to as *she/woman*. But having ascertained their female identity women must constantly be available – again – for clues as to whether or not they are encompassed in a reference, for sometimes they are included in the symbol *he/man*, and sometimes they are not. What the dominant group can take for granted is problematic to the muted group and this could be another means whereby they are kept muted.

## There's many a slip ...

It is not just that women do not see themselves encompassed in the symbol *he/man*: men do not see them either. (It is unlikely that any male, not just those in Martyna's sample, would have an image of female to accompany the symbol *he/man*.) The introduction of *he/man* into the structure of the language has helped to ensure that neither sex has a proliferation of female images: by such means is the *invisibility* of the female constructed and sustained in our thought systems and our reality.

That males do not see females in the symbol *he/man* is an hypothesis that has been put to the test and has been supported. Muriel Schulz (1978) examined the writings of many leading sociologists – past and present – who ostensibly included females in their analyses of mankind and she found that in many instances there was a consistent image in language, thought – and reality – and it was a male-only image. If female imagery impinged at all upon the thought processes of the following lecturer – who was delivering a lecture entitled 'The Images of Man' – he would not have been able to make the statements that he did (1978:1):

'How does Man see himself? As a salesman? A doctor? A dentist?' (So far the speaker could be using Man generically, referring to women as well as to men.) 'As far as sexuality goes,' he continued, 'the Kinsey reports on the activities of the American male surely affect his self-image in this regard ...' (It becomes clear that the reference has been masculine all along.)

It is these unintentional disclosures which are an index to the imagery which is operating, for few writers/speakers who are concerned with *mankind* would make specific statements that they do not include women; on the contrary, my experience has been that of being patronizingly informed on many occasions that 'Of course I mean women as well when I say *men*: it's just a figure of speech. *Everyone knows* that *man embraces woman*.' Everyone might be *told* that man embraces woman but everyone certainly does not operate this rule, as many examples can illustrate.

The effect of this rule that *man* means *woman* is to put women on the 'defensive' – not just because they are required to glean additional information, but also because in the process of gathering that information – for example, 'Are you including *women* in your discussion of *mankind*?' – they are frequently treated as unreasonable. Given the ambiguity of the symbols *he/man* for women, it is most reasonable to clarify the context, but their efforts are not always viewed in this light and on more than one occasion I have been treated as 'stupid' when I made the reasonable request to determine whether I was included in a reference.

The 'slips' where speakers reveal that it is male and male-only imagery which accompanies *he/man* are not isolated and rare. As Muriel Schulz indicates, examples abound in almost any collection of reputable writings. Alma Graham has also done research in this area and indicates that many males 'give themselves away', for even while they are protesting that they are including females their usage reveals quite the opposite (1975:62):

In practice, the sexist assumption that man is a species of males becomes the fact. Erich Fromm certainly seemed to think so when he wrote that man's 'vital interests' were 'life, food, access to females etc.' Loren Eisley implied it when he wrote of man that 'his back aches, he ruptures easily, his women have difficulties in childbirth ...' If these writers had been using *man* in the sense of the human species rather than males, they would have written that man's vital interests are life, food and access to the opposite sex, and that man suffers backaches, ruptures easily and has difficulties in giving birth.

It is because *man* evokes male imagery that the very statement of Graham's that 'man has difficulties in giving birth' strikes us as unusual. Like the statement from Elaine Morgan that the first ancestor of the human race had not yet developed *her* mighty brain when she descended from the trees, we encounter this clash of images. If *man* did encompass female imagery, there would be no such clash.

This provides another means for testing the validity of the assertion that *man* includes *woman*. Theoretically, if *man* does represent the species then the symbol should be applicable to the activities of all human beings. On the other hand if *man* does mean male then there will be a violation of the semantic rules when the term is applied to activities that are uniquely female. This test is not difficult to undertake and it yields some interesting data.

We can say that 'man makes wars' and that 'man plays football' and that 'he is an aggressive animal' without there being any clash of images even though we recognize that such statements generally only apply to half the population. But the human species does a great deal more than make wars and play football, and half the population, at least in our society, has been labelled 'passive' rather than aggressive. The human species also produces children and cares for them, yet what happens when we use *man* to refer to these equally human activities?

Can we say without a clash of images that *man* devotes more than forty hours a week to housework or that *man* lives an isolated life when engaged in child rearing in our society? A note of discord is struck by these statements and it is because *man* – despite the assurance of male grammarians – most definitely means male and evokes male imagery. (Miller and Swift, 1976:25–6):

> One may be saddened but not surprised at the statement 'man is the only primate that commits rape.' Although as commonly understood it can apply to only half the human population, it is nevertheless semantically acceptable. But 'man being a mammal breastfeeds his young' is taken as a joke.

The joke is the incongruity which is inherent in *man* performing a specifically female task. There would be no joke at all if *man* were a genuine generic and included the female instead of being a pseudo-generic. Unfortunately, the 'joke' is on women who have been systematically eliminated from language, and consequently from thought and reality. I would suggest that if it were ordinarily possible to make statements such as 'man has been engaged in a constant search to control his fertility', we would have a very different language and a very different reality. We would have one where females were visible – and audible – and we would not be able to divide the sexes into dominant/muted groups.

The effects of *he/man* language are considerable – though different – for both sexes. This is literally a man-made product which serves to construct and reinforce the divisions between the dominant and muted groups. Such a small 'device', such a little 'tampering' with the language – but with what enormous ramifications for the inequality of the sexes!

Through the introduction of *he/man*, males were able to take another step in ensuring that in the thought and reality of our society it is the males who become the foreground while females become the blurred and often indecipherable background. *He/man* makes males linguistically visible and females linguistically invisible. It promotes male imagery in everyday life at the expense of female imagery so that it seems reasonable to assume the world is male until proven otherwise. It reinforces the belief of the dominant group, that they, males, are the universal, the central, important category so that even those who are not members of the dominant group learn to accept this reality. It predisposes us to see more male in the world we inhabit, so that we can, for example, project male images on to our past and allow females to go unnoticed; we can construct our theories of the past, including evolutionary ones, formulating explanations that are consistent only with male experience. (Elaine Morgan, 1972, shows just what different knowledge is constructed when a female image is kept in the foreground.)

*He/man* also makes women outsiders, and not just metaphorically. Through the use of *he/man* women cannot take their existence for granted: they must constantly seek confirmation that they are included in the *human* species.

## The outsiders

Sheila Rowbotham (1973a) has touched upon this problem. 'Now *she* represents a woman but *he* is mankind', says Rowbotham, and 'If *she* enters mankind *she* loses herself in *he*' (p. 33). As Gilman has also pointed out, this 'simple' device of having the name of half the population serve for the whole population as well makes it very difficult for the half who are excluded for they are without a full name, without a full identity. The only way women can achieve humanity is by labelling themselves as *man* and as Rowbotham indicates this means losing their identity as *woman*.

'Reversal of roles' has often been useful as a consciousness-raising device, as a means of getting beyond the limitations of the language trap, and, in order to elaborate on the significance of being unable to assume full membership of humanity, a few researchers have attempted to reverse the situation and to find out what happens when the dominant group encounter this – for them, unusual and artificial – situation, of being excluded from a reference. As Casey Miller and Kate Swift found, the men did not like it. They protested vigorously. And of course they invoked the argument invented and used by their forefathers, that it was grammatically incorrect to leave men out.

Miller and Swift (1976) have documented the affront to male dignity which was the outcome of referring to elementary and secondary schoolteachers as *she*. During the 1960s the minority of males in the elementary schoolteaching profession began to protest loudly about this injustice and were 'complaining that references to the teacher as *she* were responsible in part for their poor public image and consequently in part, for their low salaries' (p. 33). One remedy for this situation would have been to work towards enhancing the image of women, for, after all, the majority of the profession were female. But this solution did not seem to occur to the angry male schoolteachers who were concerned with getting themselves, and their concomitant male prestige, into the picture. One such teacher, speaking at the National Education Association Representative Assembly, stated that referring to men as *she* was 'incorrect and improper use of the English language', and that while *she* continued to be used when there were males in the profession, 'the interests of neither the women, nor of the men, in our profession are served by grammatical usage which conjures up an anachronistic image of the nineteenth century school marm' (Miller and Swift, 1976: 33–4).

These male teachers wished to completely dissociate themselves from the negative female imagery that was evoked with the use of *she*: it was positive male imagery which they wanted and so they proposed on 'objective', 'correct' grounds that the women should be referred to as *he*. (Miller and Swift, 1976:34):

> There is the male-as-norm argument in a nutshell. Although the custom of referring to elementary and secondary school teachers as *she* arose because most of them were women, it becomes 'grammatically incorrect and improper' as soon as men enter the field ... Women teachers are still in the majority but it is neither incorrect nor improper to exclude them linguistically.

I have also observed that males are likely to become distressed when they are excluded from a reference. Perhaps this is because the situation is unfamiliar, or perhaps it is because they are not used to dealing with the ambiguity ('Do you mean men when you use the term *sisterhood*?'), or perhaps it is because they appreciate that in a society predicated on male primacy it is a subversive act to promote female imagery at the expense of males. Regardless of the reason, however, there is little doubt in my mind that males are generally distressed when they are excluded from a reference, and yet those same males will often not acknowledge that female exclusion from a reference could cause comparable difficulties for females.

Within the classroom I have set up my own experiments (see Spender, 1980). I gave a mixed-sex class of thirteen- and fourteen-year-olds grammatical 'exercises' in which the point was, at first, to remove females from the reference. During this period the class was quite co-operative and both sexes appeared to have no difficulties with the task. But then I modified the exercise and asked the students to remove males from the references and, at this, the male students protested. They became hostile and some of them left the class rather than continue with what they rationally declared to be stupid and unfair exercises. They too were very affronted when rendered invisible.

Socially, it is quite difficult to exclude males from linguistic references because so rare is this occurrence that listeners assume that any speaker who refers to males as *she/woman* is mentally disturbed. Given our language and resultant thought and reality it would be such a fundamental and profound error to refer to males as *she/woman* that no speaker could do it unintentionally. Such usage does violate the semantic rules and people who do not follow the semantic rules do not make sense. This is an example of yet another sanction for the perpetuation of the use of *he/man*.

The dice are loaded against women. Almost every reasonable protest

that women can make about the use of *he/man* can be countered
conveniently by man-made objective rules – such as grammatical rules
of correctness. And frequently women have bowed to the wisdom which
is ostensibly enshrined in those rules. But how logical, rational, or
objective are these rules which men have devised for eliminating
females from language, thought and reality?

## Male subjectivity

Males made up the rules of prescriptive grammar and males are still in
the main the custodians of those rules; it is therefore unlikely that male
grammarians will issue a review of their own inadequacies. Happily,
however, Julia Penelope (Stanley, 1975) has developed a feminist
critique of the work of male grammarians and has provided many useful
insights in the process.

One of the basic assumptions of the male grammarians has been that
the English language possesses *natural* gender. When a language has
*natural* gender, objects are labelled according to their sex – that is, they
can be feminine, masculine or neuter – and this is in contrast to
languages which possess *grammatical* gender (French and German, for
example) where there is no relationship between the sex of the object
and the gender to which it is linguistically allocated.

For example, in German, where there is grammatical gender, a tree
is referred to as masculine, a tomcat as feminine and a wife as neuter.
English used to have grammatical gender (the Anglo-Saxon gender
allocation was similar to that of modern German), but it has given way
to natural gender which the male grammarians have frequently posited
as an improvement because it eliminates the confusion that can arise
when sex and gender are not correlated.

But one significant factor which has been overlooked by male
grammarians is that English possesses *natural* gender only *if one is
male!*

It is easy to see how male grammarians could have fallen into this
language trap of their own making, for their *he/man* symbol has
worked not only with the rest of the population, but with them as well.
They have assumed the centrality of the male and built their theories
upon it, and those theories do not look nearly so objective and
reasonable when their assumptions are revealed as mistaken. English
does *not* have natural gender unless the population is composed
exclusively of males.

There is nothing *natural* in being a female and being referred to as *he/man*. There is just as much confusion, and just as much 'artificiality' as there is in referring to a tomcat as *she*. In fact, it could be argued that for the female half of the population there is even greater confusion than that caused by grammatical gender, because they have constantly been informed by grammarians that English possesses natural gender and there is an expectation that sex and gender should correspond.

There may be no confusion for males with the gender system of the English language because they are always referred to as *he/man*, and so for them natural gender may indeed be an improvement. There is no ambiguity created for males by the use of *he/man* to refer to men and sometimes to woman, so it is understandable that this has never been raised as an issue by male grammarians for whom *natural* gender has been *male*. But it should suggest to females that unless they are prepared to believe that the language is the property of males they should have little regard for the male grammarians' subjective invention of grammatical correctness.

That the natural gender of the English language is male gender constitutes yet more evidence that, for females, the only semantic space in English is negative. Female gender is not natural, in theory or in practice in language, and when women find themselves missing from the range of positive symbols which the language offers, and invisible in the reality which language constructs, they are witnessing the results of male control of semantics.

This is one more cog in the machine of dominant/muted groups. In order to fabricate and justify the superiority of the male, the dominant group has been obliged to spin a web of rationalizations. It is an old proverb that one lie leads to another and there can be few better examples of this than the lie of masculine supremacy.

In order to sustain their grammatical justifications, grammarians have produced many edicts which speakers of the language are required to take into account. Many of these edicts, and not just the ones associated with the construction of male supremacy, are absurd – it was writers such as Dryden and Swift, for example, who declared that it was incorrect to finish a sentence with a preposition, because you could not do it in Latin (Guth, 1973: pp. 97–8) – and some of them are contradictory.

While the male grammarians have assiduously argued that a pronoun must agree with its antecedent in number and gender, they have been able to overlook the infringement of this rule which is occasioned by *he/man* being the *correct* form of address in the presence of just one male! If there are thirty women in a group and one man, the members of that group must be referred to as *he*, which certainly breaks the rule of agreement of number.

We could ask why it is that for so long male grammarians have been unaware of the falsities of their own laws. It does not seem to be necessary to look far for the answer. In a language where women have been encoded as invisible, the knowledge which is constructed assumes this invisibility – this non-existence – and proceeds accordingly. And new knowledge which is constructed compounds this invisibility.

For women to become visible, it is necessary that they become linguistically visible. This is not such a huge obstacle as it may at first appear: there are no uses of *he/man*, for example, to refer to women in this book. There is no ambiguity here about *man* for when I use the symbol *man* I use it only in reference to male images. But other changes are also required. New symbols will need to be created and old symbols will need to be recycled and invested with new images if the male hold of language is to be broken. As the language structure which has been devised and legitimated by male grammarians exacts ambiguity, uncertainty, and anomie for females, then in the interests of dismantling the muted nature of females, that language structure and those rules need to be defied.

I do not think the world will end if we deliberately break those rules – but there might be a fissure forged in the foundations of the male supremacist world.

# · 6 ·

# The Politics of Naming

❀

In order to live in the world, we must *name* it. Names are essential for the construction of reality for without a name it is difficult to accept the existence of an object, an event, a feeling. Naming is the means whereby we attempt to order and structure the chaos and flux of existence which would otherwise be an undifferentiated mass. By assigning names we impose a pattern and a meaning which allows us to manipulate the world.

But names are human products, the outcome of partial human vision and there is not a one-to-one correspondence between the names we possess and the material world they are designed to represent. We are dependent on names but we are mistaken if we do not appreciate that they are imperfect and often misleading: one of the reasons that people are not led to the same view of the universe by the same physical evidence is that their vision is shaped by the different names they employ to classify that physical evidence.

Naming, however, is not a neutral or random process. It is an application of principles already in use, an extension of existing 'rules' (Sapir, 1970) and of the act of naming. Benjamin Whorf has stated (1976:256) that it is

> no act of unfettered imagination, even in the wildest flights of nonsense, but a strict use of already patterned materials. If asked to invent forms not already prefigured in the patternment of his [*sic*] language, the speaker is negative in the same manner as if asked to make fried eggs without eggs.

Names which cannot draw on past meanings are meaningless. New names, then, have their origins in the perspective of those doing the naming rather than in the object or event that is being named, and that perspective is the product of the prefigured patterns of language and thought. New names systematically subscribe to old beliefs, they are locked into principles that already exist, and there seems no way out of this even if those principles are inadequate or false.

All naming is of necessity biased and the process of naming is one of encoding that bias, of making a selection of what to emphasize and what to overlook on the basis of a 'strict use of already patterned materials'. Theoretically, if *all* members of a society were to provide names and these were to be legitimated, then a variety of biases could be available; the speakers of a language could 'choose', within the circumscribed limits of their own culture. Practically, however, difficulty arises when one group holds a monopoly on naming and is able to enforce its own particular bias on everyone, including those who do not share its view of the world. When one group holds a monopoly on naming, its bias is embedded in the names it supplies and these 'new' names help to maintain and strengthen its initial bias.

It is relatively easy to see how this is done. John Archer (1978) has documented this process at work in the construction of knowledge about sex roles, and he quotes one example of the work of Witkin *et al.* (1962). Witkin and his colleagues wanted to find out whether there were sex differences in the perception of a stimulus in a surrounding field and they designed an experiment where the subjects could either *separate* the stimulus (an embedded figure) from the surrounding field or else they could see the *whole*, they could see the stimulus as part of the surrounding field.

In many of these experiments Witkin and his colleagues found that females were more likely to see the stimulus and surrounding field as a whole while males were more likely to separate the stimulus from its context.

Witkin of course was obliged to name this phenomenon and he did so in accordance with the principles already encoded in the language. He took the existing patterns of male as positive and female as negative and objectively devised his labels. He named the behaviour of males as *field independence*, thereby perpetuating and strengthening the image of male supremacy; he named the female behaviour as *field dependence* and thereby perpetuated and strengthened the image of female inferiority.

It is important to note that these names do not have their origins in the events: they are the product of Witkin's subjective view. There is nothing inherently dependent or independent in seeing something as a whole, or dividing it into parts. Witkin has coined names which are consistent with the patriarchal order and in the process he has extended and reinforced that order.

There are alternatives. With my particular bias I could well have named this same behaviour as positive for females and negative for males. I could have described the female response as *context awareness* and the male response as *context blindness* and though these names would be just as valid as those which Witkin provided they would no doubt have been seen as *political* precisely because they do not adhere to the strict (sexist) rules by which the names of our language have traditionally been coined.

From this it can be seen that those who have the power to name the world are in a position to influence reality. Again, if more than one set of names were available, users of the language could elect to use those names which best reflected their interests; they could choose whether to call males field independent or context blind and the existence of such a choice would minimize the falseness which is inherent in but one or other of the terms. But because it has been males who have named the world, no such choice exists and the falseness of the partial names they have supplied goes unchecked.

The English language is a rich repository of these partial and false names which are designed to construct male supremacy and female subordination. As it would be impossible to examine the whole language I have confined myself to two areas – the language of religion and of sex – to show the way in which language constructs a sexist reality. It is not just what the dominant group has put into these names, it is also what they have left out, which makes such a study so very interesting.

## Man creates a male god

Mary Daly, a feminist theologian, has been at the forefront of the debate on the politics of naming within religion, for she sees the names of religion – which are still so influential in structuring our reality – as a paradigmatic case of the male naming of the world. She methodically analyses the meanings as they are encoded within the Bible and reveals how males have named themselves as superior and have classified women in negative terms from non-spiritual to evil, from deviant to other.

Before pursuing some of Mary Daly's arguments, however, it is necessary to place the Biblical record we have inherited in context and to appreciate that these man-made records have been 'carefully' edited and translated. It is in some of this editing and translating that we can locate the politics of naming. For example, the imagery of Adam and Eve that has percolated through our culture usually takes the form of Adam being created first, and then Eve being made from Adam's rib (this gross distortion of the male 'giving birth' to the female is an archetypal example of false naming by males); although this is the popular narrative it must be noted that it was not the only narrative available when the editing of the Bible was being undertaken. 'The bible does not give us one creation story but several', states Chiera (1938) (quoted in Stone, 1977:24) and 'the one which happens to be featured in chapter one of Genesis appears to be the one which had the least vogue among the common people'. Chiera then goes on to add that this particular version in which males play a superior role and which became the 'standard' version was evidently produced in scholarly circles, and there is no need to ask what sex these scholars were.

There are obvious reasons for the suppression of some of the other versions of the Creation which were available at the time. They did not uphold the image of masculine supremacy and would have made little or no contribution to the patriarchal order. There would have been little to gain as far as males were concerned by propagandizing the version which had God make human beings in God's image – female and male! Given this imagery of equality, Adam would have had to share his place with Eve and we would have had the opportunity to imagine God the Mother as well as God the Father. Religion could have developed along very different lines had this been the case.

Just as with the symbol *he/man* there are many who would try and point out that the symbol *God* also encompasses women, but we think male when we use *he/man* and we think male when we use *God*. As Elaine Pagels (1976) has indicated, the actual language which is used 'daily in worship and prayer gives the distinct impression that God is thought of in exclusively *masculine* terms' (p. 293). This belies the assurance that women are to consider themselves encompassed in the image of God.

The effect of making the Deity masculine should not be underestimated because it establishes one of the primary categories of our world as a male category. It immediately casts females into a negative position which can be further exploited. There was no basis for naming the Deity in this way, indeed, as Mary Daly comments 'Why ... must *God* be a noun? Why not a verb – the most active and dynamic of all?' (1975:167), but for those who were performing the naming it was a clever political move which helped to ensure their own supremacy. There was considerable advantage for males in naming God the Father (who 'gave birth' to the male Adam who in turn 'gave birth' to the female Eve); man made God in his own image (plus extras) and not the other way around as the self-conscious writers and editors of the Bible consistently and insistently would have us believe.

There were writers who named the Deity as feminine/masculine or as predominantly feminine, but their literary efforts were rejected by the editors of the Biblical anthology who were concerned with reinforcing the patriarchal order. Elaine Pagels (1976) outlines the many versions in which God was named as unisexual, androgynous or female – and these versions by far outnumbered those in which God was named male. She indicates the way in which these versions were edited, were 'sorted and judged by the various Christian communities', so that 'By the time this process was concluded, probably as late as the year AD 200, virtually all the feminine imagery for God (along with any suggestion of an androgynous creation) had disappeared from "orthodox" Christian tradition' (1976:299).

Males selected the names and they checked with other males to verify their selection and by this process female names were eliminated from the classification of the Deity. Of this Mary Daly states that (1974:130)

> it is necessary to grasp the fundamental fact that women have had the power of naming stolen from us. We have not been free to use our own power to name ourselves, the world, or God. The old naming was not the product of a dialogue – a fact inadvertently admitted in the Genesis myth in which Adam names the animals and women. Women are now realizing that this imposing of words was false because partial. That is, partial and inadequate words have been taken as adequate.

Males have 'massaged the evidence' so that it reinforces the male view of the world with themselves as central and in the process they have banished women to the periphery. Linked with the Creation is the myth of the Fall and here too males have named the world to their own advantage. Gail Shulman (1974) exposes the inherent bias in interpreting Adam's eating of the apple as a sign of his strength and superiority and says: 'Rather than blaming the man for his weakness in yielding to temptation, the woman is branded as a dangerous, irresistible temptress' by the male namers. This, says Shulman, 'is a masterpiece of male manipulation' which begins with the creation of Eve from Adam's rib and which constitutes 'the first inversion of fact – man is born from woman's body not woman from man's (1974:155).

Had women been involved in the production of these names they would no doubt have pointed to the error of the men's ways. But women were not represented, their meanings were not encoded, and the result has been that we have been required to live under gross distortions produced by males.

There were even alternative versions of the Fall available (see Chiera, 1938; Pauline, 1977; Stone, 1977) but those who compiled the Bible were biased reporters and only one side of the story is presented in the Biblical anthology. There has been no right of reply offered either. There has not even been any general acknowledgment that the story is one-sided, rather, in patriarchal fashion, the male naming of reality has been presented as the only reality once again.

From the particular version of the Fall which the Biblical anthology has popularized we categorize Eve (and the female) as evil. The asymmetry of the sexes is reinforced as man is elevated and associated with the masculine God and Eve is denigrated and associated with evil, with minus male and minus God. As Mary Daly says, this 'exclusively male effort in a male dominated society' reinforced the superiority of the male and the inferiority of the female so 'that woman's inferior place in the universe became doubly justified. Not only did she have her origin in the man: she was also the cause of his downfall and all his miseries' (1973:46).

It is this superiority/inferiority dichotomy which is a principle encoded in our language. It is the prefigured pattern of our language which serves as the source of new names for men and women. It is a pattern which we must break if women are to cease having deviancy and deficiency projected upon them. Sometimes it seems to me that these sexist (the word is not strong enough: we need a new name) principles are so deeply embedded in language and so pervasive in our reality that the task of eliminating them is almost overwhelming. But then I am encouraged for I appreciate that we are beginning to identify these principles, they are no longer entirely hidden from us, and once they have been exposed they can no longer continue to work so efficiently.

However, it is still a mammoth job. Mary Daly indicates how deeply entrenched and how extensive these false names are as they are encoded in religious myths (1973:47):

> The myth of the fall can be seen as the prototypic case of false naming ... the myth takes on cosmic proportions since the male's viewpoint is metamorphosed into God's viewpoint. It amounts to a cosmic false naming. It misnames the mystery of evil casting it in the distorted mold of feminine evil ... Implied in this colossal misnaming of evil is the misnaming of women, of men, of God.

Daly goes on to say that there *was* 'a fall' in the myth of the Fall, for 'in a real sense the projection of guilt upon woman *is* patriarchy's fall, the primordial lie', and women are only now beginning to grasp the distortion that has been perpetrated as 'women have been the primordial scapegoats' of a patriarchal religion in which *only* males do the naming (1973:47).

The men's Bible – as Elizabeth Cady Stanton called it – is another male feat which denies any positive symbolism and imagery to women. Religious myths live on and inform our consciousness long after they have been intellectually repudiated and within the structure of those myths women have been named as that which is not male, not divine, not 'normal', not central.

From the initial distortions of naming God as male and females as evil, many more distortions have flowed. As records came up for exclusion or inclusion in the Biblical anthology, males tampered again and again with the evidence in order to sustain the existence of their initial categorization. Accounts which revolved around males were glorified and extended while those in which women were the central figures were often defiled or dismissed. On the basis that only the affairs of males could be praiseworthy, male activities were named as *religion* while comparable female activities were named as *cult*.

By naming religious activities that women were engaged in as a *pagan cult*, accounts of the female Deity which told of her magnificence and splendour, her creation of the world, and her wisdom, could be classified as the very antithesis of religion. In early Christian times it was the duty of all good Christians to seek out and destroy pagan idols and it was no coincidence that '*most pagan idols had breasts*' (Stone, 1977:7). The injunction that 'Thou shalt have no other gods before me' takes on specific sexual meanings when God is a male.

The translators too played their part and the Biblical anthology reveals some ingenious practices for making women invisible. For example, for some 'strange' reason the Hebrew language has no word for *Goddess* and this absence of a name opened the way for many male malpractices under the guise of linguistic necessity. Although surrounded by accounts of female deities in other languages, the patriarchal translators showed little compunction about performing a quick sex change so that whenever female goddesses are mentioned they are referred to as males. Records coming before the editors which named a female deity were subjected to alteration so that *she* 'was named Elohim, in the masculine gender, to be translated as a god' (Stone, 1977:7). Merlin Stone comments on the 'efforts of the biblical scribes to disguise the identity of the Goddess by repeatedly using the masculine gender' (1977:26), and she deplores the fact that during all the years she spent in Sunday school she never learnt that Astoreth, the pagan deity of the Old Testament, was a female. This is hardly surprising given that Astoreth is always referred to as *he*.

There are other more recent examples of translations which have been undertaken at the expense of women and Letty Russell (1974) indicates how the English patriarchs added their reinforcement to the negative names of women in the Bible. In Genesis 2:20 Eve is referred to as 'Adam's helper', and Russell points out that the Hebrew word here is *'ezer*. Says Russell (1974:55)

> In English, *helper* implies someone who is a servant or subordinate. Yet in the twenty times *'ezer* appears in the Old Testament we find that sixteen times it refers not to a subordinate but to a superior form of help and it never refers to subordination.

These are not isolated examples: they are part of a systematic process of the manipulation of language for male ends. They serve to structure thought and reality so that the speakers of the language can 'see' men only in this superior position and women in an inferior one. It is no accident that one sometimes encounters only a vacuum when trying to entertain positive images of the female, for the substance which could give rise to such images has been methodically removed. Male supremacy is at the very core of language, thought and reality and it has been allowed to develop in this way by precluding women from the process of legitimating any positive names they may have for themselves and their existence. As a muted group, the meanings females may have generated have been systematically suppressed.

This has happened both blatantly and subtly. It has been easy to pinpoint the false naming which occurs when *he* is substituted for *she* but it has been slightly more arduous to locate some of the interpretive features of translation – the occasions when, as Merlin Stone says, the sexually active Goddess is named as 'improper, unbearably aggressive or embarrassingly void of morals' despite the fact that she has forced no one to participate against their will, 'while the male deities who raped or seduced legendary women or nymphs were described as "playful" or even "admirably virile" '. The pattern that is being woven is that the sexual customs of the Goddess faith were performed by women who in their own language were named as sacred and holy, but who in translation are referred to as 'ritual prostitutes' (1977:9).

Whatever males have done, and one does not need to get entirely outside the values of the language to recognize that they have done some terrible things, has been named as positive and allowed to flourish as desirable.

But one can only fantasize on what females might have produced if the names they had provided had ever been taken into account. They were a muted group and their mutedness has been self-perpetuating. Many of the contemporary demeaning images of the female can be traced back to the names and meanings which were consigned to them by some of the Biblical writers/editors/translators. It is a very necessary task to try and change those images, and though there has been some criticism of the movement within feminism to create a spiritual matriarchy (on the grounds that it is without political consequences), I think that such an undertaking is desirable. We do not have ancient symbols of positive women and while such symbols on their own will do little to change the power structure of society, that power structure will not be fundamentally changed unless women have access to positive names for themselves and their own existence. The politics of naming has been a real and powerful activity and women must begin to reclaim the power of naming which men have stolen from them (Daly, 1975) if there is to be a change in the asymmetrical classification of the sexes.

## Sexuality: a case of compensation

Sexuality of both sexes has also been named by males and reveals their perception of themselves – and others. The names of sexuality are a good example of the way in which a reality – which contradicts the evidence of the physical world – can be constructed.

Males began by naming themselves as sexual beings and in accordance with their male subjective logic named females as minus males and minus sexuality. Starting with the male as the norm, defining the attributes of the male as sexually valid, the dominant group ensured that (Iragaray, 1977 : 63):

> the feminine is in fact defined ... as nothing other than the complement, the other side, or the negative side of the masculine; thus the female sex is defined as a lack, a *hole*. Freud and psychoanalysts ... maintain that the only desire on the part of a woman when she discovers she has no 'sex' is to have a penis ... the only sexual organ which is recognized and valued.

Only male sexual characteristics have been named as 'real' within the patriarchal framework so, despite any contrary evidence which female anatomy may reveal, there is doubt about the existence of female 'sex'. So powerful is language in structuring thought and reality that it can 'blind' its users to the evidence of the physical world; objects and events remain but shadowy entities when they are not named.

This allocation of sexuality to the dominant group — in face of the evidence to the contrary — illustrates once again how dominance and muteness are constructed. It is not just males who perceive the non-sexuality of women according to the dictates of the culture — females learn to perceive it as well. It is not their definition of themselves and it may even contrast sharply with female-generated meanings, but the language, thought and reality affords so little support or substantiation for any possible female meanings that they are likely to become 'unreal' and to be abandoned. Had women played a role in naming sexuality, they would no doubt have been able to present convincing evidence that they were not without 'sex' and they would have been able to produce more than circumstantial evidence to corroborate their case for sexuality. But women's meanings were not legitimated and males went on verifying with other males the absence of female sexuality.

The medical profession has made a considerable contribution in recent years to the naming of females as minus males and minus sexuality. Masquerading behind the claim that their subjective opinions were *science* — and therefore unchallengeable — they helped to name females as reproductive rather than sexual beings. The medical profession as an enclave of male power did not have to seek confirmation of its names through any dialogue with females and it used its unique and frequently unquestioned position as 'authority' to dictate to women about their physiology as well as their psychology.

The absence of female sexuality has been reinforced by crude anatomical diagrams in medical texts which fail to delineate female genitals. Distortions were practised – particularly during and since the Victorian era – in which the male genitals were clearly and prominently displayed while female genitals, if characterized at all, were 'symbolized' by a dash or a stroke. If accuracy of representation had been the criterion, then any diagram which displayed female genitals would necessarily have had to be more detailed and more complex than any diagram of male genitals. This was not the case however: mentally convinced that women were without sex, the medical profession dutifully reproduced diagrams which reflected their fantasies and not the facts. And in the process of propagating their mythologies, the medical profession created a difficult situation for many females, who were required to reconcile the fantasy with the facts. Once more women were required to *accommodate* their physiology to the male version of reality. They were required to transform their own meanings into those of the dominant group, often with distressing and uncomfortable results.

Many, many females grow up ignorant of their own anatomy. As Germaine Greer has said (1971:39), within the confines of the dominant reality,

> Women's sexual organs are shrouded in mystery. It is assumed that most of them are internal and hidden but even the ones that are external are relatively shady. When little girls begin to ask questions their mothers provide them, if they are lucky, with crude diagrams of the sexual apparatus, in which the organs of pleasure feature much less prominently than the intricacies of tubes and ovaries.

This denial of female sexuality in the dominant reality can lead to a belief in female deformity by females who are trying to reconcile their own meanings with the legitimated ones they are required to use. Deprived of any accurate standard of reference, there are females who have believed that their own inability to correspond with the single-line-flourish of the diagram is evidence that there is something wrong with their own anatomy. It would seem to be a human reaction to remain silent about this deformity.

*Our Bodies Ourselves* (Phillips and Rakussen, 1978:19) contains statements from women who were convinced that they were afflicted with some form of physical abnormality when they encountered the discrepancy between their own experience and the legitimated names for that experience. Women have begun to break the silence that surrounds their sexuality by setting up women's health centres where, instead of accepting that there is something wrong with *them*, they can begin to appreciate that there is something wrong with the names that the dominant group has imposed upon them. But there is a long way to go: the patriarchal names for female sexuality are so deeply entrenched that it will be an extensive and difficult task to rename women and their sexuality.

Females have had to *adjust* their bodies in order to meet the requirements of the names they have been given, and this has not been an easy task even though they have been offered assistance by the medical profession. Diana Scully and Pauline Bart (1973) reviewed medical textbooks to ascertain what the medical profession thought of women (thoughts which no doubt would be passed on to women) and found that they did not think very much about them outside their reproductive role. Among the gems which they collected were 'The fundamental biologic factor in women is the urge of motherhood balanced by the fact that sexual pleasure is entirely secondary or even absent'; that women were 'almost universally sexually frigid', and that it was a wise move to teach women to fake orgasm (1973:284).

One statement they found which appears somewhat puzzling is that males were 'created to fertilise as many females as possible' and that they have 'an infinite appetite and *capacity* for intercourse' (my emphasis). Even males must have had some difficulty verifying this aspect of sexual behaviour with other males, and understandably many females would have been confused by this meaning had they tried to reconcile it with the behaviour of male sexual partners. It is a measure of the power of language to structure reality that such examples were not perceived as absurd by the medical writers themselves. One writer unintentionally makes a most ironic statement when he says that 'the frequency of intercourse depends entirely upon the male sex drive ... The bride should be advised to allow her husband's sex drive to set the pace' (Scully and Bart, 1973:286). If intercourse is the aim, then it is undoubtedly the male who 'sets the pace', but this is not necessarily a pace which the female may find difficult to keep up with, as the medical author implies.

If the edicts of the medical profession did not have such serious ramifications for many women, they could be taken as so ludicrous as to be amusing. Bart and Scully found that in the textbooks up until their time of writing, it was common to state (contrary to the findings of Masters and Johnson (1970), which were available) that the male sex drive was the stronger and that procreation was the major function of sexual intercourse for females. They found medical statements that most women were frigid, that the vaginal orgasm was the only mature response and that 'an important feature of sex desire in the man is the urge to dominate the women [*sic*] and subjugate her to his will: in the woman acquiescence to the masterful takes a high place' (Scully and Bart, 1973:286).

This is what the dominant group have labelled as their objectivity! They have imposed these names on women and the result has sometimes been little short of anguish. For women who have experienced their own sexuality (and one assumes that many women must have had this experience) there may have been problems and few means of resolving them to their own advantage. To present oneself to a medical practitioner as a sexual being would have been to label oneself as *sick* within this context. And to try to describe one's feelings, emotions or meanings would have been virtually impossible.

As Dorothy Hage (1972:10) grimly states: '*There is no term for normal sexual power in women*'.

It is not coincidence that there is no name for a sexually healthy female: the dominant group have not seen fit to provide such a name from their own perspective. And without a name, it is difficult to believe in the reality. While women have no name for their normal, healthy, sexuality, its existence is doubted by both women and men.

There are many aspects of female experience which have been falsely named or left unnamed by males but the examples provided in the realm of sexuality are some of the most revealing. Males, for example, have named themselves as *virile* and *potent* but they have provided no comparable names for women, and not because women cannot be arduously and healthily sexual but because patriarchal order demands that males are sexually dominant: many other structures are predicated on that base. For males to engage in extensive sexual activity there are names of commendation – *virile* and *potent* enhance the male image; but for women to engage in extensive sexual activity there is only repudiation: she is a *nymphomaniac*, a *baller*, a *bitch*. This is how asymmetry is constructed, this is how the so called 'double standard' has evolved because the fundamental classification of females and males has been developed exclusively by males to ensure that no matter what females do it is negative, and no matter what males do, it is positive.

Because males have accorded themselves sexuality (erroneously) and consigned females to the category of non-sexual, there has been an interesting linguistic development. Having granted themselves sexuality, they are in need of a term to signify the condition in which male sexuality is not present and they have used the term *emasculate*. There is of course a parallel female term structurally and it is *effeminate*, but as females have never been named as sexual, there is no need for a specific name to denote the absence of sexuality, and *effeminate* is a superfluous term for females. So males have taken it unto themselves as well and *effeminate* has comparable meanings in male-dominated reality to *emasculate*.

One can of course ponder on the accuracy of naming the male as the sexual being to begin with. When *one* sex does demonstrate a greater capacity for sexual intercourse, and a greater capacity for orgasm, it does not seem logical to name the *other* sex as virile and potent. However, when one has the power to name, it appears that one can structure almost any reality without undue interference from the evidence.

The names *frigidity* and *impotence* also provide some interesting insights upon analysis. These are not parallel terms as one might first suspect and Dorothy Hage makes this point succinctly (1972:9):

> Turning to the word *frigid*, and its counterpart *impotent*, we find these definitions.
>
> *Frigid* (1) extremely cold: without heat or warmth ... (3) sexually cold: habitually failing to become sexually aroused: said of women.
>
> *Impotent* (1) lacking physical strength ... (3) unable to engage in sexual intercourse: said of men.
>
> Note that the female has *failed* while the male is simply *unable* ... Frequently women are also blamed for men's impotence, thus excusing men from all responsibility for sexual troubles.

(Hage has a point here: it seems to me that there are two aspects of male sexuality over which women have no control but for which they are made responsible – the 'primordial scapegoats' – namely impotence and rape. This is not a contradiction, it just indicates that the dominant group has been able to make up the rules to suit itself, no matter how illogical or inconsistent those rules might be. Who would point out such illogicalities and inconsistencies? Other men?)

But there is a little more to *frigid* and *impotence*. First of all it does seem absurd to name women as non-sexual and then to find another name which implies that it is their fault. Apart from this, however, the term also helps to mask a crucial difference between the non-participating female and the non-participating male, for while the impotent male is physically prevented from engaging in sexual intercourse, the female does not necessarily experience such a physical handicap. Frigid females *can* engage in sexual intercourse: impotent males cannot.

For this reason I think *frigid* is a false name. *Frigidity* could perhaps be more aptly named (from a female point of view) as *reluctance*, and reluctance to respond to male sexuality rather than a reluctance to utilize one's own. This is a very different name for a woman who does not wish to participate in sexual intercourse – which in patriarchal order is classified as *the* essential act – from that which the dominant group has encoded. Frigidity could be renamed as an autonomous and independent state, an outcome of conscious debate and decision, freely arrived at in the face of possible alternatives. It could be a form of power against an oppressor, a form of passive resistance or unavailability. In such circumstances it is very different from *impotence* which would seem not at all to be freely arrived at as a deliberate choice. If the non-participation of females and males is viewed in this light it seems reasonable to name women's behaviour as a form of self-determination and men's as a form of powerlessness. These, however, are not patriarchal names and do not adhere to the rules for formulating meaning in a patriarchal order. But they could be new names which women wish to forge: heterosexual celibacy has been underrated by the dominant group!

What the dominant group has rated highly, almost to the exclusion of everything else, is its own role in sexual intercourse. The emphasis has been on the part which males have played so that once more the female contribution has been omitted and rendered invisible. Says Germaine Greer (1971:41):

> All the vulgar linguistic emphasis is placed upon the *poking* element, *fucking*, *screwing*, *rooting*, *shagging* are all acts performed upon the passive female: the names for the penis are all *tool* names. The only genuine intersexual words we have are the obsolete *swive* and the ambiguous *ball*.

Naming heterosexual activity from the male perspective has presented some problems, particularly for 'scientists' who have observed animal behaviour and have been confronted by sexually aggressive females. Still, this has also been resolved by referring to such females as receptive! (Herschberger, 1970:9). Ruth Herschberger analyses some of the reports on the sexual behaviour of chimpanzees and notes that, even when the female takes the initiative in sex, she is still referred to as the *naturally subordinate* member of the pair and her activities are still named as those of *submission*. Even female chimpanzees are denied sexuality by those who are programmed by language for the reality of our society.

Perhaps one of the most significant names in the language of sex is *foreplay*. This reveals very clearly whose values are operating, for included in the activities of foreplay is stimulation of the clitoris and while this could well be foreplay for males it could most definitely be experienced as an end in itself for females. Because males have decreed penetration necessary for their own sexual fulfilment, they have been obliged to name other sexual activities as less important — from their point of view.

The name *penetration* also provides clues to the identity of those who have invented the names. Susan Brownmiller states (1977:334):

> The poet Adrienne Rich wrote the line *This is the oppressors' language*. I borrow her phrase now for a small diversion into male semantics ... The sex act ... has as its 'modus operandi' something men call *penetration*. Penetration however describes what the man does. The feminist Barbara Mehrhof has suggested that if women were in charge of sex and the language, the same act could well be called *enclosure* — a revolutionary concept ...

But women have not been in charge of the language and like many other activities, there are no words for sexual behaviour which encode the experience from the female perspective. The result of this is that women lack names invested with their meanings and women and men therefore 'doubt' the reality of women's meanings. There is no better example of the silence of females than in the name *rape*.

Muriel Schulz (1975b) has stated that rape is a four-letter word, but it is not one which is taboo. 'The organs and processes of sex and elimination provide us with a set of terms in English, which we designate "dirty words" ', says Schulz, but it 'is ironic that the most vicious sexual act of all is not among them. *We have no four letter word for the act of taking women sexually by force*' (my emphasis). She goes on to add that rape 'is in fact a remarkably innocuous term' (1975b:65). Despite the violent nature of the act, there is an absence of force in the name rape, which is evidenced by its usage in polite conversation and by the fact that it can also be used metaphorically without distaste, as for example in the 'rape of the countryside'. Neither has rape been subjected to euphemistic treatment – the fate of many words which make users uncomfortable. It seems that there is a form of neutrality about the word *rape*.

This apparent incongruity demands some explanation. Starting with the evidence which is irrefutable, we can state that there are at least two individuals involved in rape, the rapist and the rape victim. Their roles are sufficiently different for it to be impossible to encompass the meanings within one name. The experience of being the rapist could not match with the experience of being the rapist's victim, if these two dissimilar events are to be accurately represented in the language, then the minimum requirement would be two very dissimilar names. But there is only one name for this event, and therefore only one question to ask: whose name is it? Whose meanings are encompassed in the seemingly neutral word, *rape?*

For whom could rape be rationalized as neutral, for whom could rape be a non-event? Muriel Schulz makes a suggestion as to the answers (1975b: 68):

A man who believes that the only women who get raped are those who ask for it, or who thinks that women probably secretly enjoy being raped, or who holds that rape would be impossible if the woman really resisted – and there are many men who hold with one or more of these assumptions – such a man must invariably have a different set of images associated with the term *rape* than does a woman. Women can easily imagine the helpless paralyzed fear of an innocent victim of an attack, the pain of forcible entry, and the trauma necessarily associated with a violent assault. To a man, *rape* may possibly be considered a myth, or else an insidious lie dreamt up to entrap him, or both of these; to a woman it is neither myth nor lie, it is a frightening reality.

But it is a reality which is unnamed and which is elusive. The only word available is a *neutral* word when women wish to represent a vicious and traumatic event.

*Rape*, as it applies to women, is an event which cannot be readily symbolized in our language, for the only name which is available names the experience as males see it, as it pertains to them, and there is a huge discrepancy between the male and female experience of this event. The meanings of the dominant group are sufficiently inadequate for females as to be completely false.

Because there is no name which represents the trauma of being taken by force, the horror for the rape victim can be compounded. When an act cannot be accurately named it cannot be readily verified, to oneself, or to others. A woman who has been attacked in this way has no other name except *rape* to describe the event, but with the inbuilt neutrality of meaning, *rape* is precisely what she does *not* mean. Unable accurately to symbolize the event, rape victims can be victimized still further by the dominant reality, which may lead them to believe that they are responsible for this terrible act which they themselves do not perform.

What is needed is a name that is not neutral, that does not rationalize the ugly facts. What is required is a name which symbolizes the horror and awfulness of rape and which directs the negative meanings to males. A new reality, one which is more consistent with female-generated meanings, would emerge if sexual attacks were named by women as they applied to women, and with women central to their meaning. Susan Brownmiller has written a lengthy book which helps to encode female meanings of rape, but there is still a significant omission in our language while there is no one word which sums up these meanings for women.

While language has been produced by just one group, inadequate and false names have abounded for that particular group as well as for those who are not members of the group. The dominant group has been able to name its own sexuality falsely, to rationalize its excesses, to project the 'blame' for its defects on to the muted group. Acts of sexual violence against women are predicated on the 'reality' – constructed by males – that they possess greater sexual urges and that women are their subordinates. The name *rape*, with its current meanings, supports and perpetuates that dominant reality. Women need a word which renames male violence and misogyny and which asserts their blameless nature, a word which places the responsibility for rape where it belongs – on the dominant group.

The very structuring of sexuality in heterosexual – or heterosexist – terms itself requires further investigation. Sometimes I must admit that I am tempted to entertain the idea that sexually males have felt so vulnerable that they have been obliged to engage in fantastic 'compensation' when encoding the male supremacist reality. They have certainly named heterosexual activity as *the* activity, have evolved a web of meanings to substantiate the legitimacy of their claims (for example, that vaginal orgasm was *mature* orgasm for females: one is constantly amazed at the blatant politics) and have oscillated between consigning lesbianism to invisibility and decrying it as a threat. At best one can say that males have been very confused when it comes to naming sexuality: their own, and that of women.

I find this somewhat puzzling. I can see, for example, how only males could have coined the name *illegitimacy*, for the concept of not having a 'legitimate' parent could not arise for a woman who has just borne a child. It is only male parents who need the apparatus of the state to legitimate their role. But I cannot decode the rationale behind many of the names for heterosexual relations. Is it male fear of exclusion from relations, and from reproduction, which has prompted this repertoire of names, which from a female perspective could well be called *womb envy?*

Undoubtedly males have not been in an advantageous position and it has taken considerable effort to encode their own sexual attributes as superior. Even Freud could have been enlightened by the conversation of two four-year-olds who were discussing and comparing their anatomy in the bath:

Female: What's that?
Male: It's my dicky.
Female: What do you do with it?
Male: It's for peeing with.
Female: Doesn't it get in your way?
Male: Yes. And it hurts if it gets hit. I have to look after it a lot.
Female: Can't you tuck it up somewhere?
Male: No, I've tried, but there's nowhere for it to go.
Female: Doesn't seem much good to me ...
Male: It's for other things too.
Female: What else can you do with it?
Male: My mother says I can help to make babies with it.
Female (inspecting): I think your mother is having you on ... I don't think it will work.(33)

Neither of these two young people has yet learned about *phallocentrism* (Mary Daly's term for the exaggerated significance of the phallus in patriarchal order) and, like many young people, they are seeing the world in an acultural way because they are novitiates and are not completely familiar with the 'rules of seeing'. Nellie Morton (1974) would be sympathetic to the classification scheme that these children

were using for she creates a similar 'reversal' and provides an account
of a young man who internalized 'envy of his sister who could run and
dance and climb and ride horseback' without fear of external damage,
while he had to 'deal with her long remembered jeering at his organs,
which she said "flopped foolishly" ' (p. 31). The naming of *vagina
gratitude* is quite a good corrective in a society which has only, and
falsely, named *penis envy*, but it is possible that the renaming of
sexuality in woman centred, and not necessarily heterosexual terms,
may touch a very vulnerable area of males. Women's names will
certainly make it difficult, if not impossible, for men to retain an image
of their own supremacist sexuality, an image they have assiduously
cultivated in the past.

There are literally thousands of examples of the way men have made
the language, and thereby made the world, and I have commented on
but few of them. Within the context of the language of sex there is a
long list of names which demand closer scrutiny. Ruth Herschberger
(1970) for example has commented on the significance of males being
involved in sexual *acts* while women are involved in sexual
*relationships*. An act, she says, 'implies something done, the exercise of
power, the accomplishment of a deed. Thus the sex act for a man
implies a goal or climax'. She adds, 'A relationship on the other hand is
a condition or state of being. It does not necessitate a goal or climax.'
Herschberger (1970:19) thinks the distinction here is not
inconsequential:

> The implications of the male act vs. the female relationship are as
> subtle as they are conclusive. The male act regards itself as single
> and indivisible, relatively unaffected by time, person or place. It is
> therefore preceded by the definite article *the*; while a sexual
> relationship is feminine, diffuse, and employs the indefinite article.

Locked in as we are to the dominant reality, it is sometimes difficult
to appreciate the significance of some of these subtle variations and to
grasp the part they play in shaping our consciousness. So pervasive,
however, are the male meanings which structure our world, that I think
it wise to accept the advice of one woman who declared warningly. 'Be
wary of every word.'

## Experience without a name

Trying to articulate the meanings of names which do not exist is a difficult task and yet it is one which feminists are constantly engaged in. Trying to reveal the falseness of patriarchal terms while confined to those false terms themselves is also difficult. Adrienne Rich's words, 'This is the oppressor's language', need to be written between all the lines. Without ready-made symbols which encode women's meanings, there is no alternative but to use metaphors and similes to suggest what women's meanings might be like; even here there are traps, for those metaphors and similes frequently encompass male meanings as well. As Luce Iragaray says (1977:65): the feminine can try to speak to itself through a new language but cannot describe itself from outside or in formal terms, except *by identifying itself with the masculine*. The alternative, however, is silence: the alternative is to be a muted group. Being aware of the limitations that are inherent in the language we possess, being sensitive to its falseness and its distortions is, however, a beginning, and a beginning from which we can develop women's meanings – albeit slowly and in cumbersome fashion at first – in a new direction. Currently, women are in a state of transition when it comes to language, and while it would be unwise to underestimate how far there is to go, it would also be unwise to underestimate how far we have come.

Women are faced with the task of encoding their own meanings which can coexist with male meanings so that the language contains sufficient resources for all those who are required to use it to shape their worlds. By necessity, this demands that males abandon not only their monopoly on the production of names but their monopoly on reality as well. It is to be expected that many males may find a 'reduction' in their powers unjust but if there is to be coexistence, there can be no 'superiority'. The process of establishing women's meanings as legitimate will necessitate the questioning of many male meanings and, in the interest of carving out semantic space for women, Mary Daly has called for the *castration* of language. She means castration 'precisely in the sense of cutting away the phallus centered value system imposed by patriarchy, in its subtle as well as its more manifest expressions' (1974:131).

Although one can remark on the falseness of the meaning of *castration* – a name which has been applied to women when paradoxically there are virtually no records of a woman having castrated a man, only of men castrating each other; again, why is there no equivalent term for woman who have been deprived of their full stature? – one can also see why many males might find this call 'threatening'. I would *not* want to argue that males are not going to 'lose' as women conceptualize their new reality since there is no room in it for male supremacy, but I would argue that they are only losing what was not rightfully theirs, but that which they appropriated in the first place.

Where women have renamed part of the world it is clear that values have shifted and, with them, the balance of power. Before the naming of *sexism*, for example, it was the behaviour of women that was problematic if they were presumptuous enough to protest about the actions of some men. Without a name, the concept they were trying to present was of dubious reality, with the result that it was women's behaviour which had to be explained – and which could be explained as anything from neurotic to ridiculous. But with the name *sexism*, with the categorization that accompanies these female-centred names, the reality is accepted and it is male behaviour which demands justification and not female objections. If there were more symbols which posited a female centred reality, there would be more occasions on which male behaviour could be measured against something other than their own standards. Sexism is one foundation-stone for a woman-generated reality: more are needed.

A more recent example of women's renaming of the world is that of *sexual harassment* particularly as it applies in the workplace. In the process of carrying out research on women and work at Cornell University, Lin Farley (1978) felt that something was missing in the morass of facts and figures she had accumulated; she felt an absence of meaning and insight and she began to talk to women about it. In a CR group the women began to discuss their work experience, and she notes (1978:xi),

> when we had finished, there was an unmistakable pattern to our employment. Something absent in all the literature, something I had never seen although I had observed it many times, was newly exposed. Each one of us had already quit or been fired from a job at least once because we had been made too uncomfortable by the behavior of men.

But just as Betty Friedan had encountered a problem without a name when she began to examine the experience of women living in suburbia, so too did Farley find that the problem she was witnessing with women and work was also nameless. This *male* behaviour at the workplace as it impinged upon women, states Farley, 'required a name, and *sexual harassment* seemed to come about as close to symbolizing the problem as the language would permit' (p. xi).

Having named the problem in accordance with woman-centred meanings, one can reconceptualize the relationships of women and men at work. There are now more than a few books or articles devoted to structuring the reality of sexual harassment, and women are in a much better position to combat this aspect of male behaviour than they were when it was unnamed.

Farley maintains that the dominant group has preserved its dominance in the workplace, partly by means of sexual harassment — though that is not what males have termed it when they have expected secretaries to provide sexual favours, or from their more influential positions have made women's continued or future employment or promotion conditional upon sexual favours — which it wilfully uses as a means of sustaining job segregation, of forcing 'lack of continuity in female employment' (you leave if you do grant sexual favours and you leave if you do not) and as a means of discouraging the development of solidarity of women.

The whole practice of sexual harassment has made it difficult to sustain an image of women as serious workers. The male image of them as sex objects has been projected upon them to such an extent that there is only a fuzzy and fleeting image of women as *workers* in many workplaces. Farley sums up the force of this new name for structuring a new reality in no uncertain terms (1978:14):

> The full importance of this must not be underestimated: it is a radical change. The phrase *sexual harassment* is the first verbal description of women's feelings about this behavior and it unstintingly conveys a negative perception of male aggression in the workplace. With this new awareness, sociologists, psychologists and management experts are now reexamining the matrix of male-female relations in the workplace. Working women are becoming more outspoken and the legality of male aggression at work is being challenged. And for the first time, studies documenting a wide pattern of sexual coercion are being publicized. The significance of these developments for working women is almost unfathomable. Our understanding of men, women and work will never be the same again.

As with the word *sexism*, the locus of responsibility, and blame, has shifted with women's naming of this phenomenon. The apparatus of language and reality which has readily permitted the dominant group to 'blame the victim' (it is the woman's fault if she is prey to male aggression be it on the street or in the workplace) is unable to continue functioning when the meanings generated by women are encoded – and legitimated. That such names can enter the vocabulary is itself testimony to the distance women have travelled from their completely muted state; that more names will emerge from this stronger state is predictable.

Already there are names such as *phallocentrism* which label the world according to the way women experience it; there are words such as *chauvinism, androcentric* and even *patriarchal*, which have been invested with new woman-centred meanings and which provide the base from which a new feminist reality can be conceptualized. A language which has these meanings is one that has moved a great distance from a language which has not.

> 'There weren't any words available to describe what I meant ten to fifteen years ago when it was such a struggle. I can remember I was always talking about the male ego and that was a great big umbrella for everything. I'd call things *sexist* today, I'd say a bloke was behaving in a sexist manner, but all I could say then was that he had a bloody male ego that he expected me to bolster.
>
> It's much easier now. I know what I mean and I know others – blokes and all – know what I mean, and I don't have to defend myself. Now that *sexism* is real I can tell him to piss off for being sexist but when I was about twenty-five, no one thought it was real and I was just stupid or, unreasonable if I told him to piss off.'(34)

There are other experiences besides sexism which still require naming, and even sexist behaviour itself needs to be differentiated, subdivided and classified along more refined lines so that we can engage in more sophisticated analyses. At a meeting where women were asked to talk about experience for which there is currently no name, there were no lulls in the conversation.

M: Often I find there aren't any words that can say what I mean.

J: What's something you want a word for that there isn't a word for now?

M: I'd like a word for the next time I complain about doing the cooking, and my husband says, 'But dear, you're so good at it.' I want a word that describes what he is doing. Getting out of something by flattering me. He wouldn't dare say 'That's women's work', because we have had that one and he knows he can be shown to be unreasonable. So he tries this one instead. But he's doing exactly the same thing. He's still being unreasonable. But this way I'm the one who appears unreasonable. He's being *nice* and I'm being *nasty*. If I complain that he's not being fair, he says that I'm just irrational. There's nothing sexist about it, its just that I am so much better at it. There's no word to describe that sort of behaviour that puts me down by being so gracious and polite and leaves me in the wrong. Sometimes I think he's probably right and then I really get mad. And that's it, isn't it. He *is* right. I'm irrational.(35)

It seems that to find a name for the automatic classification of women as *wrong* is important. Almost all the women shared an experience of this, of being in the wrong by virtue of the fact that they were women, and yet there is no name for this phenomenon. All were obliged to resort to a description of the circumstances in which this experience arose because there is no ready-made name by which to label it. No woman present needed to have the experience itself explained or elaborated: they knew what it felt like, they simply had no means of classifying it.

We start off as male and female so he has an advantage because he is more 'right' than I am to begin with. But this is just a beginning. His background is science and mine is social science and that makes him more right again. Just once I would like to have a discussion with him when I didn't start out in the wrong. He always wants my views substantiated but he thinks the rightness of his own is self-evident. I would just love to be able to say to him you're being 'X', you're behaving in a particular way that our society has labelled 'X'. Then he would have to defend his views and I could just sit back and relax. It *would* help put me in the right.(36)

Because these women offered support for each other's meanings there was no personal questioning of the 'realness' of the problem they were trying to describe. Everyone understood the meanings even if there were no convenient names for labelling that meaning. This is unusual, for traditionally it has been accepted that the absence of a name means the absence of a concept (Hage, 1972). Perhaps this is but another sexist maxim in that it refers only to males who have had the opportunity to encode at will, while females, who have been denied the opportunity to encode their own meanings permanently, have many concepts which they can convey without the aid of formulated names. This encoding is a difficult and cumbersome activity for women, however, and is not likely to persist.

When one wants to describe an object or event for which there is no name, doubt can arise as to the validity of that object or event. If it is real, why has no one needed a name for it before? Could it be possible that I am the first person to encounter this experience? For males, this might still be a reasonable question to ask, but it is most unreasonable from the perspective of a female. If the dominant group has not experienced it, then there is no reason why a name should exist. And the dominant group have not experienced being defined as wrong, for example: that's why there is no name.

Betty Friedan (1963) touched on this when she investigated, with women, their experience of living isolated in the suburbs. Commenting on the way in which males named women's existence as they perceived it, she says (1963: 16–17):

> For fifteen years, the words written for women and the words women used when they talked to each other ... were about problems with their children, or how to keep their husbands happy, or to improve their children's school, or cook chicken or make slippers ... But on an April morning in 1959, I heard a mother of four having coffee with four other members in a suburban development fifteen miles from New York, say in a quiet tone of desperation, 'The problem'. And the others knew, *without words*, that she was not talking about a problem with her husband or her children or her home. Suddenly they all realized they shared the same problem, the problem that has no name!

A similar description could be written of the women who understood what it meant to start from *being in the wrong*. There are still many names to be coined.

It is not essential that a whole new range of word coinages should be put forward for, in some cases, as Mary Daly has pointed out, words can be *recycled*, and an old symbol can be invested with a new meaning.

'We can't just occupy existing words,' says Sheila Rowbotham. 'We have to change the meanings of words before we take them over' (1973a: 33), and it would be a mistake, says Mary Daly, 'to imagine that the new speech of women can be equated simply with women speaking men's words'. There is no need for an entirely new set of words in a material sense of new sounds or letters, but rather that 'words which, materially speaking, are identical with the old become new in a semantic context that arises from qualitatively new experience'. From Daly's point of view this qualitatively new experience comes when women break the silence and violate patriarchal meanings by talking to each other. 'What is happening,' she says, 'is that women are really *hearing ourselves* and each other, and out of this supportive hearing emerge *new words*' (1973: 8).

One example Daly quotes is that of sisterhood, where women have taken an old patriarchal symbol and invested it with feminist meaning so that it 'no longer means a subordinate mini-brotherhood, but an authentic bonding of women on a wide scale for our own liberation' (p. 8).

To feminists such as Mary Daly, Adrienne Rich and Sheila Rowbotham (and many more) it is important that language be liberated. To them it is important that women cease to be muted, that they find their voices. 'The development of this hearing faculty and power of speech involves the dislodging of images that reflect and reinforce the prevailing social arrangements' (Daly, 1973: 10). Among the many rules which women need to break (Adrienne Rich urges them to be disloyal to civilization) are the semantic rules. In a patriarchal society we make sense of the world by dividing it into male/female, right/wrong, superior/inferior and while we continue to divide the world according to these man made rules we contribute to our own muted state. Our oppression 'makes sense' because of the reality we have had imposed upon us.

Only within a monodimensional reality would it be possible to construe women 'rising up to name – that is, to create – our own world' (Daly, 1973: 9) as a *replacement* for patriarchal names. It is not the fact that males have names for their version of experience which is at issue – but that they have insisted that even those who do not share that same experience should be obliged to use those names. Males may still keep – if they wish – some of their own names, but women must also have the power to name, and when there is a choice, when the objects and events of the world are accepted as being available to pluralist perception, there may also be the opportunity for closer approximations, for more accurate classification of the world.

'As soon as we learn words we find ourselves outside them,' says Sheila Rowbotham (1973a:32). This makes us aliens. This makes us silent. This makes us vulnerable. We need a language which constructs the reality of women's autonomy, women's strength, women's power. With such a language we will not be a muted group.

# · 7 ·

# Women and Writing

✳

That women constitute a muted group in terms of the written word is an assertion which many people would be quick to challenge. They could point to the number of women writers and the volume of women's writing as testimony to the fact that women have not been restricted in this sphere. But such evidence ignores the basic issue in the division of dominant/muted groups, it ignores the issue of power. Since women have been able to write, women have written; some of them have achieved publication particularly in specific areas (though it may have necessitated the ruse of a male pseudonym) and some who have been published have enjoyed prestige. But this does not constitute a denial that women are a muted group in terms of writing: it may be nothing other than an indication that some women writers have been able to please some influential men.

## The public/private dichotomy

The dichotomy of public/private becomes significant in any consideration of writing and the sexes: males are associated with the public sphere (as is published writing) while females are associated with the private sphere. Females who take up their pen have, at least, the potential to enter the public sphere and thereby to cross – and confound – classification boundaries. This makes the woman writer, like the woman speaker, a contradiction in terms, and a contradiction which not only has to be accommodated by patriarchal order, but by women writers as well.

The silence which is required of women within a patriarchal order extends to writing, a point which Cora Kaplan (1978) makes in her introduction to Elizabeth Barrett Browning's poem 'Aurora Leigh': 'Public writing and public speech, closely allied,' says Kaplan, 'were both real and symbolic acts of self-determination for women' (p. 10). This is why the woman writer who writes for a public audience is a contradiction: it is why there has been a taboo on such writing. Kaplan suggests that Barrett Browning knew exactly what she was doing when she wrote her epic poem which took a woman poet as its subject matter: 'Barrett Browning uses the phrase "I write" four times in the first two stanzas of Book I, emphasising the connection between the first person narrative and the "act" of women's speech' (Kaplan, 1978:10).

Not only do women contradict the image and the status which is allocated to them in patriarchal order by such 'defiant' acts, they also become a potential source of danger, for they are in a position to articulate a subversive doctrine, and to be heard. To speak and to write publicly threatens the patriarchal order, a point not overlooked by John Stuart Mill who observed in 1859 that 'women who read, much more, women who write, are in the existing constitution of things a contradiction and a disturbing element' (1974:460).

But it has not been possible completely to *prevent* women from writing. It has been necessary for the dominant group to find a means of resolving this contradiction, and one strategy has been to distinguish between public and private writing – for women. The taboo on public writing for women has in essence been to exclude them from writing – for men! The dichotomy of male/female, public/private is maintained by permitting women to write for private audience (which can be extended to encompass other women) but discouraging them from writing for a public audience, that is, men. In the 'private' sphere, women have been permitted to write for themselves (for example, diaries) and for each other in the form of letters, 'accomplished' pieces, moral treatises, articles of interest for other women – particularly in the domestic area – and even novels for women (during the nineteenth century, women were the mainstay of the novel-reading public). There is no contradiction in patriarchal order while women write for women and therefore remain within the limits of the private sphere; the contradiction arises only when women write for men. So the taboo is on women's *public* writing, a taboo which gains in strength the further the woman writer ascends the literary hierarchy, with its presence being most felt in drama and poetry. Says Cora Kaplan (1976) 'the language most emphatically denied to women is the most concentrated form of symbolic language – poetry' (p. 29). Poetry is a male domain.

This division of women's writing into the 'proper private' sphere and the 'improper public' sphere is one which does not operate for men. As with speech, the determining factor is not always what is stated, or how it is stated, but *who* states it, and the public/private distinction which is made in women's writing comes not from the writing but the sex of the writer. The diaries and letters of men – particularly influential men – are not necessarily classified as private, and those of male politicians, for example, have frequently been published, treated with serious consideration, and even revered as the 'real' facts. There is no taboo against men writing for men, regardless of the form the writing takes: the taboo is against women writing for men – regardless of the form *their* writing takes. So while women have encountered a split between private and public writing, with the attendant difficulties this may give rise to, men have experienced no such split and have enjoyed the benefit of a continuum. (One wonders how many males have actually written 'private' documents with thoughts to possible publication, even posthumously.) Cora Kaplan acknowledges this split for women who are encouraged to perceive only certain audiences and forms of writing as appropriate, while no such distinction prevails for men who may view *all* audiences and *all* forms of writing as open to them. 'For male speakers after puberty', says Kaplan, 'the distinction between public and private speech is not made in nearly such a strong way, if at all.' (1976:21). The same is true of writing.

In any sphere where the audience is considered a public one – and this merely means a male one – women have come up against the taboo. Harriet Martineau, one of the first women political economists, found out what happened to women who wrote on matters that were considered significant to men. They were ridiculed. After her treatise on population control, according to Margaret Walters, the *Quarterly Review* in 1833 rewarded her with the following remarks: 'Poor innocent! She has been puzzling over Mr. Malthus's arithmetical and geometric ratios, for knowledge which she should have obtained by a simple question or two of her mamma' (1976:331). But Martineau continued to write, and continued to be published and the contradiction that she posed required resolution. This was not easy. As Walters has pointed out, it called for 'a splendidly contorted piece of reasoning', but one reviewer the same year in the *Edinburgh Review* was up to the task and able to preserve the classification scheme of public/private and male/female:

Political economy is to do with the poor: women are traditionally charitable to the poor: therefore a woman may express interest in political economy – with the proviso that 'the less women usually meddle with anything which can be called public life out of their village, we are sure the better for all parties' (1976: 332).

This counsel – to keep away from writing for men – was given to Harriet Martineau after she was published. Charlotte Brontë received similar counsel before she was published. When she wrote to Robert Southey, seeking advice, he replied in terms of the way in which a serious commitment (that is, one which is comparable to a male commitment) would be harmful to her 'femininity'. Margot Peters (1977: 54) quotes Southey's letter:

The day dreams in which you habitually indulge are likely to induce a distempered state of mind; and, in proportion as all the ordinary uses of the world seem to you flat and unprofitable, you will be unfitted for them without becoming fitted for anything else. Literature cannot be the business of a woman's life and it ought not to be. The more she is engaged in her proper duties, the less leisure she will have for it, even as an accomplishment and a recreation ...

Even private writing – as an accomplishment and recreation – should not be taken too seriously, not allowed to interfere with the business of being a woman.

Where there have been no individual rebukes, however, women have still often been made conscious of the taboo on their writing. Implicitly and explicitly they have been warned to 'keep out' so that as early as the seventeenth century Anne Finch, Countess of Winchilsea [*sic*] (1661–1720), wrote that 'a woman who attempts the pen' is most definitely 'an intruder on the rights of men' (Goulianos, 1974: 71). Appreciating the censure which would be the outcome of writing in areas not designated as their particular sphere, it is understandable that many women writers should have experienced considerable conflict; no doubt some of them were even persuaded not to write. They could not ignore the repercussions that followed their writing, and Cora Kaplan (1976: 29) states that

The consciousness of the taboo and its weight seemed to press heavily on the women who disobeyed it, and some form of apology, though tinged with irony, occurs in almost all of the women poets, as well as in many prose writers, whether avowed feminists or not, as an urgent, perhaps propitiating, preface to their speech.

Anne Finch knew what the response to her poetry would be, and she felt bitter about it. There is little apology and much anger – albeit controlled – in her words (Goulianos, 1974:71):

> Did I my lines extend for publick view,
> How many censures, wou'd their faults persue,
> Some wou'd, because such words they do affect,
> Cry they're insipid, empty, uncorrect.
> And many, have attain'd, dull and untaught
> The name of Witt, only by finding fault.
> True judges, might condemn their want of witt,
> And all might say, they're by a Woman writt.

Women knew that their fault lay in being women and was not necessarily inherent in their writing. It was the act of writing for 'publick view' which gave offence because 'the right to write was closely concerned with every wider choice that women might wish to make' (Kaplan, 1978:9); such an act was not in keeping with the position of a muted group and it was the infringement of the dominant definition of reality which gave offence.

That women should restrict their writing to the private realm may have been an understanding that was constructed by males and one which may have been policed by males, but it is nonetheless one which women have been obliged to share, to come to terms with, and even perhaps to internalize. This has had implications for their writing. Some women may have accepted this decree as 'natural', they may have 'chosen' not to write for public view and not to risk compromising their femininity; some may have sought publication and addressed themselves to men with either apology or defiance. But no matter which form of accommodation women made, it was an accommodation not required of males for whom there were no restrictions on writing, be the audience female or male.

Elizabeth Gaskell was certainly aware of the prohibition against 'public appearances', which was perhaps why she chose to write novels. It enabled her to take a stand without necessarily being personally visible: 'She maintained that she could hold a point of view in a book but not expound it in a preface because it "would involve so much personal appearance as it were before the public" ' (Walters, 1977:13). Perhaps this is why many women writers turned to fiction which permitted them a certain degree of anonymity, as it were. Perhaps this is why fiction itself has come close to being identified with the private sphere.

Women writers have had to 'rationalize' their acts. From the seventeenth century onwards when women began to enter the literary ranks, women 'comment in moods which range from abnegation to outright anger on the culture's prohibition against women's writing' (Kaplan, 1976:29). Told that they ought not to write, and that they could not write, women had to contend with many difficulties that were not experienced by men.

Partly because women's writing of fiction has been well documented – and partly because it is one of the most visible achievements of women writers – much of this discussion on women and writing is confined to the literary world. However, the world of letters does not exist in isolation and many of the points which can be made about the literary world apply to other areas of writing as well. There is a comparable situation in the media world where the distinction of private/public and female/male has been maintained by making it permissible for women to write for other women – for example, women's magazines or the women's page in the newspaper – but where it is still unusual for women writers to address themselves to men. There are also similarities in the academic world where, because women recognized that this 'bias' was operating and that male reviewers were selecting material for publication which 'coincidentally' perpetuated the tradition of giving prominence to male scholars from prestigious universities, women have begun to insist upon anonymity (as their predecessors made use of male pseudonyms) in order to be given a fair evaluation. The *New York Times* (14 August 1979: p. CI) has stated that 'there is increasing interest in a system of anonymous submissions that some scholarly journals are adopting to shield the identities of the authors from the reviewers, who are given articles with the names of the authors deleted.' Some of the 'interest' has taken the form of resistance, and this is not surprising because without knowing the sex of the writer it is impossible to determine which standard of the double standard should operate for an evaluation of the writing. As we have learnt from the past examples of Currer Bell (Charlotte Brontë), George Eliot (Marian Evans), Cotton Mather Mills (Elizabeth Gaskell) and George Egerton (Mary Chavelita Dunne), women understood that they got 'a better hearing' if it was thought they were males; seeking publication while concealing that one is female (as in scholarly journals) is another attempt to pre-empt the operation of the double standard which has been used to ensure that women are not encouraged to address themselves to men.

## The double standard

While there may be some speculation as to the consequences of the taboo against public writing for women writers, what is not at issue is that the woman writer who intends her words for the public confronts a different set of problems from a man when she begins to write. This is partly because she will be judged as a woman and not just as a writer: as Julia Stanley (1977) has pointed out, *the* writer is a male with the semantic space of this term occupied by a plus male reference, as are the terms *poet* and *journalist*, *dramatist* and *academic*. By appropriating legitimation as writers for themselves and by judging women against a background of minus male and minus writer, the dominant group exercised indirect control over women's writing and contributed to the construction of their muted position.

This double standard which men have created has been shared by women, a factor which Philip Goldberg (1974) seems to find surprising. Using professional literature from six fields, he made up two sets of booklets in which 'the same article bore a male name in one set of booklets, a female name in the other' (p. 39) and asked girls [*sic*] to rate them. Although the six professional fields covered traditionally masculine and traditionally feminine areas, the girls rated the male author, John T. McKay, as superior to the female author, Joan T. McKay, in all areas. 'Women', says Goldberg, 'seem to think that men are better at everything' (1974:40–1):

> On all nine questions, regardless of the author's occupational field, the girls consistently found an article more valuable – and its author more competent – when the article bore a male name. Though the articles themselves were exactly the same, the girls felt that those written by the John T. McKays were definitely more impressive, and reflected more glory on their authors, than did the mediocre offerings of the Joan T. McKays.

Goldberg continues with a naïve interpretation of his results: 'for reasons of their own,' he states, 'the female subjects were sensitive to the sex of the author' and they used this 'apparently irrelevant information' about the author's sex to make their biased judgments. 'Women – at least these young college women – are prejudiced against female professionals', he concludes (p. 41). What he has indicated, though he may not be fully aware of it, is that women have learnt their lesson well and that they too operate the double standard which has facilitated the construction and maintenance of the dominant group.

Women writers have known – and still know – that being evaluated by a woman is not of itself necessarily an advantage precisely because women have been required to take on male definitions of the world and themselves (for further discussion, see p. 21). When it came to seeking publication they did not put their trust in being evaluated by women – which would have been most misplaced given that there were, and are, still few women in positions to make such decisions – but in male pseudonyms. Much as this practice of seeking publication by means of male pseudonyms must have disconcerted and even outraged some men, who saw it as 'dishonest', it did allow some women to penetrate the male controlled net of publishing. It may also have caused some embarrassment to some males for, as G. H. Lewes said of *Adam Bede* after it had been revealed that the author was a woman, 'It is quite clear that people would have sniffed at it had they known the writer to be a woman but they can't now unsay their admiration' (Stern, 1972 : 57).

Charlotte Brontë believed she would get a better hearing if it were thought she was a male, and she was right. After the publication of *Jane Eyre* a literary debate arose as to whether Currer Bell was a male or a female and there was some agreement that if the novel had been written by a man it was a marvellous achievement, but if written by a woman it was scandalous. 'If Currer Bell *were* a woman, she violated ... [the] sense of what was proper in a good daughter, wife, or woman of England' (Peters, 1977 : 205).

Women writers have been judged foremost as women and although they may have had best-selling books this could always be explained in some way that 'minimized' their contribution or their person. Having written something considered 'praiseworthy', they could always have the prize taken away. Sometimes it was their 'womanhood' that was attacked: they could be called 'odious' or else informed they had 'transcended the limitations of their sex'. Either way they were branded as not *real* women.

Denying the real womanliness of a successful female writer has been one means of accommodating the contradiction. Even women who have been celebrated within the world of letters have frequently been singled out for their difference from other women. This may have served the interests of patriarchal order but it has hardly served the interests of women writers who have been obliged to cope with a complex set of problems about their identity as women, as well as the purpose of their writing.

If their difference from other women was not cause for congratulation, then it could be cause for condemnation. While women could be relied upon to write about feelings and emotions – perhaps with even greater clarity and force than some men – they could not be expected to deal with the more significant intellectual issues in their writing. Women may move their readers to sympathy for this is perfectly consistent with their role in the private sphere, but they cannot stimulate their readers towards an understanding of the 'higher' goals. This is a 'fundamental attitude' towards women writers, states Anna Walters (1977), and it persists 'to the present day. It rests on the assumption that having discovered any writer to be a woman, we may expect to find a profound exploration of feeling but a singular lack of coherence on the level of ideas' (p. 19).

Such assumptions, which have been shared in varying degrees by women themselves, have served as one form of control over women's writing, but if these notions of the women writer being an aberration were insufficient to intimidate women and prevent them from writing, other ploys could be called upon. As with speech, the prevailing belief has been that it is best if women do not write at all, but if they do then there are ways of discounting their words and making them 'invisible'. The way in which publishing processes and the institution of literary criticism has been set up has facilitated the task of keeping women writers a muted group.

It is males of a particular class who have decreed what constitutes good writing and they have done so without reference to females of any class. Dorothy Smith (1978) outlines the role that males have played in the construction of our culture and emphasizes 'that the forms of thought we make use of to think about ourselves and our society originate in special positions of dominance' occupied almost exclusively by men, and 'this means that our forms of thought put together a view of the world from a place women do not occupy. Hence, the means that women have had available to them to think, image and make actionable their experience have been made for us and not by us' (p. 282). It is the dominant group which has determined the ideas, the vocabularies, the images and the beliefs; that has decreed and promulgated the ideologically sanctioned form of social relations; that has developed the criteria of 'authoritative ideological sources (what kind of books, newspapers, etc., to credit, what to discredit, who are the authoritative writers or speakers and who are not)' (pp. 286–7). Into this framework, women have been required to fit. It is men primarily who have determined whether or not they have 'passed the test' and they have often been men who have operated from the initial hypothesis that women should not be in the framework anyway.

That males have determined the criteria of what constitutes good writing, that they have then also controlled the means of making decisions about what good writing gets published and what does not, and that they have also had the power to rank published writing, making or breaking the reputation of women writers, means that there is a virtual labyrinth which women writers must attempt to find their way through if they are to gain any stature in the culture. That some women occupy influential positions as publishers, editors or critics cannot be taken as evidence of women's emancipation from male control. The sense of what is suitable, of what is laudable – they were all encoded before women made their appearance in the world of letters. Women who enter such positions share these models which men have ordained (see Philip Goldberg, 1974) and, at best, if they were aware of this and desired to bring about change, they could undertake only peripheral modifications. But women in these 'unusual' positions are not always secure: as women they run the risk of being automatically 'in the wrong' and they are more likely to be labelled as incompetent, as incapable of making *proper* aesthetic judgments than they are to be praised for their innovation, their freshness of vision or their formulation of a new perceptual framework, if they attempt to express values that do not conform to the male-decreed standards.

Such women – like all women in influential positions in the public domain – are there under sufferance, and are themselves likely to feel *outsiders* and to be intent on demonstrating their fitness for the task. This may necessitate dissociating themselves from other women, and of subscribing vehemently to male definitions, sometimes enforcing them with a vengeance in the attempt to 'prove' that they are more male than the males.

There are occasions when some individuals – Philip Goldberg being one of them – can express surprise that women can be 'prejudiced' against other women, but this strategy of divisiveness has been used in the patriarchal order to isolate women and to pre-empt the development of solidarity that could be threatening. Women writers themselves have often felt betrayed by women publishers, editors and critics who have treated them unjustifiably harshly. But this behaviour is to be expected, although not condoned, and anyone who expects otherwise is ignoring the basic power configurations of our society: women are muted – be they publishers, editors, critics or writers! And as a muted group they have frequently made decisions which support the dominance of men.

Writing may be a difficult task – although I am somewhat suspicious of this judgment, given that it has its origins in the dominant group – but men writers do not confront the same range and depth of problems which women writers must overcome. Men have a right to write which women do not; they operate from a basis of shared subjectivity with publishers, editors and critics which women do not; they are encouraged and made confident which women are not; they have linguistic resources which enhance their image and support their values which women do not; they can write for men without jeopardizing their human – 'masculine' – identity while women cannot without jeopardizing their human – 'feminine' – identity. If men write with the idea of other men looking over their shoulder then it can be a source of confirmation. When women write with men looking over their shoulder it is a source of inhibition, of diminishment. Adrienne Rich has said (1979:37–8):

> No male writer has written primarily or even largely for women, or with the sense of women's criticism as a consideration when he chooses his materials, his themes, his language. But to a lesser or greater extent every woman writer has written for men even when, like Virginia Woolf, she was supposed to be addressing women.

She is referring to *A Room of One's Own*, *Women and Fiction* and *Professions for Women*. In each of these Virginia Woolf is ostensibly addressing women (and thereby confining herself to the proper *private* sphere) about writing, and at times is even taking the male censure of women's writing as her subject. But she is also looking over her shoulder in order to gauge the reaction that her words will have on influential men. She is extremely *careful* with her criticism, so careful in fact that J. Christine Salem (1980, in press) who has done a linguistic analysis of Woolf's work, claims that her manipulation of the sentence focus allows her to be critical without naming names: her 'use of the truncated passive ... obscures the agenitive role men have played in the oppression of women' and indicates her 'unwillingness to name the agents of women's oppression', presumably on the grounds that she does not wish to give offence to men. While women may have been writers, it has been men who have indirectly controlled what women write; while men retain that control, women remain a muted group.

When the medium is speech it is possible to detect the direct control which males exercise over the definition of reality in mixed-sex groups – that is, when women talk to men. The way in which males intervene directly to decree what is real, what is worthwhile, what is relevant is readily discernible. Because the mixed-sex nature of interaction between writers and readers is not so immediately obvious it is possible to lose sight of the operation of this same – though indirect – control in writing. Males are still able to determine what is real, worthwhile and relevant when it comes to writing, but women must rely more on the internalization of these values – if they wish to be accepted by men – rather than the direct feedback which can be forthcoming in speech contexts. In commenting on this male control Virginia Woolf (1972) has stated that order is imposed by convention and that 'men are the arbiters of that convention' (p. 45). She says, 'the values of a woman are not the values of a man' (1972:146), and

> when a woman comes to write a novel, she will find that she is perpetually wishing to alter the established values – to make serious what appears insignificant to a man, and trivial what is to him important. And for that, of course, she will be criticized; for the critic of the opposite sex will be genuinely puzzled and surprised by an attempt to alter the current scale of values, and will see in it not merely a difference of view, but a view that is weak, or trivial, or sentimental, because it differs from his own.

Women writers can attempt to pre-empt such criticisms by careful reproduction of the male scale of values but to do so would be to accept external demands that play no role for the male writer. And it is possible that such demands take their toll, that they introduce a 'translation' factor which distorts what it is that the writer wishes to say: this is what Tillie Olsen (1978) has referred to as 'telling it slant'.

But the ramifications of dominant/muted divisions go beyond even these considerations in a comparison of the task of writing for females and males. For if women writers are intimidated by male models of the world and male control of their reputation as writers, male writers have had their image enhanced not just by the linguistic resources, by the models of the world, but also by their reception by females. Whereas to women writers the opposite sex represents a source of censure, to men writers the opposite sex can very often represent a source of praise and affirmation. Women, as speakers and writers, can reinforce the tunnel vision of men.

In *Professions for Women*, Virginia Woolf discusses her own feelings about reviewing the writing of men, and she invokes the figure of The Angel in the House to make her point. 'It was she who used to come between me and my paper when I was writing', she states, and then goes on to describe The Angel of the House in mocking terms (1972:285):

> [She] was intensely sympathetic. She was immensely charming. She was utterly unselfish ... She sacrificed herself daily. If there was chicken, she took the leg; if there was a draught she sat in it – in short she was so constituted that she never had a mind or a wish of her own, but preferred to sympathise always with the mind and wishes of others. Above all – I need not say it – she was pure.

This was the phantom who slipped between Virginia Woolf and the page when she took up her pen to write comments on the work of a male. It was a phantom which symbolized women's muted position and epitomized their subordinate and dependent place in society. For women, praise lies in praising their 'masters'. Woolf acknowledged the necessity of banishing The Angel in The House if she were to write with integrity; some would suggest she was not entirely successful. She describes (1972:285) the way in which The Angel attempted to 'seduce' her by whispering:

> 'My dear, you are a young woman. You are writing about a book that has been written by a man. Be sympathetic, be tender; flatter; deceive, use all the arts and wiles of our sex. Never let anyone guess that you have a mind of your own. Above all, be pure!'

One need not look far for parallels with the spoken word, for this is but the literary version of 'the art of conversation'. It is another example of the powerlessness of the muted group who can come to depend upon pleasing their 'superiors' in order to survive. Woolf may be commenting on male control of women's writing but she is doing it 'ever so nicely' and in a form which males may find acceptable. There is little sting in her words, for the criticism is modulated and masked by deprecatory references to the female sex. Of course, her intention was to satirize, but for those who share the dominant group's model of humour, there is also something to be laughed at in the caricature of the female Angel of the House. Ironically, in the very act of rebelling against male control, Woolf defers to male power.

It would be unjust to be unduly harsh upon Virginia Woolf for couching her message in these terms. Given the muted position of women, it was a courageous act for her to go as far as she did and it is understandable that she wished to seek a compromise which would allow her to retain her reputation while still striking 'soft' blows at those who were responsible for it: she did 'nibble' at 'the hand that fed her'. But while women do defer to males when they write they also support the restrictions under which they write; seeking confirmation in a male stamp of approval means being 'overshadowed by male cultural imperialism' (Showalter, 1977:4).

It is a mark of how far women have moved from that muted position that Adrienne Rich can state without hint of cajolery or flattery, 'This is the oppressor's language'. Such actions break women's silence and are not open to legitimation by men for they are the beginnings of women developing their own scale of values, their own definitions of what is real, worthwhile or relevant. Women readers can confirm women writers and deny that they are not the public sphere.

## The fading of the printed word

But even if every obstacle were overcome and a woman found the courage to write, the confidence to write, the chance of publication and the conquest of the literary and public world in her own age, her efforts could still be minimized with the passage of time and her writing fade till it disappeared entirely from public view. Many women writers have gone this way partly because male-controlled publishing institutions have 'allowed them to go out of print', and partly because literary history, as other forms of history, has been written by men with men's concerns in mind (D. Smith, 1978:286). One of the fundamental tasks facing contemporary women is the unearthing of these 'lost' writers and their work.

This excision of women from our literary heritage helps to reinforce the confines of our muteness. As women we look at the past and find few other women and our suspicions, inculcated by patriarchal order, are fed, and we question our own abilities. As writers we have our doubts multiplied. We have been denied the full knowledge of the contribution made by other women writers and this hinders our own efforts. It is a situation in which every woman writer has found herself.

Elaine Showalter (1977) states that 'each generation of women writers has found itself, in a sense, without a history, forced to rediscover the past anew, forging again and again the consciousness of their sex' (pp. 11–12). This silence has been man made. It is not that women have not written, nor that they have not broken through some of the restrictions and been heard: it is that their contributions have been suppressed through a variety of social institutions which men have created and controlled.

While a select group of men have controlled these institutions which apportion blame and fame and which decree what will continue to be heard and what will not, 'women's literary history has suffered from an extreme form of ... "residual Great Traditionalism" which has reduced and condensed the extraordinary range and diversity of English women novelists to a tiny band of the "great", and derived all theories from them' (Showalter, 1977:6–7). The claim that women have succeeded in the male literary world, says Showalter, is based on four or five women writers, the Brontës, Jane Austen, George Eliot and Virginia Woolf, and 'even theoretical studies of the "woman novelist" turn out to be endless recyclings and recombinations of insights about "indispensable Jane and George" ' (1977:7). It would seem that English literature has also had its token woman for each age; one wonders how significant it is that all of them were novelists.

The 'residual Great Traditionalism' has resulted in the elevation of the few and the elimination of the many. While a small group of women have almost continuously 'enjoyed dazzling literary prestige during their own lifetimes' they have then almost vanished 'without trace from the records of posterity' (Showalter, 1977:11) as they 'fail to be remembered', as they are permitted to go out of print, as they are considered less worthy of scholarly consideration by those who are in a position to decree what the literary landscape should look like. The result has been that neither women nor men have been aware of the continuum of women's writing and while this may have served to reinforce confidence for men writers it has contributed to the undermining of confidence for women writers. 'Having lost sight of the minor novelists who were the links in the chain that bound one generation to the next,' says Showalter, 'we have not had a very clear understanding of the continuum of women's writing', and their meanings have more often been lost than passed on to the next generation. So the world of letters – despite the apparent success of a few women within it – has played its part in producing the silence of women; it has created yet another barrier to be broken, another means of promoting self-doubt, another area of male control which women are subjected to.

The means by which women writers are consigned to the periphery is an enlightening area of study. Such a process requires considerable ingenuity particularly if, at first, the author is thought to be a man or the sex is unknown, and there has been praise and enthusiasm for the writing. It is well worth examining the shift from adulation to virtual oblivion, and, in her case study of Elizabeth Gaskell, Anna Walters (1977) traces this process and provides many valuable insights.

Anna Walters documents the way in which Elizabeth Gaskell, who was initially highly acclaimed for her innovation and independence in the 1850s becomes by 1910 – in the hands of the men of letters – a woman who, according to Chadwick (1910), 'never wrote anything without her husband's approval'; and by 1934 David Cecil said of Gaskell that her most distinguishing feature was that she was a married woman with 'feminine sensibility'. This is little short of damnation in literary circles (Walters, 1977:31).

David Cecil helps to ensure Elizabeth Gaskell's place as a minor and almost forgotten novelist when he commends her for her marital status; Anna Walters indicates the lengths to which he was prepared to go: 'Charlotte Bronte's admirers do not think of her as Mrs Nicholls, George Eliot's admirers would wonder whom one meant if one referred to her as Mrs Cross', she states, quoting Cecil, 'but Elizabeth Cleghorn Stevenson is known to the world as Mrs Gaskell. This is just as it should be' (Walters, 1977:31).

Although during her own lifetime it was possible that Elizabeth Gaskell could have been praised for transcending the limitations of her sex, just over three generations later she has become the archetype of the limitations of her sex. Designated primarily as a married woman, *with children*, it becomes 'understandable' that this should dictate the standard by which her work should be judged; it becomes 'understandable' that she should not be considered central to the literary tradition – regardless of her contribution – but should be treated as something of an historical curiosity by the occasional scholar.

In 1848 *Mary Barton* was published, and Elizabeth Gaskell had departed from the convention of writing a pleasant tale of people of good breeding with a happy ending. An 'anonymous tale of Manchester life', it ventures into previously uncharted territory. Before the sex of the author was known, it received favourable reviews, and Anna Walters quotes the *Athenaeum* (1848: 1050) which commended it for breaking new frontiers and for exposing social evils (1977: 18):

> But we have met with few pictures of life among the working classes at once so forcible and so fair as *Mary Barton*. The truth of it is terrible. The writer is superior to melodramatic seductions, and has described misery, temptation, distress and shame as they really exist. Only twice has (he?) had recourse to the worn out machinery of the novelist and then he has used it with a master's hand.

But that is almost the pinnacle: once the sex of the writer is known, the reviews begin to take on a subtly different note. Her *diffidence* and *modesty* begin to be cause for commendation, she is praised for her ability to move her readers to sympathy. If she has entered the arena of politics and economics and elaborated on points of significance, then in typical patriarchal fashion where women are robbed of their creativity and intelligence (Clarricoates, 1980) it must have been by accident, for it could not have been by design. Some reviewers even go further and begin to criticize her for her lack of 'objectivity', another patriarchal ploy. The process of elimination has begun, and Walters shows the role played by the various reviewers in reducing Gaskell, when she quotes (1977: 18) from the *Prospective Review* (1849: 54):

> From intense interest in her subject and complete self abandonment to it the sympathies of the authoress are for the time perhaps too exclusively enlisted on behalf of a particular class, and dispose her to view all events too much from the point of view in which she has placed herself. It is unfortunate for the general correctness of the impression produced by her tale that the only occasion on which the masters are brought on the scene presents them in a harsh and repulsive light.

When the author was given the benefit of the doubt and thought to be a man, 'he' showed things 'as they really exist'; but now that it is known she is a woman, she gives an 'incorrect impression'. There can be no mistaking who has the right to define reality. As a woman she has been too lenient with the 'humbler classes' and too harsh with the 'masters'. This, according to the masters, is a distortion and a deficiency and they are displeased: an author*ess* who is critical of class oppression and who also subtly portrays the oppression of women; an authoress who breaks new ground and introduces politics into literature; but, of course, an authoress who understandably has got much of it out of proportion and who cannot be aware of the significance of her 'achievement'.

In 1853 *Ruth* was published, and this time the reviewer in *The Athenaeum* knew that the author was a woman. Perhaps this is why it escaped his attention that Elizabeth Gaskell had once more been innovative, this time by presenting a heroine who departed radically from the Victorian ideal of femininity in a narrative of seduction, betrayal, illegitimacy and injustice; the reviewer, however, is able to classify this novel with religious tracts – a proper sphere, for a woman.

Rather than perceiving the novel as a protest against injustice and hypocrisy – a reading which is certainly possible and indeed easy – the reviewer chose to interpret it as a story with a moral: the 'fallen woman' who 'gets what she deserves' and serves to reinforce the desirability of not straying from 'the straight and narrow'. And of course it was not only male reviewers who felt obliged to accommodate Gaskell's words. As Walters reports, Mrs Oliphant, herself the writer of many novels designed to while away the hours pleasantly and to provide 'uplifting' messages, decreed that *Ruth* was 'a great blunder in art', that Elizabeth Gaskell had made a 'mistake in choosing such a heroine at all' and that really she, Mrs Oliphant, did 'not believe that there is any such woman as Ruth' (Walters, 1977:22). Mrs Oliphant played her part in upholding the decreed standards.

Surveying the reviews which Elizabeth Gaskell's novels received and juxtaposing them alongside the novels themselves, it is possible to see a systematic pattern of misreading, a phenomenon which is hardly surprising. *Sylvia's Lovers* appeared in 1863, and in it Gaskell 'set out to describe the havoc wrought by love, the deadening of once acute feelings, the failure of human relationships and, by implication, the precarious bonds of marriage' (Gerin, 1976:229) – subversive images in a Victorian context. But again the critics try to render her views harmless and their reading of the novel reflects the role played by their own interests as they predictably invoke the double standard which makes *love* a woman's responsibility and vocation. While completely ignoring the despicable actions of the hero, the *Spectator* (1863) finds the heroine 'hard, selfish and unforgiving'. Jill Lewis (1977) has spoken of 'love as an oppressive ideology' for women; *Sylvia's Lovers* could serve as an apt illustration of this thesis, but the reviewers of *Sylvia's Lovers* pointed their finger not at love but at a selfish and unnatural woman.

And so it was with *Wives and Daughters* (serialized in the *Cornhill* in 1865). By this stage, Elizabeth Gaskell, despite her success as measured by her popularity and sales, had been given a niche as a writer: it was one which 'unites two strands of criticism which we have seen emerging, the tendency to relegate women writers to the realm of feeling rather than intellect, coupled with an inability to understand what is happening to the image of the heroine in the novel' (Walters, 1977:27) – able to *move* the reader but not really responsible for what she was doing.

Henry James, writing for the *Nation* in 1866 (p. 247) sums it up, and in the process, reports Walters (1977:27), puts Gaskell 'in her place': 'But genius is of many kinds,' he says,

> and we are tempted to say that of Mrs. Gaskell strikes us as being little else than a peculiar play of her personal character. In saying this we wish to be understood as valuing not her intellect the less, but her character the more. Were we touching upon her literary character at large, we should say that in her literary career as a whole she displayed considering her success a minimum of head.

This is a *woman* writer. She has plenty of heart (subjectivity, emotion, the *private* realm) and little *head* (objectivity, reason, the *public* realm), who may have achieved remarkable results but who cannot really be given credit for them, for what were they but the product of 'the peculiar play of her personal character'?

The stage is set for the excision of *Mrs* Gaskell. She is to be known for her heart, her morality, her ability to promote sympathy. Her originality, her intellectual achievement, her artistic achievement, all are to be veiled by 'feminine accomplishment'. Blatant as this strategy has been, it has also been successful. By 1929, the seeds had blossomed and Stanton Whitfield can survey her work and declare that her writings are 'sweet and fragrant', that they are a 'nosegay of violets, honeysuckle, lavender, mignonette and sweet briar' (Whitfield, 1929:209). New generations finding their way into the world of letters are unlikely to be inspired by these words and to seek out Elizabeth Gaskell's novels; rather, they will pass her by, another innocuous Victorian 'lady novelist', a definition itself in need of examination. They will be led to believe that she has little to offer today. Such judgment could not be farther from the truth.

This transformation of reputation from a writer (sex unknown) who wrote of the terrible truth of working-class life to a writer whose work shows affinity (sex known) with 'floral decorations' is one way to deal with the words of women. However, it does not just consist of a shift in emphasis – although this lays the foundation – but involves the construction of false facts. By 1934 David Cecil was able to paint a picture of Elizabeth Gaskell's life and work which was in complete contradiction to the evidence; needless to say, there were no protests.

Cecil begins from perfectly predictable patriarchal assumptions: *Mrs* Gaskell was a *woman* and a *married* woman, with *children*. This sets the narrow and private limitations of her writings. If she is to be praised, then it is in terms of her femininity and, in patriarchal terms, this is damnation. Walters reports that, with flagrant disregard for the evidence, Cecil states that Mrs Gaskell 'performed with decorous enthusiasm the duties expected of a Unitarian minister's wife' and 'looked up to her man as her sex's rightful and benevolent master' (Walters, 1977:37). This is complete fabrication, but it was useful for consigning Gaskell to the ranks of the minor novelists.

Walters points out that Mr and Mrs Gaskell 'pursued increasingly independent paths', that 'Mrs Gaskell was perfectly able to conduct her own life and affairs', including her financial affairs – and, indeed, did so – and that 'it is clear that she had some of her most significant experiences without her husband' (1977:33–4). It is also clear that 'she no sooner settled in Manchester than she steadily and consistently objected to her time being considered as belonging in any way to her husband's congregation … What she did was of her own choice and desire' (Rubenius, 1950:22). As early as 1849 she 'looks back nostalgically at the unthinking lack of responsibility of the submissive wife as a state to which she can never return' (Walters, 1977:37). This is not a woman who writes nothing without her husband's approval, who looks to him for guidance and inspiration; it is a woman of remarkable independence and spirit for Victorian times. But Walters indicates that the way in which Cecil distorted and fabricated the legitimated version of Elizabeth Gaskell's life and work is mind-boggling. For example, he states:

Cloistered like a young girl in her convent of peaceful domesticity, she never lost the young girl's eager-eyed response to the world. Mrs. Gaskell had not a chance to grow blasé. Her mental palate, fed always as it was on the fruit and frothing milk of her nursery days, kept a nursery simplicity and gusto. And in consequence her whole picture of life is touched with a peculiar dewy freshness, shimmers with a unifying, softening light.

And, as Anna Walters says, 'we might well ask what this critic has been reading' (1977: 38). She suggests that in order to make this statement – and others equally absurd – David Cecil must have refrained from reading the novels at all! Likewise, he could not possibly have explored the realities of Elizabeth Gaskell's life. But perhaps it is too harsh to accuse him of intentional malpractice; perhaps he was familiar with her life and work but merely wished to render an objective, unbiased, rational account in patriarchal style.

Whatever his motives, however, it is possible to see the contribution the male literary establishment has made towards ensuring the invisibility of Elizabeth Gaskell. By treating her virtually as a child – she 'kept a nursery simplicity and gusto' – by constantly minimizing, diminishing and undermining her achievement – she had 'not of course a great style. Mrs. Gaskell's feminine sensibility shows itself', says Walters (pp. 38–9) quoting Cecil. By suggesting that she really had very little to say, Cecil helps to dissuade future generations from reading her. By this process, women are denied the knowledge of the extensive contribution other women have made to the literary world. The male literati have played a considerable role in manipulating and controlling the words of women writers and in the construction of women's silence.

## Contradiction and resolution: eliminating the male/public

Why women should have enjoyed such relative success as novelists and yet have been so invisible as essayists, historians, dramatists and poets is a question which presents some puzzles and a few explanations. Virginia Woolf (1974) has her own explanation. Women were latecomers to the literary scene – as they were latecomers to education – and by the time they made their entry, 'all the older forms of literature were hardened and set' and 'the novel alone was young enough to be soft in their hands' (p. 77). This explanation is feasible – though not perhaps complete – in terms of the literary world, for while the essay, poetry and drama have a history which can be traced for many centuries, the novel is only a comparatively recent genre: it was in the process of being patterned and structured when women began to take up their pens in appreciable numbers. In the absence of a codified set of understandings and prescriptions about the form and mores of the novel, women writers may not have felt intimidated, not self-conscious about their absence of a 'good classical education', not unsure because of their lack of systematic knowledge of what had gone before.

'All women who write are pupils of great male writers', said John Stuart Mill (1974:512), commenting on the way women have been required to function in forms and genres which were not of their own making and which may have even been destructive of their purpose. When they came to write they found 'a highly advanced literature already created' (p. 512) – with the exception of the novel – and they had little alternative but to attempt success in the terms already laid down by men. If women writers wanted acceptance from 'the men of letters', then they were obliged to internalize the values that had been encoded by males, and to adhere to them, regardless of the accommodations and transformations which could be demanded of them in the process. Perhaps because of its relative freshness as a form, the novel demanded the least compromise of them; perhaps there are qualities, intrinsic to the novel itself, that made it a more hospitable genre.

But this can only be part of the answer. Recent efforts have revealed that women did write drama and experience success: Aphra Behn, 1640–89, was a professional playwright who was acclaimed as 'the English Sappho' (Goulianos, 1974:87). They did write poetry: Elizabeth Barrett Browning, 1806–61, wrote poetry and 'was a prominent candidate for poet-laureate when Wordsworth died at mid-century'. (Kaplan 1978:5). And there have been many women writers of non-fiction from Mary Wollstonecraft (1759–97) to Mary Somerville (1780–1872), who was 'the best known science popularizer of her time' and whose highly successful books 'were *The Connexion of the Physical Sciences* (1834), *Physical Geography* (1848) and *Molecular and Microscopic Science* (1869). Her expertise was very broad, ranging from astronomy and physics to meteorology, oceanography and zoology' (Schacher, 1976:29–30). There was Harriet Martineau (1802–76) who wrote 'books on economics, culture, history, philosophy and travel as well as novels, short stories and an extensive autobiography' (Goulianos, 1974;199). These are only a few, some of whom have only become 'known' in the last few years as a result of the feminist search to locate them. There can be no doubt that given time we will be able to mention many more and to delineate a 'literature of their own' (Showalter, 1977) in non-fiction, as well as the novel. There is:

> a rich and complex literature by women that goes back to the Middle Ages, a literature that consists of diaries, of autobiographies, of letters, of protests, of novels, of poems, of stories, of plays – a literature in which women wrote about their lives ... When women wrote, they touched upon experiences rarely touched upon by men, they spoke in different ways about these experiences, they often wrote in different forms ... [But to find it takes] massive researching (Goulianos, 1974:xi).

What requires explanation is not why women have not written non-fiction, and drama and poetry – for they have – but why only token women novelists (the four 'greats') have been allowed to find favour among the 'men of letters'. Why has there been a taboo against the 'public' writing of women which has led to their excision from our literary heritage, with the exception of a few novelists? Why were Jane Austen, Charlotte Brontë, George Eliot and Virginia Woolf allowed to remain visible while everyone else, from Hannah More to Elizabeth Barrett Browning and Elizabeth Gaskell, was rendered invisible?

Cora Kaplan offers an explanation (1976:29–30):

> If fiction has been the most successful genre for women writers it is not, as has often been suggested, because the novel makes a use of the domestic scene, or the life of the feelings, or 'trivial' observation, all those things supposedly close to women's experience, but because its scene is that world of social relations, of intersubjectivity, in which the author can reconcile to some extent her speech and her silence ...

For some reason, perhaps not completely understood, patriarchal order has been able to accommodate the contradiction of speech and silence in occasional women novelists and has been able to preserve the dichotomy of private/public, female/male with the novel. And in this dialectic process, as the accommodation has been made and the contribution of some women confirmed, more women perhaps have felt more confident about entering the realm of fiction and have come to accept it as their forte. The patriarchal expectation that some women can write novels, but that no woman can write poetry — that is acceptable to men — is fulfilled.

Kaplan provides a convincing example of the way in which the literati dealt with Elizabeth Barrett Browning's poem 'Aurora Leigh', and although it required comparable actions to those used to deal with Elizabeth Gaskell, it is more extreme and did call for even greater distortions. To Kaplan, poetry is part of *high language* in a way that the novel is not (a distinction I do not completely share) and 'control of high language is a crucial part of the power of dominant groups'; we must 'understand that the refusal of access to public language is one of the major forms of the oppression of women within a social class as well as in trans-class situations' (1976:21). Women, she says, are aware of this exclusion and the reasons for it: 'the language most emphatically denied to women is the most concentrated form of symbolic language — poetry' (p. 29) and, because of this, women poets have devoted a large part of their poetry to the right to speak and write. Writing poetry constitutes an act of defiance and threatens their identity as 'feminine' (silent and private) in patriarchal order (1976:22):

> To be a woman and a poet presents many women poets with such a profound split between their social, sexual identity (their 'human' identity) and their artistic practice that the split becomes the insistent subject, sometimes overt, often hidden or displaced, of much women's poetry.

The male/public will not confirm them in their role as *women poets*, the contradiction is too great, and both their womanliness ('femininity') and their poetry are called into question by this act. Hence the taboo against women poets.

'The taboo,' says Kaplan (1978), 'it is stronger than prejudice against women's entry into public discourse as speakers or writers, was in grave danger of being definitively broken in the mid-nineteenth century as more and more educated literate women entered the arena as imaginative writers, social critics and reformers' (p. 9), and the boundaries were shifted in order that the taboo could be preserved. Fiction became permissible, became clustered with the private, and women were allowed to retain some measure of success. But poetry was preserved — ultimately — as a male stronghold.

In 1857 'Aurora Leigh' was published: it was an immense success. By 1873 there had been thirteen editions of this poem in which the protagonist was a woman and a poet. Where *now* are Elizabeth Barrett Browning and 'Aurora Leigh'?

'Aurora Leigh' posed a considerable threat to patriarchal order; it was a contradiction which was difficult to accommodate and preferable to remove (Kaplan, 1978:10):

> In the first person epic voice of a major poet it breaks a very specific silence, almost a gentleman's agreement between women authors and the arbiters of high culture in Victorian England, that allowed women to write, if only they would shut up about it.

An epic poem, by a woman, about the contradictions of being a woman poet obliged to address herself to men? It had to be removed and removed it was.

Barrett Browning wrote this poem in defiance of the myth that women could not write poetry, and particularly not epic poetry, but she could not destroy that myth. By excising her from the literary canon in a relatively short time (Virginia Woolf was lamenting her absence in 1932) the myth that women cannot write poetry, and certainly not epic poetry, has been preserved. Men did not want to be addressed by a woman poet who threatened their view of the world and, while they could not control her initial popularity, they could − almost − control her eventual popularity. The belief that women cannot write *any* poetry is still not uncommon today and it is indicative of the successful nature of the suppression of Barrett Browning's contribution.

I do think that there are difficulties for women writers, difficulties that are not shared by men, but I would not want to subscribe to the patriarchal myth that these difficulties are insurmountable, with the consequence that women cannot write, and have not written in the past. I acknowledge that women have frequently been excluded from a sense of authorship, that they have been obliged to conform to male models and to utilize male semantics, that their products have been controlled and manipulated by the dominant group and that women − as well as men − know that there is a contradiction in being a woman writer. But they *have* written, and they can be united as women in an 'imaginative continuum' in which there is 'the recurrence of certain patterns, themes, problems and images from generation to generation' (Showalter, 1977:11). Elaine Showalter has uncovered this tradition in fiction, Cora Kaplan in poetry. In time there will be more 'discoveries' in other genres. It would be little short of collusion with patriarchal order to deny women's achievements with reference to writing; it would

exacerbate many of those difficulties which women writers encounter
because it would reinforce their sense of exclusion from authorship, it
would strengthen the taboo against their writing. But it would be equally
culpable, however, to deny the existence of those difficulties.

The crux of these difficulties for many women writers is that they
must write for men. They are doubly dependent on men in that they
depend upon the dominant group's definition of them as women and
they depend upon the dominant group's evaluation of their writing.
Both their womanliness and their writing, in patriarchal order, requires
confirmation from men, and yet the dominant group has insisted on the
mutual exclusivity of the categories of *woman* and *public writing*, that
is, writing for men. The dilemma for the woman writer has been,
traditionally, that she must write for men, but that she is prohibited
from doing so.

A double bind? A double bind that can paralyse and lead her to not
writing at all? Perhaps.

A very similar situation occurred with speech. Women have solved
that contradiction by talking to other women and no longer seeking
confirmation from men. The taboo does not apply when women write
for women: that has long been acceptable – such an audience has also
been discounted in patriarchal order. This is where women have
generated a transformation, and it applies just as much to writing as it
does to speech.

Once women ceased to seek approval and confirmation of their talk
by males alone, they deconstructed part of their muted condition and
were free to explore and name their own experience. There is evidence
that a comparable shift is occurring with women's writing. Women
have begun to by-pass males and to establish their own autonomy as
*women* and as *writers* and, in this context, there is no contradiction.

Part of the process has been the establishment of feminist presses, for
not only have they helped to break the male control over publishing, but
they have also helped to validate women's writing by their very
existence (Jan Clausen, 1976). The move from seeking affirmation
solely from males to that of seeking it from females is summed up by
June Arnold (1976), who argues for the exclusion of males from the
entire process – publishing included – in much the same way as women
have insisted upon the exclusion of males from consciousness-raising
groups. Let women control women's words and confirm women's
existence, argues Arnold: 'In 1970 we marched wearing aprons which
read: Is this uterus the property of New York State? In 1976 we

should wear headbands which state: My words will not be sold to "his master's voice".' (1976: 24).

Although not always advocating the same measures as June Arnold, many women writers have appreciated the potential of seeking validation from other women. Adrienne Rich (1979) believed that we were beginning to reach this stage, a stage of autonomy, where women were no longer obliged to replicate the definitions of the dominant group and no longer required to seek validation of their words and experiences from the male/public (1979: 38):

> If we have come to the point when this balance might begin to change, when women can stop being haunted, not only by 'convention and propriety' but by internalized fears of being and saying themselves, then it is an extraordinary moment for the woman writer — and reader.

Since Rich first wrote these words in 1971, there has been a virtual explosion in women's writing which is addressed primarily to women. The existence of women's presses has helped to 'prove' that there is a market for such writing and the commercial presses have been quick to follow it up, with the result that books on women, by women, be they fiction or non fiction, are being produced at an ever-increasing rate. She suggested that the 'balance might begin to change' for women writers, and it can now be stated, with some degree of assurance, that the balance *has* changed. Many women writers no longer engage in the covert practice of looking over their shoulders in order to gauge the response of the male/public; many women writers no longer feel the 'split' between being a woman and a writer; indeed, many women writers no longer write for males for they no longer seek legitimation from that quarter (this does not preclude their writing from being of interest to males, or of being of value to males, it simply means that males are not the prime consideration).

Women readers are providing the audience for women writers and within patriarchal order this can be tolerated: the difference in the current — and usually, though not always, feminist context — is that women readers are no longer considered a substitute audience, no longer held to be second best: this *cannot* be readily tolerated. The dominant group's dichotomy of female/male and private/public has remained intact, but it has also been undermined as feminists have revalued and reclassified. Women can talk to women, women can write for women and it can no longer be discounted as 'not the *real* thing'.

The male control of women's writing has been subverted in much the same way as the male control of women's talk, and although it cannot be stated that women writers are no longer muted — for it is still a struggle to escape the male-dominated structures, from the language itself to the conditions in which writing takes place — neither can it be asserted that women are completely muted. They are beginning to take control of their own words.

It is a beginning, but it may not be a permanent gain. Women have begun writing for women and, initially, this poses little threat to patriarchal order, since such writers and readers are classified as the *private* domain and therefore do not count. It is akin to gossip, trivial talk about *women's* business. But once it is recognized that women writing for women is not harmless, that it is not under male control, we can begin to expect a very different reaction. There will be resistance by men as there has been resistance to consciousness-raising. We will be urged in our writing to 'extend our horizons', to leave behind women's business and to tackle topics of a more *universal* nature, that is, topics about men. The categories of private/public and female/male will be violated if women begin to be counted, and there is little reason to suspect that patriarchal order will be pleased by such developments. As June Arnold (1976: 26) has said, 'The first feminist movement was briefly just as popular as ours, just as sought after' by commercial presses, and it evaporated. There was more literature in the nineteenth and early twentieth centuries on 'the woman question' than there was on socialism and there was probably more feminist material then than there is, yet, today. But it 'disappeared'. There is no reason that this could not happen again.

## Working conditions

Writing is work. In patriarchal order women and men have different working conditions; men, including professional men writers, traditionally have had only *one* job (Glastonbury, 1978) and women, who have been writers, have traditionally had *two*. This makes a significant difference: it has facilitated access to written discourse for males, it has reduced it for females.

*Time* is an important consideration in any discussion of men's and women's writing, for writing takes time, and women in our society do not usually have as much of it as men. It takes sustained and uninterrupted time to work at writing, and with the sexual division of labour we have been 'blessed' with women have been required to produce time – for men! (Leghorn, 1980; Rose, 1979). Women have produced time for men to write (Glastonbury, 1978) and in the process they have reduced their own amount of time in which to write. Another variation on 'the art of conversation', another development of male words at the expense of their own, another form of *shitwork* (see p. 49) for Pamela Fishman's comment on women as the *shitworkers in conversation*).

Almost every woman writer has commented on the demands made on her time as a woman and the consequences this has had for her writing. Much has been made of the fact that Charlotte and Emily Brontë, Jane Austen, George Eliot and Virginia Woolf had no children (Woolf herself comments on this in the other writers) for this helped to 'explain' the time they had for writing[1]. (It might also help to explain why they have been tolerated as reputable woman writers in patriarchal order: without children, they were not demonstrably 'real' women. Elizabeth Gaskell did have children, she was a writer, but she was excised.)

Virginia Woolf comments on the demands which are made on women's time, and even quotes Florence Nightingale who so vehemently complained that 'women never have half an hour ... that they can call their own' (1974: 67). Although time has frequently been mentioned as a factor in reducing women's opportunity to write, it is one which I still feel is very much underestimated. It is not just unfortunate, it is not just coincidence, it is very much part of the pattern of pre-empting women's participation from the public sphere and encompasses far more than writing.

Adrienne Rich has made this point quite explicitly: (1979: 43):

1 Tillie Olsen (1978: 31) has made the point that 'until very recently, almost all distinguished achievement has come from childless women; Willa Cather, Ellen Glasgow, Gertrude Stein, Edith Warton, Virginia Woolf, Elizabeth Bowen, Katherine Mansfield, Isak Dinesen, Katherine Anne Porter, Dorothy Richardson, Henry Handel Richardson, Susan Glaspell, Dorothy Parker, Lillian Hellman, Eudora Welty, Djuna Barnes, Anais Nin, Ivy Compton-Burnett, Zora Neale Hurston, Elizabeth Maddox Roberts, Christina Stead, Carson McCullers, Flannery O'Connor, Jean Stafford, Mary Sarton, Josephine Herbst, Jessamyn West, Janet Frame, Lillian Smith, Iris Murdoch, Joyce Carol Oates, Hannah Green, Lorraine Hansberry.'

To whom one would want to add: Jane Austen, Elizabeth Barrett Browning, Simone de Beauvoir, Aphra Behn, the Brontës, George Eliot, Anne Finch, Harriet Martineau, Olive Schreiner.

Such a proportion of women without children is hardly representative of the population as a whole.

I want to make it clear that I am *not* saying that in order to write well, or think well, it is necessary to become unavailable to others, or to become a devouring ego. This has been the myth of the masculine artist and thinker; and I repeat, I do not accept it. But to be a female human being trying to fulfil traditional female functions in a traditional way *is* in direct conflict with the subversive function of the imagination. The word traditional is important here. There must be ways and we will be finding out more and more about them, in which the energy of creation and the energy of relation can be united.

Traditionally, women writers have been *women* and judged as women in their lives and in their writing; they have been obliged to produce time for men (to write and to engage in other serious matters) and this has meant that they have been required to assume the 'burden' of servicing the home and the children. Elizabeth Gaskell indicates how 'available' she was in a letter to a friend (Chapple and Pollard, 1966: 489):

> If I had a library like yours all undisturbed for hours, how I would write. Mrs. Chapone's letters should be nothing to mine! I would out do Rasselas in fiction. But you see everybody comes to me perpetually. Now in this hour since breakfast I have had to decide on the following variety of important questions. Boiled beef — how to boil? What perennials will do in Manchester smoke, and what colours our garden wants. Length of skirt for a gown. Salary of a nursery governess and stipulations for a certain quantity of time to be left to herself. Settle twenty questions of dress for the girls ... and it's not half past ten yet.

In contrast, *Mr* Gaskell 'trots off to his study, whoever is here all the same' (Rubenius, 1950: 25). Mrs Gaskell wrote in the dining room (Jane Austen wrote in the drawing room), which had three doors leading from it and from which she could supervise the household. Independent Elizabeth Gaskell may have been for her time, but this did not include abdication from *any* of her feminine duties. On the contrary, it was even more important that she be seen as a proper wife and mother. Men may have the right to write, to go off as they please to attend to their writing, for when men write, it is usually a serious business. But women? I suspect that women still feel they must *steal* time to write (Buchan, 1979), they feel guilty about neglecting their 'duties'. And there are many 'duties' which they as women, simply cannot neglect (Olsen, 1978: 32–3):

> Motherhood means being instantly interruptable, responsive, responsible. Children need one *now* (and remember, in our society, the family must often try to be the center for love and health the outside world is not). The very fact that there are needs of love, not duty, that one feels them as one's self; *that there is no one else to be responsible for these needs*, gives them primacy. It is distraction, not meditation that becomes habitual; interruption not continuity; spasmodic, not constant toil ...

And the chances of this changing seem to be remote. Says Olsen, 'the fundamental situation remains unchanged. Unlike men writers who marry, most will not have the social equivalent of a wife – nor (in a society hostile to growing life) anyone but themselves to mother their children' (p. 32).

That men are serviced while women do the servicing is a crucial consideration in the working conditions for writing. Marion Glastonbury (1978) presents a forceful case for men writers not only being provided by women with more time in which to write, not only being provided with numerous secretarial services to make writing less difficult, but also being provided with a shield from the 'daily business of living'. Men have more time and more 'assistance', but they also operate from a different context in which servicing itself remains invisible and unknown. They are severed from this aspect of existence, she argues, they 'are sincerely ignorant of the processes that supply their comforts, strangers to blisters and back aches. So housework is missing from our literature ...' (1978: 45).

Not for them the daily toil; not for them the interruptions and demands of child-rearing: 'Few literary men have ever lived with their children: the poor, like Rousseau sent them to the foundling hospital; the prosperous, like A. A. Milne, consigned them to the nursery' (1978: 36). But the situation for women who are writers, is very different: 'no authoress ever finds a means of delegating drudgery which has the natural fit, the social convenience, the effortless spontaneity of the author's reliance on his wife' (p. 39). Under such circumstances women will write differently, they will have a different world view grounded in a very different reality. For them it is not possible to ignore the servicing, nor the implications of it (1978: 44–5):

When Mrs Carlyle told her husband that on a previous occasion she had thought of leaving him, he replied, 'I don't know that I would have missed you. I was very busy with Cromwell just then'. He would of course have missed her as soon as he felt hungry or needed a change of clothes. But the master can afford the luxury of forgetting his reliance on the slave, whereas the condition of slavery can never be forgotton. It is permanently present to the mind.

But what may be permanently present in the minds of women may be non-existent in the minds of men. The servicing of which Glastonbury speaks, the drudgery, may be invisible. Women are not only required to perform it, but it is 'unreal' if they wish to centre it in their writing. And so their mutedness is constructed and reinforced. Their different material conditions make it more difficult for them to write, erect obstacles in their access to discourse; they also ensure that the position from which women view the world and from which they write is one which is discounted and not legitimated by the dominant culture.

Under the traditional sexual division of labour the tunnel vision of males is reinforced. They do not see what every woman knows. There is an omission in their life and their work and it is a significant one. And from a muted position women cannot tell them, for their words could be meaningless, their experience unreal. Men will need to know for themselves. And this will mean an end to the traditional division of labour, it will be a new way 'in which the energy of creation and the energy of relation can be united' (Rich, 1979: 43). Currently, however, the traditional division prevails.

The way that men's writing has itself been serviced by women – and understated in the acknowledgment – has been well documented by Glastonbury. From Dr Spock to Carlyle and Tolstoy – and the seven drafts of *War and Peace* which his wife copied out – we see the pattern of men using the labour of women. Hilary Simpson (1979) has taken us even further by revealing the way in which male writers have *appropriated* – often without any acknowledgment at all – the writing of women. D. H. Lawrence, for example, 'solicited notes and reminiscences from Jessie [Burrows], from his wife Frieda, from Mabel Dodge Luhan and others ... he also took over women's manuscripts and rewrote them, as in the cases of Helen Corke and Mollie Skinner ...' (Simpson, 1979: 155). In *Sons and Lovers*, 'It is clear that some of the most vivid scenes in the novel derive from Jessie's reminiscences. Lawrence often takes sentences directly from her manuscript; some of the descriptions of nature, especially, go into *Sons and Lovers* almost exactly as Jessie wrote them' (p. 162). And Lawrence is not an isolated case: there is Samuel Richardson, Thomas Hardy, Scott Fitzgerald and William Wordsworth, to name but a possible few.

Such appropriations may not be aberrations. They may be the logical outcome of a world view in which the work that women do – including writing – is seen as a reasonable service, to men. It is not a *leap* but a *slight shift* when women's writing, like women's time and energy, is made available to men. The conditions under which men produce writing makes this a logical outcome; those same conditions also result in a different product (Glastonbury, 1978: 29):

> If you believe, as Karl Marx and Jean-Paul Sartre and I do, that 'the mode of production of material life generally dominates the development of social, political and intellectual life', then the maintenance of the writer's work place and the divisions of labour within it are far from irrelevant.

The conditions in which the writing is produced have a decided bearing on what is written, and the conditions of work are generally very different for women and for men.

In insisting that women needed money and a room of their own in which to write, Virginia Woolf was claiming for women writers the same material conditions for writing that prevailed for many men. She was claiming time: time in which they were not automatically available to men; time in which they were not required to service *other* healthy adult human beings; time in which they were not required to assume the responsibility for males of caring for and the nurturing the young, the old and the sick; time which they did not have to pay for their economic dependence.

She was also claiming space. William Gaskell had his study while Elizabeth Gaskell had the dining room and there are many contemporary counterparts of this arrangement.

But perhaps she should also have insisted that men begin to service themselves so that men too would be unable 'to disregard the contrast between the interminable repetition of work that sustains life, and the crystallization of experience that culminates in art' (Glastonbury, 1978: 38). Perhaps she should have insisted that men begin to engage in supportive and nurturing tasks so that writers of both sexes share comparable working conditions. In this context the tunnel vision of men may begin to recede; the muteness of women might begin to be dismantled (Rich, 1972: 25):

> I am curious and expectant about the future of the masculine consciousness. I feel in the work of men whose poetry I read today a deep pessimism and fatalistic grief; and I wonder if it isn't the masculine side of what women have experienced, the price of masculine dominance. One thing I am sure of; just as woman is becoming her own midwife, creating herself anew, so man will have to learn to gestate and give birth to his own subjectivity – something he has frequently wanted woman to do for him. We can go on trying to talk to each other, we can sometimes help each other, poetry and fiction can show us what the other is going through; but women can no longer be primarily mothers and muses for men; we have our own work cut out for us.

## Breaking the boundaries

But even with the abolition of the dichotomy of female/male, private/ public, with the elimination of the double standard, the end of male control of the printed word and the beginning of comparable working conditions for women and men writers, the problem of *man-made language* still remains. We must still deal with a symbolic system constructed by men to ensure the primacy of men: we must still contend with this aspect of our muteness.

Women writers are exploring and transforming this symbolic system but it is a delicate and extended task. Able to perceive the limitations which have been imposed upon them by male models of the world, they have begun to focus on the construction of *woman-centred* meanings and to structure a *woman-centred* symbolic framework. They have an ideal but it is one which is not yet near to realization. Today's women writers who are writing for women stand at the threshold in the creation of metapatriarchal meanings: they are retrieving women's experience, bringing it to the surface, looking at it with fresh eyes and naming it in accordance with a new perceptual framework. When this task has been accomplished, then it can be said that our muted state has been transformed.

One of the first tasks which confronts us is to symbolize *woman*:

we are in need of self-definition. Although women writers have in the past portrayed women, it has been self-conscious act rather than one of self-definition (Showalter, 1977). Women writers have at times told the male/public what they wanted to hear and have reinforced the dominant group's definition of reality in the process. They have supported the tunnel vision of males and have been accomplices in the reproduction of patriarchal order by portraying females in the distorted forms in which males have cast them, even while they, as women writers, were aware of the falseness of this image. 'The greater part of what women write about women', declared John Stuart Mill, 'is mere sycophancy to men' (1974: 456). Contemporary women writers, particularly feminist writers, are no longer motivated by the desire to provide men with what they want to hear, but there is no ready-made alternative available. It is a struggle to construct self-defined images and it is a struggle in which many women writers are engaged (Maitland, 1979: 205):

> Sexist ideology is so well developed that it has a wide ranging series of frequently totally contradictory symbols and images on which a writer can draw. To some extent we are still at the stage of challenging, denying, exposing, destroying this tight web of meaning. This is hard enough in itself, rebuilding is infinitely harder. Even as we struggle valiantly against the image of 'woman as the source of evil, the gateway of the devil, the whore', we discover that we are condoning the opposite (and equally destructive) image of the 'woman as pedestaled Goddess, as Virgin redemptorix'.

There are enormous gaps in our symbolic structure and we need to locate them; there are vacuums that we need to fill. In her essay, 'The best kept secret – how working class women live and what they know', Marion Glastonbury (1979) reveals the awesome extent of some of the omissions from literature. One absence is that of working-class women.

'Women of the labouring classes', she states, 'are mute figures in our cultural landscape' who if noticed at all are portrayed in idyllic or idealized form. 'Seen and not heard, their exertions supply writers and artists with a source of symbolism, sensuality and satire. On the rare occasions when they speak for themselves, they do so under a special pressure ...' (p. 171). It is as a murderess (a case she quotes) or in some other sensational capacity that they appear. For the daily routine of their lives, the condition of their existence, there is no legitimated voice. Yet if women writers are to construct a symbolic framework for women, it must be one in which the voices of all women are represented. It must be multidimensional.

'Working class women, literate or illiterate, play virtually no part', in the conversion of raw material into literature, states Glastonbury, 'since their preoccupations are not convertible into the accepted currency of truth' in patriarchal order (1979: 172). The prevailing definition of reality necessarily makes working-class women and their lives *invisible*.

For women writers, the dominant definition of what constitutes experience that is worthy of portrayal in literature will not suffice: it excludes the lives of most women. On such practices the primacy, the visibility, the universality of male experience rests, and it is these very practices which need to be subverted. 'Women fail to speak, not because they are personally disqualified, nor because the substance of their days is inherently intractable in its refusal to lend itself to literature', states Glastonbury, but because, in patriarchal order, any 'direct view from the social position which [the women] occupy, cannot be accommodated within the perspectives of the educated public' (p. 172).

It would be too much to ask of readers who share the dominant group's definitions of the world to identify with those whose invisibility and anonymity is essential for the perpetuation of those definitions. The world has been ordered from a position which women do not occupy, and a position from which women are consigned to the periphery: to make women and their lives central considerations is to challenge the validity of that view. It is imperative that women be invisible, that they be silent (Glastonbury, 1979: 173):

> Mutedness and invisibility are not incidental by-products of female labour; they are what women are paid for, part of the service, the pre-requisites of privacy, ease and confidentiality for men. For women, economic survival within marriage, in domestic service, in prostitution and in all analogous occupations, depends directly on keeping a civil tongue in your head and divulging nothing to outsiders. This requires ... [a] chameleon strategy ...

This is why women are missing from the literary canon that men have constructed – muteness and invisibility suit male purpose; they establish the primacy of the male and the authenticity of the male view of the world. Visible, autonomous women do not suit male purpose; they undermine the primacy of the male and they challenge the authenticity of a world view in which women are mute and invisible. To explore in literature that which, of necessity, must remain hidden for the maintenance of male defined world order would be foolish – for males.

To construct and validate this literary canon, men of letters have checked with a select group of other men and have had their views and values confirmed; they have been commended for their discrimination, lauded for their good taste and sound judgment. Those who may have protested have not been consulted; their views and values not acknowledged or ever taken into account. Traditionally we have developed an *exclusive* literature, and this has no place in a feminist scheme of values. Women need to consult *all* women, to develop an inclusive literature, if we are not to replicate the mistakes made by males. We have not always avoided them and we must be careful.

It is distressing to know that whole areas of women's lives have been excluded from literature, that women themselves have been unable to see their existence confirmed and given resonance in literature, but it is also distressing to know that where some women have set down their experience, it has been passed over by women as well as men. We cannot afford to have the writing of some women going unheard by other women. Barbara Smith (1979) writes of the 'massive silence' which surrounds the writing of Black feminist lesbians and emphasizes that it is not only the male literary establishment which has ignored them. 'Black women's existence, experience and culture,' she says, 'and the brutally complex systems of oppression which shape these are in the "real world" of white and/or male consciousness beneath consideration, invisible, unknown' (1979: 183). She goes on to say of her own work and writing:

> It seems overwhelming to break such a massive silence. Even more numbing, however, is the realization that so many of the women who read this have not yet noticed us missing from either their reading matter, their politics, or their lives.

The male-defined hierarchical world view that we possess is so deeply engrained that, if we are to avoid replicating the injustices of classism, racism and sexism we must deliberately seek to give recognition and validity to those areas of experience that have been expressly denied in the male version of literature and of *truth*. Women's writing, if it is to make a contribution to the elimination of oppression, must encompass the diversity of women's experience. It must be multidimensional or it falls short of the goals to which we aspire.

Clearly no *one* woman writer will accomplish this task and provide a complete, ready-made symbolic framework – although Mary Daly, for example, has made a fundamental and fantastic contribution to the development of such a framework – and it would be unfair to expect her to do so. In commenting on fiction, Sara Maitland discusses the demands that women may place on women writers when they insist on a comprehensive symbolic form for the vast repertoire of women's unspoken experience (1979: 206):

> It seems to me that feminists are so hopeful and desperate to resolve the dilemma quickly that they are laying exorbitant demands on those writers they identify as their own. We are asking each individual feminist work, to some extent, simultaneously to overturn a deep-rooted symbolic structure and to replace it immediately with a brand new one of universal validity. When I look at the symbols, myths and icons that the women's movement is currently producing I see how slow and delicate this work is going to be.

There are many emerging images, but at the moment, says Maitland, 'none on their own can carry the symbolic meaning of the women's movement' (p. 206). While cautioning against expecting too much, too soon, she emphasizes the significance and the responsibility that is entailed in helping to formulate a new symbolic framework for women's expression.

Among women writers there are already many examples of the restructuring of the symbolic order and they range from new conceptualizations of *woman* right through to new conceptualizations of appropriate *forms* for holding and developing the weight of new meanings. The struggle to find a perceptual order in which woman is central is reflected in the re-emergence of non-fiction, a form which has its antecedents in Mary Wollstonecraft, Elizabeth Cady Stanton and Simone de Beauvoir, for example, and a form which defies male categorization. The last ten years have witnessed a resurgence in the non-fiction writing of women, which is neither philosophy, politics, history nor sociology, but containing elements of all of these; the evolution of a genre all of their own, perhaps best referred to as *metaethics* (Daly, 1978). In the writing of Betty Friedan (*The Feminine Mystique*, 1963), Germaine Greer (*The Female Eunuch*, 1971), Elizabeth Janeway (*Man's World: Woman's Place*, 1971), Sheila Rowbotham (*Women's Consciousness: Man's World*, 1973),

Shulamith Firestone (*The Dialectic of Sex*, 1970), Anne Summers (*Damned Whores and God's Police*, 1976), Mary Daly (Gyn/Ecology, 1978) and Adrienne Rich (*On Lies, Secrets and Silence*, 1979), the primary goal has been to explore and create a new symbolic framework in which women are represented. Such writing is an indication of the extent to which women are moving outside their muted confines and articulating a new reality. They are in the process of transforming the man-made language, and thereby of defining themselves.

## The problem is power, not women

Difficulties still persist. The dominant reality in which women are diminished and in which their mutedness and invisibility are constructed and maintained is still the prevailing reality, the one which is legitimated and generally accepted. New members of society are initiated into it and no one can remain immune from its influence, even though many of us reject its premises and struggle to break free of its limitations. The dominant reality remains the reference point even for those of us who seek to transform it. Not only does this mean that we internalize many of its precepts, which are damaging and demoralizing to women, it also means that there is a danger that the formulation of an alternative runs the risk of being a reaction, a mirror image, an opposing schema which is still rooted in the symbolic order as defined by the dominant group. The difficulties are compounded for women writers.

But in examining these difficulties which confront women writers we must be extremely careful. The dominant reality would have us accept that it is difficult for women to write because they are *inferior*, not because they are women who have been denied access to the production of our cultural forms and are a *muted* group without a voice. There are two sets of difficulties and we need to distinguish between them, denying the validity of one set and overcoming the problems posed by the other. It would be a contribution to the maintenance of patriarchal order if we were to accept that for women writing is difficult, too difficult, and we were therefore dissuaded from attempting it.

We need to make distinctions. There are those difficulties which are put upon us within the patriarchal order and which relate to our ostensible inadequacies as women. They are meant to undermine us. They are designed to control our language and to discourage us from

writing and virtually every woman who 'takes up the pen', from Anne
Finch to today's women students writing dissertations for male
supervisors, has encountered these 'man-made' difficulties:

> 'My supervisor is constantly telling me what an awful writer I am.
> He says I let my imagination run loose and I have no style. He
> insists on looking at my work before I send it off anywhere. He
> always keeps it for weeks (very frustrating, particularly if you have
> a deadline to meet) and it always comes back covered with red
> pencil cross outs. Am I such an awful writer? It really is
> beginning to worry me'.(37)

Such ploys play their part in pre-empting women's participation in
the public sphere. Discouraged and disillusioned, they can be defeated
before they begin:

> 'Unfortunately I seem to have a writer's block. I always do.
> Although I'd describe myself as reasonably confident in lots of
> situations, I have no confidence when it comes to writing. There
> always seems to be a voice hovering around, making sarcastic
> remarks. It's always a male voice and it's always full of
> ridicule.'(38)

This is a predictable response in our culture. It is one that has been
desired and one that has been engineered. These are the threads that
weave the taboo against women's public use of language; they intimate
that this is not a proper place for women. They have no right to be
here:

> 'Every time I sit down to write, I get an almost overwhelming
> sense of inadequacy. Who am I to be so presumptuous? What
> possible evidence do I have that this is something I can expect to
> do?'(39)

The definitions of the dominant group have been designed to
perpetuate that dominance; because women's writing threatens that
dominance, the dominant group has declared that women cannot write.
It is too difficult for them. They lack the necessary aptitude. Clever –
but false.

There is no substance to these claims. The problem lies not in the
male defined reality that woman are deficient and cannot write, but in
the male monopoly on reality. The source of women's difficulty as
writers is that males have appropriated the means for constructing *our*

world view and the mechanisms for insisting on its legitimacy. It is the power configurations, the relationship of female/male, that the dominant group has decreed – and that women can change – that make writing (temporarily) problematic for women in a way that it is not for men. It is male control – and the myriad means of maintaining that control – which inhibits women's writing, which constrains, coerces and censors (Olsen, 1978: 44):

> These pressures toward censorship, self censorship, toward accepting, abiding by entrenched attitudes, thus falsifying one's own reality, range, vision, truth, voice, are extreme, for women writers (indeed, have much to do with fear, the sense of powerlessness that pervades certain of our books, the 'above all, amuse' tone of others). Not to be able to come to one's truth, or not to use it in one's writing, even in telling the truth having to 'tell it slant,' robs one of drive, of conviction: limits potential stature; results in loss to literature and the comprehensions we seek in it.

This is where the difficulty lies. It is not the deficiency of women, but the deficiency of a social order, a symbolic system, in which they are not represented, in which they have been denied the means to produce and to sanction. We had better not believe that there is something *wrong* with women.

Zoë Fairbairns (1979) is a writer who is concerned about a current trend in the discussion of the problems which confront women writers. In her review of *Woman as Writer*, a book in which women write about writing, Fairbairns says that 'the book makes me uneasy because of the uses to which it might be put: as fodder for the increasing number of feminist discussions on the "problems" of women writers' (1979: 247). This is a dangerous practice she argues, because focusing on the 'problems' not only takes up time which could be used for writing, but also serves as an excuse for not writing at all. Women can construct a reality in which they perceive writing as too difficult and not worth the effort. Such a reality hardly serves feminist ends.

Few women writers would want to underestimate the problems inherent in writing, for *both* sexes. As Fairbairns says, it takes time and energy. 'You have to begin it and stick at it through many long and solitary hours and at that point *every* writer feels unsure, voiceless and guilty' (p. 247). And few women writers would want to underestimate the particular problems faced by women. Tillie Olsen states (1978: 27):

> How much it takes to become a writer. Bent (far more common than we assume), circumstances, time, development of craft – but beyond that: how much conviction as to the importance of what one has to say, one's right to say it. And the will, the measureless store of belief in oneself to be able to come to, cleave to, find the form for one's own life comprehensions. Difficult for any male not born into a class that breeds such confidence. Almost impossible for a girl, a woman.

Almost impossible while women remain a muted group: not nearly so difficult once those constraints are shed. And let us be perfectly clear about the origin of those difficulties. They come from being consigned to a muted group: paradoxically the most constructive thing women can do in these circumstances is to write, for in the *act* of writing we deny our mutedness and begin to eliminate some of the difficulties that have been put upon us.

Our efforts will not go unchallenged. Patriarchal order can be ever-accommodating and, as we disentangle ourselves from one constricting layer, another is already being constructed to ensnare us. As we try and formulate our own meanings, there are forces at work to discredit us and to name us in patriarchal terms (Rich, 1979: 195):

> A literary critic, reviewing two recent anthologies of women's poetry, declares that 'the notion that the world has been put together exclusively by men, and solely for their own benefit and that they have conspired together for generations to discriminate against their mothers and sisters, wives and daughters, lovers and friends, is a neurosis for which we do not yet have a name.'

We have gained the initiative by naming the world from our vantage point, by naming *patriarchy* and *sexism*, and here is an attempt to wrest that power from us, to wrench it away from our grasp, to name us once more as deficient, abnormal, as *neurotic*. 'It is striking that, even in his denial', adds Adrienne Rich, 'this writer can describe women only as appendages to men' (1979: 195), as mothers, sisters, wives, daughters, lovers and friends – of men.

But we can also be encouraged by this response because it would not be forthcoming if women were genuinely muted. The resistance is a measure of the threat: here is male 'objectivity' responding to a reality which women have created, despite the obstacles: here is a literary critic who is shocked by the existence of women's voice and who is confounded by the presentation of a symbolic structure which he cannot comprehend. His is not a reaction to a muted group but a protest against the loss of mutedness in women. He still insists on man-made language as his reference point, and he clearly feels that his male symbolic order is under attack.

This is one context where I have no reservations in stating – he is right!

# Transcripts

✹

The means of documenting these transcripts has presented me with
some problems, for while wishing to indicate the source, I have also
been concerned to preserve the anonymity of the women whom I have
quoted. In my compromise I may have pleased no one, but the general
context in which I made the tapes is noted, while the means to identify
time, place and person is not.

1   Feminist conference, 'Women in Literature', Bristol, 1976.
2   Feminist research group, University of London Institute of
    Education, 1976.
3   Feminist research group, University of London Institute of
    Education, 1977.
4   The Politics of Education conference, London, 1978.
5   Private social gathering, 1979.
6   Private social gathering, 1978.
7   Feminist research group, 1976.
8   Feminist research group, 1977.
9   Consciousness-raising group, England, 1978.
10  Postgraduate seminar, University of London Institute of
    Education, November 1978.
11  Language sex conference, Germany, 1979.
12  Language sex conference, Germany, 1979.
13  Private social gathering, 1976.
14  Consciousness-raising group, Australia, 1976.
15  Consciousness-raising group, Australia, 1974.

16  Feminist research group, 1977.
17  Consciousness-raising group, England, 1979.
18  Consciousness-raising group, Australia, 1975.
19  Consciousness-raising group, North America, 1979.
20  Feminist research group, 1976.
21  Feminist research group, 1977.
22  Consciousness-raising group, Australia, 1975.
23  Feminist research group, 1978.
24  Private social gathering, North America, 1979.
25  Feminist research group, 1976.
26  Consciousness-raising group, North America, 1979.
27  Consciousness-raising group, England, 1979.
28  Consciousness-raising group, England 1978.
29  Feminist research group, 1977.
30  Feminist research group, 1976.
31  Ibid.
32  The Politics of Education conference, London, 1978.
33  Private social gathering, Australia, 1978.
34  Feminist research group, 1976.
35  Feminist research group, 1977.
36  Ibid.
37  Documentation for Women's Research and Resources Centre seminar, 'Women and Writing', February 1979. Quotes from personal correspondence.
38  Ibid.
39  Ibid.

# Bibliography and Further Reading

✣

Adix, Shauna, 1979, private correspondence.

Allen, Pam, 1970, *Free Space: A Perspective on the Small Group in Women's Liberation*, Times Change Press, New York.

Archer, John, 1978, 'Biological explanations of sex role stereotypes: conceptual, social and semantic issues', in Jane Chetwynd and Oonagh Hartnett (eds), *The Sex Role System: Psychological and Sociological Perspectives*, Routledge & Kegan Paul, pp. 4–17.

Ardener, Edwin, 1975, 'Belief and the problem of women', in Shirley Ardener (ed.), *Perceiving Women*, Malaby, pp. 1–28.

Ardener, Shirley, 1975, Introduction, pp. vii–xxiii, and 'Sexual insult and female militancy', pp. 29–54 in Shirley Ardener (ed.), *Perceiving Women*, Malaby.

Argyle, Michael, Mansur Lalljee and Mark Cook, 1968, 'The effects of visibility on interaction in a dyad', *Human Relations*, 21, pp. 3–17.

Aries, Elizabeth, 1976, 'Interaction patterns and themes of male, female, and mixed groups', *Small Group Behavior*, 7, pp. 7–18.

Arnold, June, 1976, 'Feminist presses and feminist politics', *Quest: a Feminist Quarterly*, 3, no. 1, summer, pp. 18–26.

Baird, John E., Jr, 1976, 'Sex differences in group communication: a review of relevant research', *Quarterly Journal of Speech*, 62, pp. 179–92.

Bate, Barbara, 1975, 'Generic man, invisible woman: language, thought and social change', *Michigan Papers in Women's Studies*, 2, summer.

Beechey, Veronica, 1979, 'On patriarchy', *Feminist Review*, 3, pp. 66–82.

Berger, Gertrude and Beatrice Kachuk, 1977, *Sexism, Language and Social Change*, US Dept of Health, Education and Welfare, National Institute of Education.

Berger, Peter L. and Thomas Luckmann, 1972, *The Social Construction of Reality*, Penguin.

Bernard, Jessie, 1972, *The Sex Game*, Atheneum, New York.

Bernard, Jessie, 1973, 'My four revolutions: an autobiographical history of the A.S.A.', in Joan Huber (ed.), *Changing Women in a Changing Society*, University of Chicago Press, pp. 11–29.

Bernard, Jessie, 1975, *Women, Wives, Mothers: Values and Options*, Aldine, Chicago.

Bodine, Ann, 1975, 'Androcentrism in prescriptive grammar: singular *they*, sex indefinite *he* and *he* or *she*', *Language in Society*, 4, no. 2, pp. 129–56.

Bolinger, Dwight, 1975, *Aspects of Language*, Harcourt, Brace, Jovanovich, New York, 2nd ed.

Brend, Ruth, 1975, 'Male-female intonation patterns in American English', in Barrie Thorne and Nancy Henley (eds), *Language and Sex: Difference and Dominance*, Newbury House, Rowley, Mass., pp. 84–7.

Britton, James, 1975, *Language and Learning*, Penguin.

Brownmiller, Susan, 1977, *Against our Will: Men, Women and Rape*, Penguin.

Buchan, Lou, 1978, private correspondence.

Buchan, Lou, 1979, private correspondence.

Burns, Elizabeth and Tom (eds), 1973, *Sociology of Literature and Drama*, Penguin.

Carden, Maren Lockwood, 1974, *The New Feminist Movement*, Russell Sage Foundation, New York.

Carrol, John B. (ed.), 1976, *Language, Thought and Reality: Selected Writings of Benjamin Lee Whorf*, MIT Press, Cambridge, Mass.

Cassell, Joan, 1977, *A Group Called Women: Sisterhood and Symbolism in the Feminist Movement*, David McKay, New York.

Chadwick, Esther, 1910, *Mrs. Gaskell: Haunts, Homes and Stories*, Pitman.

Chalmers, A. F., 1978, *What is this Thing Called Science?: an Assessment of the Nature and Status of Science and its Methods*, Open University Press, Milton Keynes.

Chapple, J. A. V. and A. Pollard, 1966, *The Letters of Mrs Gaskell*, Manchester University Press.

Cherry, Louise, 1975, 'Teacher–child verbal interaction: an approach to the study of sex differences', in Barrie Thorne and Nancy Henley (eds), *Language and Sex: Difference and Dominance*, Newbury House, Rowley, Mass., pp. 172–83.

Chesler, Phyllis, 1971, 'Marriage and psychotherapy', in Radical Therapist Collective (eds), *The Radical Therapist*, Ballantyne, New York, pp. 175–80.

Chiera, Edward, 1938, *They Wrote on Clay*, University of Chicago Press (Quoted in Merlin Stone, *The Paradise Papers*, Virago, 1976, p. 24.)

Clarricoates, Katherine, 1980, 'All in a Day's Work', in Dale Spender and Elizabeth Sarah (eds), *Learning to Lose: Sexism and Education*, pp. 69–80.

Clausen, Jan, 1976, 'The politics of publishing and the lesbian community', *Sinister Wisdom*, 1, no. 2, Fall, pp. 95–115.

Cornillon, Susan Koppelman, 1972, 'The fiction of fiction', in S. K. Cornillon (ed.), *Images of Women in Fiction: Feminist Perspectives*, Popular Press, Bowling Green, Ohio, pp. 113–30.

Coser, Rose Laub, 1960, 'Laughter among colleagues', *Psychiatry*, 23, pp. 81–95.

Daly, Mary, 1973, *Beyond God the Father*, Beacon Press, Boston.

Daly, Mary, 1974, 'Theology after the demise of God the father: a call for the castration of sexist religion', in Alice Hageman (ed.), *Sexist Religion and Women in the Church*, pp. 125–42.

Daly, Mary, 1975, 'God is a verb', in Uta West (ed.), *Woman in a Changing World*, McGraw-Hill, New York, pp. 153–70.

Daly, Mary, 1978, *Gyn/Ecology: the Metaethics of Radical Feminism*, Beacon Press, Boston.

de Beauvoir, Simone, 1972, *The Second Sex*, Penguin.

Delamont, Sara and Lorna Duffin (eds), 1978, *The Nineteenth Century Woman: her Cultural and Physical World*, Croom Helm.

Densmore, Dana, 1971, 'On communication', in *No more Fun and Games*, 5, pp. 66–81.

Densmore, Dana, n.d., *Speech is a Form of Thought*, Know, Inc., Pittsburgh.

Dreifus, Claudia, 1973, *Women's Fate: Raps from a Feminist Consciousness-Raising Group*, Bantam, New York.

Dubois, Betty Lou and Isobel Crouch, 1975, 'The question of tag questions in women's speech: they don't really use more of them, do they?', *Language in Society*, 4, pp. 289–94.

Edelsky, Carole, 1981, 'Who's got the floor?', *Language and Society*, 10, pp. 383–421.

Eichler, Margrit, 1979, 'The origin of sex inequality: a comparison and critique of different theories and their implications for social policy', *Women's Studies International Quarterly*, 2, no. 3, pp. 329–46.

Fairbairns, Zoë, 1979, review of Jeanette Webber and Joan Grumman (eds), *Woman as Writer*, Houghton Mifflin, New York, 1978, *Women's Studies International Quarterly*, 2, no. 2, pp. 246–7.

Farley, Lin, 1978, *Sexual Shakedown: the Sexual Harassment of Women on the Job*, McGraw-Hill, New York.

Finch, Anne, Countess of Winchelsea, 1974, 'The Introduction', in Joan Goulianos (ed.), *By a Woman Writt*, NEL pp. 71–3.

Firestone, Shulamith, 1970, *The Dialectic of Sex: the Case for Feminist Revolution*, William Morrow, New York.

Fishman, Pamela, 1977, 'Interactional shitwork', *Heresies: a Feminist Publication on Arts and Politics*, no. 2, May, pp. 99–101.

Flexner, Stuart, 1960, Preface, Harold Wentworth and Stuart Flexner (eds), *Dictionary of American Slang*, Thomas Crowell, New York.

Foster, Brian, 1976, *The Changing English Language*, Penguin.

Freeman, Jo, 1975, *The Politics of Women's Liberation*, David McKay, New York.

Friedan, Betty, 1963, *The Feminine Mystique*, Penguin.

Gagnon, T. H. and W. Simon, 1974, *Sexual Conduct*, Hutchinson.

Gardiner, Jean, 1976, *A Case Study in Social Change: Women in Society*, D302, Patterns of Inequality, unit 32, Open University Press, Milton Keynes, pp. 33–82.

Gearhart, Sally, 1979, 'The womanization of rhetoric', *Women's Studies International Quarterly*, 2, no. 2, pp. 195–202.

Gerin, Winifred, 1976, *Elizabeth Gaskell: a Biography*, Clarendon Press, Oxford.

Gershuny, H. Lee, 1974, 'Sexist semantics in the dictionary', *Etc: a Review of General Semantics*, 31, pp. 159–69.

Gilman, Richard, 1971, 'Where did it all go wrong?', *Life*, 13 August, pp. 40–55.

Glastonbury, Marion, 1978, 'Holding the pens', in *Inspiration and Drudgery: Notes on Literature and Domestic Labour in the Nineteenth Century*, Women's Research and Resources Centre Publications, pp. 27–46.

Glastonbury, Marion, 1979, 'The best kept secret – how working class women live and what they know', *Women's Studies International Quarterly*, 2, no. 2, pp. 171–83.

Goffman, Erving, 1972, 'The nature of deference and demeanor', in E. Goffman,

*Interaction Ritual: Essays on Face-to-Face Behaviour*, Penguin, pp. 47–96.

Goldberg, Philip, 1974, 'Are women prejudiced against women?', in J. Stacey, S. Bereaud and J. Daniels (eds), *And Jill Came Tumbling After: Sexism in American Education*, Dell Publishing, New York, pp. 37–42.

Goulianos, Joan (ed.), 1974, *By a Woman Writt: Literature from Six Countries by and about Women*, NEL.

Graham, Alma, 1975, 'The making of a non-sexist dictionary', in Barrie Thorne and Nancy Henley (eds), *Language and Sex: Difference and Dominance*, Newbury House, Rowley, Mass., pp. 57–63.

Greer, Germaine, 1971, *The Female Eunuch*, MacGibbon & Kee.

Greer, Germaine, 1974, 'Flying pigs and double standards', *The Times Literary Supplement*, 26 July, p. 784.

Guth, Hans, 1973, *English for a New Generation*, McGraw-Hill, New York.

Hage, Dorothy, 1972, 'There's glory for you', *Aphra: the Feminist Literary Magazine*, 3, no. 3, summer, pp. 2–14.

Hageman, Alice (ed.), 1974, *Sexist Religion and Women in the Church: No More Silence!*, Association Press, New York.

Hamilton, Cicely, 1909, 1981, *Marriage as a Trade*, The Women's Press, London.

Hardwick, Elizabeth, 1974, *Seduction and Betrayal: Women and Literature*, Weidenfeld & Nicolson.

Harrison, Linda, 1975, 'Cro-magnon woman – in eclipse', *Science Teacher*, April, pp. 8–11.

Hartman, Maryann, 1976, 'A descriptive study of the language of men and women born in Maine around 1900 as it reflects the Lakoff hypothesis in *Language and Women's* [sic] *Place*'., in B. L. Dubois and I. Crouch (eds), *The Sociology of the Languages of American Women*, P.I.S.E. Papers, IV, Trinity University, San Antonio, Texas, pp. 81–90.

Haupt, Enid, 1970, *The New Seventeen Book of Etiquette and Young Living*, David McKay, New York.

Henley, Nancy, 1975, 'Power, sex and nonverbal communication', in Barrie Thorne and Nancy Henley (eds), *Language and Sex: Difference and Dominance*, Newbury House, Rowley, Mass., pp. 184–203.

Herschberger, Ruth, 1970, *Adam's Rib*, Harper & Row, New York.

Hochschild, Arlie Russell, 1975(a), 'Inside the clockwork of male careers', in Florence Howe (ed.), *Women and the power to Change*, McGraw Hill, pp. 47–80.

Hochschild, Arlie Russell, 1975(b), 'The sociology of feeling and emotion: selected possibilities', in M. Millman and R. Kanter (eds), *Another Voice: Feminist Perspectives on Social Life and Social Science*, Anchor/Doubleday, New York, pp. 280–307.

Howe, Florence, 1977, *Seven Years Later: Women's Studies Programs in 1976*, Report of the National Advisory Council on Women's Educational Programs.

Hubbard, Ruth, 1979, 'Reflections on the story of the double helix', *Women's Studies International Quarterly*, 2, no. 3, pp. 261–74.

Iragaray, Luce, 1977, 'Women's exile' (trans. Couze Venn), *Ideology and Consciousness*, no. 1, May, pp. 62–76.

Isles, Susan, 1978, 'Guilty men and sick women: the medicalization of female deviancy', available from Women's Research and Resources Centre.

Janeway, Elizabeth, 1971, *Man's World, Woman's Place: a Study in Social*

*Mythology*, Delta, New York.

Janeway, Elizabeth, 1975, *Between Myth and Morning: Women Awakening*, William Morrow, New York.

Jenkins, Lee and Cheris Kramer, 1978, 'Small group processes: learning from women', *Women's Studies International Quarterly*, 1, no. 1, pp. 67–84.

Jenkins, Lee and Cheris Kramer, forthcoming, 'Linguistics', in Dale Spender (ed.), *Men's Studies Modified*.

Jespersen, Otto, 1922, *Language: its Nature, Development and Origin*, Allen & Unwin.

Jespersen, Otto, 1923, *The Growth and Structure of the English Language*, Blackwell, Oxford; Appleton, New York.

Kaplan, Cora, 1976, 'Language and gender', in, *Papers on Patriarchy*, Women's Publishing Collective, pp. 21–37.

Kaplan, Cora, 1978, Introduction to *'Aurora Leigh' and other Poems: Elizabeth Barrett Browning*, The Women's Press, pp. 5–36.

Key, Mary Ritchie, 1972, 'Linguistic behavior of male and female', *Linguistics*, 88, 15 August, pp. 15–31.

Key, Mary Ritchie, 1975, *Male/Female Language*, Scarecrow Press, Metuchen, N.J.

Kirkby, John, 1746, *A New English Grammar*, Scolar Press Facsimile, 1971.

Klein, J., 1971, 'The family in "traditional" working class England', in Michael Anderson (ed.), *Sociology of the Family*, Penguin.

Kolodny, Annette, forthcoming, 'Dancing through the minefield', in Dale Spender (ed.), *Men's Studies Modified*.

Komarovsky, Mirra, 1962, *Blue Collar Marriage*, Random House, New York.

Korda, Michael, 1975, *Male Chauvinism: How it Works at Home and in the Office*, Hodder & Stoughton.

Kramer, Cheris, 1975, 'Women's speech: separate but unequal', in Barrie Thorne and Nancy Henley (eds), *Language and Sex: Difference and Dominance*, Newbury House, Rowley, Mass., pp. 43–56.

Kramer, Cheris, 1977, 'Perceptions of female and male speech', *Language and Speech*, 20, no. 2, April/June, pp. 151–61.

Kramer, Cheris, 1978, 'Resistance to the public female voice', paper presented to Sociolinguistics: Language and Sex (Ninth World Congress of Sociology), Uppsala, Sweden, 14–20 August.

Kramer, Cheris, Barrie Thorne and Nancy Henley, 1978, 'Perspectives on language and Communication', *Signs: Journal of Women in Culture and Society*, 3, no. 3 spring, pp. 638–51.

Kramarae (Kramer), Cheris (ed.), 1980, *The Voices and Words of Women and Men*, Pergamon Press, Oxford.

Kramarae (Kramer), Cheris, 1981, *Women and Men Speaking*, Newbury House, Rowley, Mass.

Kuhn, Thomas, 1972, *The Structure of Scientific Revolutions*, University of Chicago Press, 2nd ed.

Lakoff, Robin, 1975, *Language and Woman's Place*, Harper & Row, New York.

Langer, Susanne K., 1976, *Philosophy in a New Key: A Study in the Symbolism of Reason, Rite and Art*, Harvard University Press, 3rd ed.

Lawrence, Barbara, 1974, 'Dirty words can harm you', *Redbook*, 143, May, p. 33.

Leach, Penelope, 1979, *Who Cares?*, Penguin.

Leech, Geoffrey, 1968, *Towards a Semantic Description of English*, Indiana University Press.

Leghorn, Lisa, 1980, private correspondence.

Leonard, Diana, 1979, 'Is feminism more complex than the W L M realises?', paper presented to the Radical Feminist Day Workshop, White Lion Free School, London, 8 April.

Lewis, Jane, forthcoming, 'History', in Dale Spender (ed.), *Men's Studies Modified*.

Lewis, Jill, 1977, 'Love as an oppressive ideology', WRRC Seminar, London, 6 January.

Liddington, Jill and Jill Norris, 1978, *One Hand Tied Behind Us: the Rise of the Women's Suffrage Movement*, Virago.

Lovenduski, Joni, forthcoming, 'Political science', in Dale Spender (ed.), *Men's Studies Modified*.

Luchsinger, R. and G. E. Arnold, 1965, *Voice, Speech, Language!*, Constable.

McConnell-Ginet, Sally, Ruth Borker and Nelly Furman (eds), 1980, *Women and Language in Literature and Society*, Praeger, New York.

McDowell, Margaret B., 1971, 'The new rhetoric of woman power', *Midwest Quarterly*, no. 12, pp. 187–98.

Mack, Joanna, 1974, 'Women's studies in Cambridge', *New Era*, 55, no. 6, July/August, pp. 162–4.

MacRobbie, Angela and Jenny Garber, 1975, 'Girls and subcultures', in S. Hall and T. Jefferson (eds), *Resistance through Rituals: Youth Subcultures in Postwar Britain*, Hutchinson, pp. 209–23.

McWilliams, Nancy, 1974, 'Contemporary feminism, consciousness raising and changing views of the political', in Jane S. Jaquette (ed.) *Women in Politics*, Wiley, New York, pp. 157–70.

Maitland, Sara, 1979, 'Novels are toys not bibles, but the child is mother to the woman', *Women's Studies International Quarterly*, 2, no. 2, pp. 203–8.

Marine, Gene, 1972, *A Male Guide to Women's Liberation*, Holt, Rinehart & Winston, New York.

Martyna, Wendy, 1978, 'Beyond the he/man approach: the case for language change', private correspondence (forthcoming article).

Masters, William and Virginia Johnson, 1970, *Human Sexual Inadequacy*, Little, Brown, Boston.

Mattingly, Ignatius C., 1969, 'Speaker variation and vocal tract size', paper presented to Acoustical Society of America (abstract: *Journal of Acoustical Society of America*, 39, p. 1219).

Mill, John Stuart, 1974, *On Liberty, Representative Government, the Subjection of Women* (Intro. Millicent Garrett Fawcett), Oxford University Press.

Miller, Casey and Kate Swift, 1976, *Words and Women: New Language in New Times*, Anchor/Doubleday, New York.

Miller, Jean Baker, 1976, *Toward a New Psychology of Women*, Beacon Press, Boston.

Mitchell-Kernan, C, 1973, 'Signifying', in A. Dundes (ed.) *Mother Wit from the Laughing Barrel*, Prentice-Hall, Englewood Cliffs, N.J.

Moers, Ellen, 1977, *Literary Women: the Great Writers*, Anchor/Doubleday, New York.

Moore, H. T. 1922, 'Further data concerning sex differences', *Journal of Abnormal and Social Psychology*, 4, pp. 81–9.

Morgan, Elaine, 1972, *The Descent of Woman*, Souvenir Press, London; Stein & Day, New York.

Morton, Nellie, 1974, 'Preaching the word', in Alice Hageman (ed.), *Sexist Religion and Women in the Church*, pp. 29–46.

Moulton, Janice, 1975, 'The myth of the "neutral" man', paper presented to Eastern Division Meeting, American Philosophical Association, Washington, DC, December.

Murray, Jessica, 1973, 'Male perspective in language', *Women: a Journal of Liberation*, 3, no. 2, pp. 46–50.

Nilsen, Alleen Pace, 1973, 'Grammatical gender and its relationship to the equal treatment of males and females in children's books', unpublished Ph.D. thesis, University of Iowa.

Nilsen, Alleen Pace, 1977, 'Linguistic sexism as a social issue', in A. P. Nilsen, Haig Bosmajian, H. Lee Gershuny and Julia Stanley, *Sexism and Language*, NCTE, Urbana, Ill., pp. 1–26.

Nochlin, Linda, 1972, 'Why have there been no great women artists?', in E. B. Hess and E. C. Baker (eds), *Art and Sexual Politics*, Collier-Macmillan, pp. 1–39.

Oakley, Ann, 1974, *The Sociology of Housework*, Martin Robertson.

Oakley, Ann, 1979, *Becoming a Mother*, Martin Robertson.

Olsen, Tillie, 1978, *Silences*, Delacorte Press/Seymour Lawrence, New York.

Pagels, Elaine H., 1976, 'What became of God the mother?: conflicting images of God in early Christianity', *Signs: Journal of Women in Culture and Society*, 2, no. 2, winter, pp. 293–303.

Parker, Angele, 1973, 'Sex differences in classroom intellectual argumentation', unpublished MS. thesis, Pennsylvania State University.

Pauline, 1977, 'Old Testament covenant against the goddess', *Shrew*, spring, pp. 8–9.

Peters, Margot, 1977, *Unquiet Soul: a Biography of Charlotte Brontë*, Futura.

Phillips, Angela and Jill Rakussen, 1978, *Our Bodies Ourselves: a Health Book by and for Women*, Penguin.

Pogrebin, Letty Cottin, 1972, 'Competing with women', *Ms*, 1, no. 2, p. 78.

Pogrebin, Letty Cottin, 1973, 'Rap groups: the feminist connection', *Ms*, 2, no. 9, pp. 80–3, 98–100, 104.

Poole, Joshua, 1646, *The English Accidence*, Scolar Press Facsimile, 1967.

Rich, Adrienne, 1972, 'When we dead awaken: writing as re-vision', *College English*, 34, no. 1, October, pp. 18–30.

Rich, Adrienne, 1977, *Of Woman Born: Motherhood as Experience and Institution*, Virago.

Rich, Adrienne, 1979, *On Lies, Secrets and Silence: Selected Prose: 1966–78*, Norton, New York.

Robbins, Susan, 1978, 'Gender and agency in Indo-European languages', paper presented to Sociolinguistics: Language and Sex (ninth World Congress of Sociology), Uppsala, Sweden, 14–20 August.

Roberts, Cathy and Elaine Millar, 1978, 'Feminism, socialism and abortion', *Women's Studies International Quarterly*, 1, no. 1, pp. 3–14.

Roberts, Helen, forthcoming, 'Sociology', in Dale Spender (ed.), *Men's Studies Modified*.

Roberts, Joan, 1976, *Beyond Intellectual Sexism: a New Woman, a New Reality*,

David McKay, New York.

Rose, Hilary, 1979, private correspondence, September.

Rosen, Harold, 1972, *Language and Class: a Critical Look at the Theories of Basil Bernstein*, Falling Wall Press, Bristol.

Rosen, Harold, 1975, 'Towards a language policy across the curriculum' (discussion document prepared and introduced by Harold Rosen on behalf of the London Association for the teaching of English), in Douglas Barnes *et al.*, *Language, the Learner and the School*, Penguin.

Rowbotham, Sheila, 1973a, *Woman's Consciousness: Man's World*, Penguin.

Rowbotham, Sheila, 1973b, *Hidden from History*, Pluto Press.

Rubenius, Aina, 1950, *The Woman Question in Mrs. Gaskell's Life and Works*, Harvard University Press.

Russell, Letty, 1974, 'Women and ministry', in Alice Hageman (ed.), *Sexist Religion and Women in the Church*, pp. 17–62.

Ruth, Sheila, forthcoming, 'Philosophy', in Dale Spender (ed.), *Men's Studies Modified*.

Sachs, Jacqueline, Philip Lieberman and Donna Erickson, 1973, 'Anatomical and cultural determinants of male and female speech', in Roger Shuy and Ralph Fasold (eds), *Language Attitudes: Current Trends and Prospects*. Georgetown University Press, Washington, pp. 74–84.

Salem, J. Christine, 1980, 'On naming the oppressor: what Woolf avoids saying in *A Room of One's Own*', *Women's Studies International Quarterly*, 3 (forthcoming).

Sapir, Edward, 1970, *Culture, Language and Personality: Selected Essays*, ed. David G. Mandelbaum, University of California Press.

Schacher, Susan (co-ordinator), 1976, 'Hypatia's Sisters: Biographies of Women Scientists, Past and Present', developed by 'Women and Science Class', University of Washington Women's Studies Program, Feminists Northwest, Seattle, Washington.

Schneider, J. and Sally Hacker, 1973, 'Sex role imagery and the use of the generic man', *American Sociologist*, 8, no. 1, February, pp. 12–18.

Schneider, Michael J. and Karen A. Foss, 1977, 'Thought, sex and language: the Sapir–Whorf hypothesis in the American women's movement', *Bulletin: Women's Studies in Communication*, 1, no. 1, spring, pp. 1–7.

Schulz, Muriel, 1975(a), 'The semantic derogation of women', in Barrie Thorne and Nancy Henley (eds), *Language and Sex: Difference and Dominance*, Newbury House, Rowley, Mass., pp. 64–75.

Schulz, Muriel, 1975(b), 'Rape is a four-letter word', *Etc: a Review of General Semantics*, 32, no. 1, pp. 65–9.

Schulz, Muriel, 1975(c), 'Is the English language anybody's enemy?', *Etc: a Review of General Semantics*, 32, no. 2, pp. 65–9.

Schulz, Muriel, 1978, 'Man (embracing woman): the generic in sociological writing', paper presented to Sociolinguistics: Language and Sex (Ninth World Congress of Sociology), Uppsala, Sweden, 14–20 August.

Scott, Hilda, 1985, *Working your Way to the Bottom*, Pandora Press, London.

Scully, Diana and Pauline Bart, 1973, 'A funny thing happened on the way to the orifice: women in gynecology text books', in Joan Huber (ed.), *Changing Women in a Changing Society*, University of Chicago Press, pp. 283–8.

Searle, Chris, 1973, *The Forsaken Lover: White Words and Black People*, Penguin.

Sharpe, Sue, 1976, *'Just Like a Girl': How Girls Learn to be Women*, Penguin.

Showalter, Elaine, 1977, *A Literature of their Own: British Women Novelists from Brontë to Lessing*, Princeton University Press.

Shulman, Gail, 1974, 'View from the back of the synagogue: women in Judaism', in Alice Hageman (ed.), *Sexist Religion and Women in the Church*, pp. 143–66.

Simpson, Hilary, 1979, 'A literary trespasser: D. H. Lawrence's use of women's writing', *Women's Studies International Quarterly*, 2, no. 2, pp. 155–70.

Smith, Barbara, 1979, 'Toward a black feminist criticism', *Women's Studies International Quarterly*, 2, no. 2, pp. 183–94.

Smith, Dorothy, 1978, 'A peculiar eclipsing: women's exclusion from man's culture', *Women's Studies International Quarterly*, 1, no. 4, pp. 281–96.

Smith, Frank, 1971, *Understanding Reading: A Psycholinguistic Analysis of Reading and Learning to Read*, Holt, Rinehart & Winston, New York.

Spender, Dale, 1980, 'Disappearing tricks' in Dale Spender and Elizabeth Sarah (eds), *Learning to Lose: Sexism and Education*.

Spender, Dale, 1982(a), *Invisible Women; the Schooling Scandal*, Writer's and Readers, London.

Spender, Dale, 1982(b), *Women of Ideas and What Men have Done to Them – From Aphra Behn to Adrienne Rich*, Routledge & Kegan Paul, London.

Spender, Dale, (ed.), 1983(a), *Feminist Theorists; three centuries of women's intellectual traditions*, The Women's Press, London; Pantheon, New York.

Spender, Dale, 1983(b), *Therre's Always Been a Women's Movement This Century*, Pandora Press, London.

Spender, Dale (ed.), forthcoming, *Men's Studies Modified: the Impact of Feminism on the Academic Disciplines*, Pergamon, Oxford.

Spender, Dale and Elizabeth Sarah (eds), 1980, *Learning to Lose: Sexism and Education*, The Women's Press.

Stanley, Julia, 1973, 'Paradigmatic woman; the prostitute', paper presented to South Atlantic Modern Language Association, 1972; American Dialect Society, 1972; *Linguistic Society of America*, 1973.

Stanley, Julia, 1974, 'What's in a label: the politics of naming', symposium on Sexism in Language, Northeastern Illinois University, Chicago, 6 April.

Stanley, Julia, 1975, 'Sexist grammar' paper presented to South Eastern Conference of Linguistics, Atlanta, Georgia, 7 November.

Stanley, Julia, 1977, 'Gender marking in American English', in A. P. Nilsen *et al.*, *Sexism and Language*, NCTE, Urbana, Ill., pp. 44–76.

Stern, Jenny, 1972, 'Women and the novel: the nineteenth century explosion', *Women's Liberation Review*, Falling Wall Press, Bristol.

Stoll, Clarice Stasz and Paul T. McFarlane, 1973, 'Sex differences in game strategy', in C. S. Stoll (ed.), *Sexism: Scientific Debates*. Addison-Wesley, Reading, Mass., pp. 74–85.

Stone, Merlin, 1977, *The Paradise Papers: the Suppression of Women's Rites*, Virago.

Strodtbeck, Fred, Rita M. James and Charles Hawkins, 1957, 'Social status in jury deliberations', *American Sociological Review*, 22, pp. 713–19.

Summers, Anne, 1976, *Damned Whores and God's Police: the Colonization of Women in Australia*, Penguin, Melbourne.

Susan, Barbara, 1970, 'About my consciousness-raising', in Leslie B. Tanner (ed.), *Voices from Women's Liberation*, Signet, New York, pp. 238–43.

Swacker, Marjorie, 1975, 'The sex of the speaker as a sociolinguistic variable', in Barrie Thorne and Nancy Henley (eds), *Language and Sex: Difference and Dominance*, Newbury House, Rowley, Mass., pp. 76–83.

Thorne, Barrie and Nancy Henley, 1975, 'Difference and dominance: an overview of language, gender and society', in Barrie Thorne and Nancy Henley (eds), *Language and Sex: Difference and Dominance*, Newbury House, Rowley, Mass., pp. 5–42.

Thorne, Barrie, Cheris Kramarae and Nancy Henley (eds), 1983, *Language, Gender and Society*, Newbury House, Rowley, Mass.

Tobias, Sheila, 1978, 'Women's studies: its origins, organization and prospects', *Women's Studies International Quarterly*, 1, no. 1, pp. 85–98.

Toth, Emily, 1970, 'Can a woman MAN the barricades? – or – linguistic sexism up against the wall', *Women: a Journal of Liberation*, Fall, p. 57.

Trudgill, Peter, 1975(a), *Sociolinguistics: an Introduction*, Penguin.

Trudgill, Peter, 1975(b), 'Sex, covert prestige and linguistic change in the urban British English of Norwich', in Barrie Thorne and Nancy Henley (eds), *Language and Sex: Difference and Dominance*, Newbury House, Rowley, Mass., pp. 88–104.

Walker, Beverley, forthcoming, 'Psychology', in Dale Spender (ed.), *Men's Studies Modified*.

Walters, Anna, 1977, 'The value of the work of Elizabeth Gaskell for study at Advanced Level', unpublished MA dissertation, University of London Institute of Education.

Walters, Margaret, 1976, 'The rights and wrongs of women: Mary Wollstonecraft, Harriet Martineau, Simone de Beauvoir', in Juliet Mitchell and Ann Oakley (eds), *The Rights and Wrongs of Women*, Penguin, pp. 304–99.

Weisstein, Naomi, 1971, 'Psychology constructs the female and the fantasy life of the male psychologist', in Michelle H. Garskof (ed.), *Roles Women Play: Readings towards Women's Liberation*, Wadsworth, Calif., pp. 68–83.

West, Candace and Don H. Zimmerman, 1983, 'Small insults; a study of interruptions in cross sex conversations between unacquainted persons', in Thorne *et al.* (eds), *Language, Gender and Society*, Newbury House, Rowley, Mass.

Whitehead, Ann, 1976, 'Sexual antagonism in Herefordshire', in Diana Leonard Barker and Sheila Allen (eds), *Dependence and Exploitation in Work and Marriage*, Longman, pp. 169–203.

Whitfield, A. Stanton, 1929, *Mrs. Gaskell: her Life and Work*, George Routledge.

Whorf, Benjamin Lee, 1976, *see* Carrol, John B. (ed.).

Williams, Raymond, 1975, *The Long Revolution*, Penguin.

Wilson, Thomas, 1553, *Arte of Rhetorique*, Scholar's Facsimiles and Reprints, Delmar, N.Y., 1962.

Witkin, H. A. *et al.*, 1962, *Psychological Differentiation*, Wiley, New York (quoted in Archer, J., 1978).

Wood, Marion, 1966, 'The influence of sex and knowledge of communication effectiveness on spontaneous speech', *Word*, 22, nos 1, 2, 3, pp. 112–37.

Woolf, Virginia, 1972, 'Women and fiction', in Leonard Woolf (ed.), *Collected Essays: Virginia Woolf*, vol. 2, Chatto & Windus.

Woolf, Virginia, 1974, *A Room of One's Own*, Penguin.

Young, Michael F. D. (ed.), 1975, *Knowledge and Control: New Directions for the Sociology of Education*, Collier-Macmillan.

Zimmerman, Don and Candace West, 1975, 'Sex roles, interruptions and silences in conversation', in Barrie Thorne and Nancy Henley (eds), *Language and Sex: Difference and Dominance*, Newbury House, Rowley, Mass., pp. 105–29.

# Index